Critical Inquiries in the
Sociolinguistics of Globalization

ENCOUNTERS

Series Editors: **Jan Blommaert,** *Tilburg University, The Netherlands,* **Ben Rampton,** *Kings College London, UK,* **Anna De Fina,** *Georgetown University, USA,* **Sirpa Leppänen,** *University of Jyväskylä, Finland* and **James Collins,** *University at Albany/SUNY, USA*

The Encounters series sets out to explore diversity in language from a theoretical and an applied perspective. So the focus is both on the linguistic encounters, inequalities and struggles that characterise post-modern societies and on the development, within sociocultural linguistics, of theoretical instruments to explain them. The series welcomes work dealing with such topics as heterogeneity, mixing, creolization, bricolage, crossover phenomena, polylingual and polycultural practices. Another high-priority area of study is the investigation of processes through which linguistic resources are negotiated, appropriated and controlled, and the mechanisms leading to the creation and maintenance of sociocultural differences. The series welcomes ethnographically oriented work in which contexts of communication are investigated rather than assumed, as well as research that shows a clear commitment to close analysis of local meaning making processes and the semiotic organisation of texts.

All books in this series are externally peer-reviewed.

Full details of all the books in this series and of all our other publications can be found on http://www.multilingual-matters.com, or by writing to Multilingual Matters, St Nicholas House, 31–34 High Street, Bristol BS1 2AW, UK.

ENCOUNTERS: 14

Critical Inquiries in the Sociolinguistics of Globalization

Edited by
Tyler Andrew Barrett and Sender Dovchin

MULTILINGUAL MATTERS
Bristol • Blue Ridge Summit

DOI https://doi.org/10.21832/BARRET2845
Library of Congress Cataloging in Publication Data
A catalog record for this book is available from the Library of Congress.
Names: Barrett, Tyler Andrew, editor. | Dovchin, Sender, editor.
Title: Critical Inquiries in the Sociolinguistics of Globalization /
  Edited by Tyler Andrew Barrett and Sender Dovchin.
Description: Bristol; Blue Ridge Summit, PA: Multilingual Matters, 2019. |
   Series: Encounters: 14 | Includes bibliographical references and index.
Identifiers: LCCN 2018046596| ISBN 9781788922845 (hbk : alk. paper) | ISBN
   9781788922838 (pbk : alk. paper) | ISBN 9781788922876 (kindle)
Subjects: LCSH: Language and languages—Globalization. | Languages in
   contact. | Multilingualism. | Sociolinguistics.
Classification: LCC P130.5 .C75 2019 | DDC 306.44—dc23 LC record available at
https://lccn.loc.gov/2018046596

British Library Cataloguing in Publication Data
A catalogue entry for this book is available from the British Library.

ISBN-13: 978-1-78892-284-5 (hbk)
ISBN-13: 978-1-78892-283-8 (pbk)

Multilingual Matters
UK: St Nicholas House, 31–34 High Street, Bristol BS1 2AW, UK.
USA: NBN, Blue Ridge Summit, PA, USA.

Website: www.multilingual-matters.com
Twitter: Multi_Ling_Mat
Facebook: https://www.facebook.com/multilingualmatters
Blog: www.channelviewpublications.wordpress.com

Copyright © 2019 Tyler Andrew Barrett, Sender Dovchin and the authors of individual chapters.

All rights reserved. No part of this work may be reproduced in any form or by any means without permission in writing from the publisher.

The policy of Multilingual Matters/Channel View Publications is to use papers that are natural, renewable and recyclable products, made from wood grown in sustainable forests. In the manufacturing process of our books, and to further support our policy, preference is given to printers that have FSC and PEFC Chain of Custody certification. The FSC and/or PEFC logos will appear on those books where full certification has been granted to the printer concerned.

Typeset by Nova Techset Private Limited, Bengaluru and Chennai, India.

Contents

Acknowledgements — vii
Contributors — ix
Preface — xiii

1 Linguistic and Multimodal Resources within the Local–Global Interface of the Virtual Space: Critically Aware Youths in Bangladesh — 1
  Shaila Sultana

2 Linguascaping the City: A Phenomenological Inquiry into Linguistic Place-making of Toronto's Chinatown and Kensington Market Neighborhoods — 20
  Dejan Ivković, Violetta Cupial, Jamie Arfin and Tiziana Ceccato

3 'That's my Husband's sees the Smoke on this Card Bill he Doesn't like me Smoking': Service Interactions in Persian Shops in Sydney — 47
  Dariush Izadi

4 Language, Scale and Ideologies of the National in Kazakhstan — 66
  Kara Fleming

5 The Politics of Injustice in Translingualism: Linguistic Discrimination — 84
  Sender Dovchin

6 Translingualism as Resistance Against What and for Whom? — 102
  Jerry Won Lee

7 Transgrammaring Bilinguals and 'Ordinary' English in Japanese Ethnic Churchscapes — 119
  Tyler Barrett

8 The Coding Catastrophe: Translingualism and *Noh* in the
   Japanese Computer Science EFL Classroom   147
   Kim Rockell

Index   168

Acknowledgements

We would like to thank all contributing authors for their hard work, patience and promptness. Our gratitude goes to the editor of this series, Jan Blommaert, and the editorial director of Multilingual Matters, Anna Roderick, for their enduring support. Special thanks go to the anonymous reviewers who meticulously reviewed each chapter of this edited volume.

Funding: This work was supported by Australian Research Council (ARC) [grant number DE180100118], Japan Society for the Promotion of Science [grant number 17K13504].

Contributors

Jamie Arfin is an English professor at Humber College. Research interests include adult education, additional language acquisition teaching/learning, arts in education-embodied learning/drama pedagogy, post-secondary education, and internationalization of higher education. During her Master's degree, she created a drama pedagogy-based workshop for adult immigrants/international students aiding in language acquisition and focusing on identity building and student empowerment.

Tyler Andrew Barrett is an academic who teaches in the Division of Continuing Education at the University of California, Irvine, USA. His research interests include the sociolinguistics of globalization, language ideology, language policy and translingualism.

Tiziana Ceccato is a high school home economics/family studies teacher whose interests focus on early childhood education, child/adolescent development, second language acquisition, and language in social contexts. Her thesis research about beliefs between parents and teachers in Kindergarten has been presented at conferences such as HICE, ICSEI and IFHE.

Violetta Cupial is an instructor at York University whose pedagogy focuses on academic writing and research skills. As a researcher, she explores the intersections between multiple language knowledge, migration experiences, and identity. She explores migratory experiences of language teachers and International students in the context of Canadian academia.

Sender Dovchin is Senior Research Fellow at the School of Education, Curtin University, Western Australia. Previously, she was Associate Professor at the Centre for Language Research, University of Aizu, Japan. Her research focuses on the language education of young people living in globalized contexts, and she has contributed widely to international peer-reviewed journals. Her most recent publications include *Language, Media and Globalization in the Periphery: The Linguascapes of Popular Music in Mongolia* (Routledge, 2018) and *Popular Culture, Voice and Linguistic*

Diversity: Young Adults On- and Offline (co-authored with Alastair Pennycook and Shaila Sultana, Palgrave Macmillan, 2018).

Kara Fleming is Assistant Professor in the Language Center of KIMEP University in Almaty, Kazakhstan. Her research focuses on how language ideologies interact with ethnic and national identities, particularly as mediated through the education system. She received her PhD in Linguistics from the University of Hong Kong, and previously worked at the University of Hong Kong and the University of Leeds.

Dejan Ivković (Дејан Ивковић) is a scholar of language in society, multilingualism and multiliteracies from Toronto. Currently, his main projects and publishing engagements are (a) the pedagogy of linguascaping focusing on Toronto and Canada, (b) the semiotics and politics of digraphia in Serbian and Slavic, (c) the virtual linguistic landscape and multilingualism in new media and (d) critical literacies online. He also teaches at York University, the University of Toronto and the University of Guelph.

Dariush Izadi received his PhD in Linguistics from Macquarie University, Sydney, Australia. His PhD project focused on the intersection of social action, practices and discourses produced and reproduced by the shop-owners and the customers in Persian shops in Sydney and the way they are interactionally realized. In his work, he applied Mediated Discourse Analysis and Nexus Analysis to investigate the practices and methods through which participants accomplish their actions in the shops. Currently, he works at Western Sydney University, Australia, where he teaches Language and Linguistics Research Methods, Discourse Analysis and TESOL Units.

Jerry Won Lee is Assistant Professor in the Departments of English and Anthropology at the University of California, Irvine. His publications include *The Politics of Translingualism* (Routledge, 2017) and *Korean Englishes in Transnational Contexts* (co-edited with Christopher J. Jenks, Palgrave Macmillan, 2017).

Kim Rockell is Associate Professor at the Centre for Language Research, the University of Aizu, Japan. He is a PhD graduate of the University of Canterbury in Christchurch, New Zealand. His research interests encompass sociolinguistics, ethnomusicology and the music/language nexus in language EFL education. He is also active performing as a classical guitarist throughout the Asia-Pacific region.

Shaila Sultana is Professor of English Language, Institute of Modern Languages, University of Dhaka. She has been educated at Jahangirnagar

University (Dhaka), Monash University (Melbourne), King's College (London) and the University of Technology, Sydney. Her research interests include trans approaches to language and identity, sociology, critical geography and the historical and sociocultural significance of English in postcolonial countries. She has authored articles in many international peer-reviewed journals. Her most recent book is *Popular Culture, Voice and Linguistic Diversity: Young Adults On- and Offline* (co-authored with Sender Dovchin and Alastair Pennycook, Palgrave Macmillan, 2018).

Preface

Studies in this collection seek to contribute to the recent research in the debate on 'sociolinguistics of globalization' (Blommaert, 2010) that has problematized hybridity/bi/multilingualism/code-switching for falling short in addressing contemporary linguistic repertoires constructed out of a diversity of linguistic and cultural resources. We seek to expand knowledge in the critical discussions of 'sociolinguistics of globalization' by demonstrating how language users may (re)localize, (re)negotiate and (re)make certain available linguistic and cultural resources to achieve their communicative aims. In fact, we argue that it is critical to see language as a practice that can be mixed with other linguistic, semiotic and cultural resources used by speakers interacting across different linguistic codes. Language users are not necessarily involved with the practices of 'codeswitching' or 'bi/multilingualism' but rather are engaged with sophisticated transcendence of the linguistic and cultural boundaries to create multiple and mixed identities, agencies, desires and expressions (Dovchin, 2018).

Studies in this collection seek to recognize the notions of 'linguistic diversity' and 'hybridity' through the lenses of critical new theories and relative theoretical frameworks embedded within the current broader discussion of sociolinguistics of globalization. The main themes include critical inquiries on online/offline languages in society, language users, language learners and language teachers who may operate 'between' languages and are faced with decisions to navigate, negotiate and invent or re-invent languages. Drawing mostly on the first-person point of view, the methodological approaches include linguistic ethnographic and 'netnographic' (Dovchin, 2015, 2017, 2018) tools such as interviews, observations and discourse and semiotic analyses of local and global and virtual spaces often with attention to phenomenological self-positioning perspectives that result in sense-making and meaning making in various contexts that include the linguistic landscapes, schools, classrooms, neighborhoods and virtual spaces of Australia, Bangladesh, Canada, Japan, Kazakhstan, Mongolia, South Korea and the US. In the following we present the abstracts from our authors outlining their chapters.

In Chapter 1, Sultana explores local and global virtual spaces of Bangladeshi youths who use multimodal semiotic resources to communicate. Through identifying processes of decontextualization, entetxualization and resemiotization in communication, she seeks to understand how these youths make meaning together. The analysis shows that Bangladeshi youths are able to claim legitimacy through transglossic interactions and multidimensional experiences in virtual spaces by using voices that linguistically challenge and by default destabilize existing societal boundaries, perceptions and practices. In addition to the fact that very little research has been done about virtual spaces in Bangladesh, the chapter expands upon the emerging concept of 'transglossia'.

In Chapter 2, Ivković *et al.* present a study about linguascaping, a term described as 'linguistic place-making', which is used to emphasize meaning-making through the phenomenological perspectives of participants in linguascapes. In an effort to explore how people perceive linguistic and semiotic resources beyond identification of static notions of meaning associated with linguistic and semoiotic artifacts at face value, Ivković *et al.* use an ethnographic approach with an Interpretive Phenomenological Analysis (Smith *et al.*, 2009) to identify how participants understand linguistic and cultural diversity in cosmopolitan areas of Toronto. The analysis shows us that through interpretive interaction people co-create the meaning of the world around us as they negotiate culturally complex discourses in cosmopolitan settings. The chapter contributes to the concept of 'linguascaping' as a construct, metaphor and heuristic as opposed to the more common conceptualization 'linguascapes' (Dovchin, 2018).

In Chapter 3, Izadi examines intercultural communication in service encounters that take place in a typical Persian shop in Sydney, Australia. He uses Mediated Discourse Analysis (Scollon, 2001) and Nexus Analysis (Scollon & Scollon, 2004) to identify communicative interactions as informed by the social identities of the participants and the physical spaces of the transactions. The study shows that traditional surface-level views of service encounters ought to be reconsidered beyond so-called traditional or typical descriptions as a result of the complexity of language practices in late-modern urban settings where participants use a wide range of cultural and semiotic resources to engage in transactions. The study identifies the complexities in service encounters, which, at face value, have been traditionally determined as mundane transactions.

In Chapter 4, Fleming examines discourses of language policy, media and individuals who participate in the discursive construction of nationalistic beliefs about the developing nation of Kazakhstan. She uses an ethnographic approach of semi-structured interviews and discourse analysis to identify scale-making as a process that produces global and local ideological perspectives and processes that impact beliefs about nationalism. In addition to the fact that very little sociolinguistic research has been conducted about Kazakhstan, this chapter highlights the use of 'scale' (Blommaert *et al.*, 2015) not as a term synonymous with hierarchical categorization, but as a term referring to the social construction of beliefs that inform identity through processes in which society members draw upon linguistic resources to make meaning about a nation and subsequent nationalism together.

In Chapter 5, Dovchin presents a study about translingualism in the context of young Mongolians who experience inequality, discrimination and prejudice based on how they speak English and other local dialects and accents. Highlighting the gap in the literature on translingualism concerned with inequality, she uses a linguistic ethnographic approach to identify how local practices and local constraints may limit translingual practices. The study expands upon the orientation of translingualism in terms of identifying instances in which local constraints lead to perspectives that produce discrimination that affects translingual speakers who do not represent clear-cut cultural or linguistic identities.

In Chapter 6, Lee examines translingualism in the context of English textbooks in South Korea. He presents a critical discourse and social semiotic analysis of an English textbook used in South Korea in an effort to understand curricular priorities yielding cultural and ideological hybridity embedded within surface-level examples of linguistic hybridity. His study suggests that resistance discourse and orientations ought to consider what is being said and who said it to better determine the intentions and consequences of presenting particular discursive artifacts in textbooks and other contexts in which values and norms are determined and disseminated. The chapter indicates the importance and potential of self-critical recursive examinations of notions such as translingualism that seek to resist the limitations of epistemological approaches rooted in the past for the sake of progress.

In Chapter 7, drawing on Dovchin's (2017) idea of 'ordinariness' distinction, Barrett presents a study about bilinguals who use 'ordinary' English in Japanese ethnic churchscapes. He uses discourse analysis and a transgrammaring lens to identify 'ordinary' English in texts produced by participants in interviews. The analysis reveals Japanese ethnic churchscape communities use 'ordinary' English that is a legitimate variety and deserves recognition. The chapter expands upon the transgrammaring orientation as a heuristic for legitimizing 'ordinary' English speakers who do not see themselves as legitimate bilingual English speakers.

As studies in this collection show, a closer look at language in society reveals semiotic hybridity (Izadi; Ivković) transglossia (Sultana) translingualism (Dovchin; Lee) and transgrammaring (Barrett), among other things, which are undeniable realities at multiple levels and scales (Fleming) in societies around the globe. While normative approaches to language and education continue to be favored for reasons that include determining and acquiring cultural and linguistic capital in a globalizing world, decisions about language use and education based upon normative preferences, standards and tradition often keep the translingual realities of millions of individuals in the periphery. The periphery deserves recognition; and if we look a little closer, as demonstrated in the chapters of this book, the evidence is there. In other words, the implication is that within these societal and educational contexts, confronting collateral forms of linguistic, semiotic and ideological hybridity is inevitable. Hence, the following chapter, the final chapter, is one final example identifying how semiotic resources and translingual realities can be effectively utilized and repurposed for pedagogical purposes.

We conclude this volume with a study on translingualism and its effectiveness in EFL classroom contexts. Rockell presents a study about *Noh* (Japanese drama) used as a pedagogical method to encourage characteristically shy Japanese students to participate in English class at a computer science university in Japan. As a participant observer he uses an ethnographic approach to analyze translingualism in semiotic resources and multilevel discourse exchanges between the instructor, staff and students. This study is novel on its own terms since it repurposes *Noh* beyond the epistemological limitations of its tradition and into an interdisciplinary approach used in English education that bridges the gap between languages and cultures through processes in which translingualism is evident at both linguistic and semiotic levels.

References

Blommaert, J. (2010) *The Sociolinguistics of Globalization*. Cambridge: Cambridge University Press.
Blommaert, J., Westinen, E. and Leppänen, S. (2015) Further notes on sociolinguistic scales. *Intercultural Pragmatics* 12 (1), 119–127.
Dovchin, S. (2018) *Language, Media and Globalization in the Periphery: The Linguascapes of Popular Music in Mongolia*. New York: Routledge.
Dovchin, S. (2017) The ordinariness of youth linguascapes in Mongolia. *International Journal of Multilingualism* 14 (2), 144–159.
Dovchin, S. (2015) Language, multiple authenticities and social media: The online language practices of university students in Mongolia. *Journal of Sociolinguistics* 19 (4), 437–459.

Scollon, R. (2001) *Mediated Discourse: The Nexus of Practice*. New York: Routledge.
Scollon, R. and Scollon, S. (2004) *Nexus Analysis: Discourse and the Emerging Internet*. London: Routledge.
Smith, J.A., Flowers, P. and Larkin, M. (2009) *Interpretative Phenomenological Analysis: Theory, Method, Research*. London: Sage.

1 Linguistic and Multimodal Resources within the Local–Global Interface of the Virtual Space: Critically Aware Youths in Bangladesh

Shaila Sultana

Virtual Space and its Significance

Virtual space or the computer-mediated multimodal environment, as a research context, has drawn the interest of applied linguists for a long time. There have been a significant number of research studies, addressing the meaning-making processes in virtual space. Various signs and symbols, such as emoticons, punctuation marks or abbreviations, specific ways of communication used by young adults in specific countries, Facebook statuses and their forms and functions, micro-blogging and individual stances, gamers and their strategies of making meaning in different gaming sites or typographic play have been explored in detail (Androutsopoulos, 2006, 2014; Leppänen & Piirainen-Marsh, 2009; Thurlow & Mroczek, 2011). These research studies allow us to understand the idiosyncrasies of virtual space, which are not solely dependent on linguistic resources, but also depend on other semiotic resources.

Drawing on insights from these research studies, this chapter explores the ways Bangladeshi youths engage with multimodal semiotic resources in virtual space. Virtual space has been chosen as the research context for three specific reasons. First, it has immense meaning potentiality in terms of linguistic and multimodal resources. Multimodal resources in addition to languages, such as images, music videos, photographs, links to online news and tag lines of characters from popular culture play a vital role in meaning-making processes. Interlocutors, even when they have limited linguistic resources, may use other sociocultural semiotic resources in order to express their opinions, values and meanings (Dovchin *et al.*, 2016). They can use dialogues from films or song titles from their favorite albums in order to engage in conversations and perform a 'cool' youth identity (Sultana, 2014). They can also express their affiliation, support and comradery by pressing the like button or sharing posts (Blommaert & Varis, 2017). All of these linguistic and multimodal resources, recontextualized in the virtual space, emerge with new meanings, based on the purposes and communicative functions they serve for the interlocutors.

Second, virtual space is specifically important to understand the agentive role of the interlocutors. Thurlow and Mroczek (2011) identified that the new media, even though it is afforded by technologies, is given social meanings by the users. On a similar note, Varis and Wang (2011: 71) define virtual space as 'a superdiverse space par excellence' that has 'seemingly endless possibilities for self-expression, individual life projects and community formation'. People have freedom and independence in arranging the physical and social environment of the space with specific resources and in selecting interlocutors with whom they want to engage in conversations. Virtual space is thus individually defined and people may express varied individual senses of self and reconfigure relationships with others.

Third, virtual space seems to provide a unique platform for socially, culturally and politically marginalized segments of the society for engaging in alternative discourses and negotiating different facets of identification. Virtual space creates a personal and private space where individuals may express themselves, while they fail to do so in a public space. Virtual space is significant for coming to terms with personal, social, cultural and ideological issues, especially for those who are marginalized in society for any specific reasons, be it socioeconomic condition, gender identity or political affiliation (Karim, 2014; Kee, 2011). Hence, it is important that we understand the process of meaning-making in the virtual space along with the function of linguistic and multimodal resources. The chapter intends to address the research questions given below:

- What kind of linguistic and multimodal resources do young adults in Bangladesh use in virtual space?
- In what ways do they use these resources?
- For what purposes do they use them?

Unraveling the relationship among youth language practices and various multimodal resources, the chapter thus explores the process of meaning-making in virtual space. It contributes to the new trend of sociolinguistics research rather than the linguistic features of these resources, which gives more emphasis on the intentions and purposes of language use and contextual realities that determine the actual meanings of these resources in the newer contexts. The chapter also captures the trajectories of these resources through time, locations, cultures and modalities. This chapter is significant for Bangladesh since virtual space has remained almost an unexplored research site. It intends to bring sociolinguistics insights into the space which has been explored only from a cultural perspective, missing the chance to develop nascent understanding of how language and other semiotic resources work as mediating tools in the meaning-making process.

Virtual Space: Transglossia, Re-entextualization and Resemiotization

In recent times, the linguistic and multimodal resources used in virtual space and the use of different codes, modes and genres in the meaning-making processes have been explored in applied linguistics research. Language is viewed as transglossic, which is an extension of Bakhtin's heteroglossia (see also Sultana, 2015; Sultana *et al.*, 2015; Dovchin *et al.*, 2017). Transglossia underscores the importance of 'voices' and the way voices engender new meanings through linguistic and multimodal resources. These studies show that voices, in mimicking dialogues, allow individuals to transgress linguistic and cultural boundaries. Hence, language no longer remains attached to any specific location and culture.

Voices adopted through the use of various modes of semiotic resources such as quotations, images, links to music videos and photographs in virtual space allow individuals to flout the boundaries of modes. Language no longer remains restricted to one specific mode or multiple modes. Voices with borrowed intonation, stress or paralinguistic features enrich language with new ideological, historical, local, discursive and interpretive elements. Meanings can no longer be deciphered without traversing the restricted meaning of the texts. Similarly, when individuals translate words from one language to another and manipulate the opacity of meaning in different languages, their voices can no longer be interpreted with reference to discreet languages. Interpretation requires thinking across the blurred boundaries between languages, a process that is compelling in translation.

Since linguistic and cultural borrowing and blending are integral to meaning-making processes, it is possible to give a better interpretation of a language by showing that the voices emerge from the mixture of codes and modes and genres. These voices decentralize the language in the complexity of *transcultural* (drawing on multiple cultural resources), *translocal* (drawing on linguistic and cultural resources from multiple locations), *transmodal* (operating across different modalities), *transtextual* (deploying a range of meaning-making practices across languages) and *translational* relations of communication (making meaning across and against codifications, manipulating the differences in meaning caused by the opacity of translation; Pennycook, 2007). Here a quotation in Bangla or English without features of any other languages can be transglossic because of its purposive use and shift in meaning.

In order to understand the formal and functional process of how meaning changes with the alteration of location and time, it is important to understand the process of 'decontextualization', 'entextualization' (Bauman & Briggs, 1990) and 'resemiotization' (Iedema, 2003). *Transculturation, translocalization, transmodality* and *transtextualization* of these resources occur because they are 'entextualizable' and 'resemiotizable' in virtual space. 'Entextualization' means 'the process of making a stretch of linguistic production into a unit – a *text* – that can be lifted out of its interactional setting. A text ... is discourse rendered decontextualizable. Entextualization may well incorporate aspects of context, such that the resultant text carries elements of its history of use within it' (Bauman & Briggs, 1990: 73). In other words, entextualization is the extraction of discourse from its original context and recontextualization of it in a newer context through integration, adaption and reorganization. The text trajectories of discourse thus get a newer dimension in recontextualization. Theodoropoulou (2016: 29) stated, 'The notion of entextualization is a useful one in the study of semiotic resources, as it allows us to track down the dynamic trajectory thereof and thus to tap into the complexities associated with meaning making in digital discourse'. On a similar note, Leppänen *et al.* (2013) identify that entextualization indicates what happens in between the decontextualization, that is, while dissociating the materials from their original context, and recontextualization, that is, during modification and adaptation of them in the newer context. As a result, entextualization allows us to explore how linguistic and multimodal resources are taken out of their original context of use and re-used in the virtual space for distinctly different purposes.

Closely intertwined with the process of entextualization is 'resemiotization'. 'Resemiotization is meant to provide the analytical means for (1) tracing how semiotics are translated from one into the other as social processes unfold, as well as for (2) asking why these semiotics (rather than others) are mobilized to do certain things at certain times' (Iedema, 2003: 29). While entextualization refers to the decontextualization and recontextualization of discourse, resemiotization brings forth the changes that have occurred in meaning because of changes in mode, modality or location and the creation of new semiotic modes and resources. It also unearths the factors that prompt resemiotization. That is why resemiotization ensures the 'socio-historical exploration and understanding of the complex processes' involved in the meaning-making process (Iedema, 2003: 48) and 'resemiotization seeks to underscore the material and historicized dimensions of representation' (Iedema, 2003: 50). Leppänen et al. (2013) and Blommaert and Varis (2015) identify that the meaning-making process in resemiotization can bring distinctly different meaning to the same linguistic and multimodal resources because of the new sets of contextualization conditions. That is why it seems useful in understanding why and how a photograph of a film star with a ridiculous gesture may be used to mock a friend; a song title may be given as an answer to a friend's question; a link to a newspaper article shared may show individual ideological affiliation; and emoticons, 'like' or 'love' buttons on Facebook may indicate sociocultural preferences.

Entextualization and resemiotization seem integral to *transculturalization* and *translocalization* too. Leppänen et al. (2013) refer to a Finnish rap video in which entextualization and resemiotization have been used by the artists in order to make the rap that embraces the spirit of the global genre of rap music culture, and make it pertinent to the local music setting and issues of young rappers themselves. They tend to demonstrate themselves as translocal and polycentric music culture members. According to Leppänen et al. (2013), the artifact itself becomes *translocal* and *transcultural* in entextualization and resemiotization.

Entextualization and resemiotization also bring to the fore the agency and freedom that individuals enjoy in virtual space. Bauman and Briggs (1990), Leppänen et al. (2013) and Blommaert and Varis (2015) identify the 'authority' people enjoy and the power of the individual agency they exert in their entextualization – 'an act of control', since they decide which resources they want to decontextualize and they show their legitimacy and competence in reusing and assessing differential values associated with various linguistic and multimodal resources. However, this authority is not valueless – it is influenced by sociocultural ideologies, eligibility and accessibility to institutional structures, legitimacy, cultural propriety and the competence to conduct decontextualization and recontextualization (Bauman & Briggs, 1990).

The decisions and choices made during the process of entextualization and resemiotization are closely related to what identity individuals prefer to perform. Since it is their decision what linguistic and multimodal resources they use within the social, cultural, spatial, and historical realities, they have more control over what identity attributes they want to perform in a given moment. On a similar note, Pennycook (2004) considered performitivity as a way of looking at the production of identity in the 'doing'. With reference to the survival strategies used by homeless women in the street for protecting themselves from criminal victimization, it was shown that their gendered performativity depended on situations, contexts and interlocutors and the ways they manipulate the semiotic resources to their favor (Huey & Berndt, 2008). Nevertheless, it should be noted that individual agency in identity performativity does not give individual sole independence in performing whatever identity they prefer. It is negotiated in relation to the ontological realities, such as gender, race and sexuality (Huey & Berndt, 2008).

The chapter adds to it by showing that entextualization and resemiotization are integral aspects of meaning-making and identity performances. These aspects give a nascent understanding of how meaning is transferred from one location to another, what purpose they serve both in formal and functional terms, and with whom and why.

Method, Context, Data Sources and Data Analysis

An ethnographic study was conducted at a university called the University of Excellence (UOE)[1] in the cosmopolitan city of Dhaka, Bangladesh. Twenty-nine participants from a number of different departments volunteered to participate in the research. They were observed outside the classroom in the student cafeteria and lounges, university clubs and favorite hangouts within the university premises. Their face-to-face conversations within their peer groups in different social situations were recorded. Of the 29 participants, 17 gave access to their Facebook (FB) accounts, from which their virtual conversations were collected. To understand the data on FB, a virtual ethnographic method, which Androutsopoulos (2011) defined as 'Internet ethnography', was adapted, and the use of English and Bangla on FB was observed. The virtual ethnography continued for several years with the consent of the research participants.

The data drawn from the Facebook were analyzed through a *transglossic framework* (Sultana, 2015; Sultana *et al.*, 2015). The data were explored for *contextual* (physical locations and participants), *pretextual* (historical trajectories of texts), *subtextual* (ideologies mobilized by texts), *intertextual* (meanings that occur across texts) and *post-textual* interpretations of the data (the ways texts are read, interpreted, resisted and appropriated; cf. also Pennycook, 2007: 53–54). Their responses in *post-textual interpretations* on why they produced their own language and how they interpreted the language of others made the data analysis not only the researcher's interpretation, but also theirs.

The entextualization and resemiotization of linguistic and multimodal resources were brought to the fore when the contextual and intertextual references were considered. Both of these references unraveled the trajectories of linguistic and multimodal resources from different locations, cultures and changes in meanings that had been brought to them along with changes in their locations and purposes. *Pretextual*, *subtextual* and *post-textual* references, in addition, disentangled the individual, political, social and cultural values that may influence the choices of these resources. Two pieces of FB conversations were selected based on the meanings rendered in and purposes served through entextualization and resemiotization.

Young Adults' Critical Awareness of Political Ideologies

The FB status given below was shared by Nayeem, a business studies student at the UOE in January 2015. He also uploaded a photograph of a truck parked in front of the office of Ms Khaleda Zia, the Chairperson of the opposition political party, the Bangladesh Nationalist Party (BNP), and shared a news link with coverage of the house arrest of Ms Khaleda Zia by the Government of Bangladesh. The photo shows one of the trucks of sand and sections of the eight platoons of police surrounding her office. Ms Khaleda Zia was stopped coming out of her office by the Government (bdnews.24, 2015). The number of sand-filled trucks barricading the roads leading to the office entrance increased to 24 (Ramany, 2015) when she, on behalf of the BNP, declared the need for organized agitation, such as demonstrations and rallies, to observe the 10th parliamentary election day as 'Democracy Killing Day' (The Guardian, 2015). The date 5 January 2014 is called 'Democracy Killing Day' because all major opposition parties boycotted the parliamentary election and the Awami League, the ruling political party of the government, ran a one-party election and won the election uncontested. Around 21 people were killed on the election day (The Guardian, 2015). This is a status which shows Nayeem's concern about the political turmoil in Bangladesh.

Extract 1

Language guide: English – regular font; Bangla – *italic*

https://bdnews24.com/politics/2015/01/05/sand-laden-trucks-close-off-road-to-khaledas-office

		Facebook status	Translation
1.	Nayeem	*গণতন্ত্রের নতুন সংজ্ঞা* !!!!!!!.........	The new definition of democracy !!!!!!!.........
		On The '*বালুর ট্রাক*', For The '*বালুর ট্রাক*', By The '*বালুর ট্রাক*' !!!!!!!.........	On The 'sand truck', For The 'sand truck', By The 'sand truck' !!!!!!!.........
		Shame George washington !!!!!!!......... u r wrong	Shame George Washington !!!!!!!......... !.........You are wrong ....
2.	XX	Keep it *দোস্ত, তথাকথিত গণতান্ত্রিক দেশ, এর চেয়ে ভাল কিছু আশাও করা যায় না।*	Keep it [up] mate, in this so-called democratic country, we can't hope anything better than this.

Nayeem voices the rhetoric of the country repeatedly represented on media. His voice *pretextually* refers to the bleakness of politics in Bangladesh. Mrs Zia was not permitted to go out of her office; no one was allowed to meet her either. The former President, Badruddoza Chowdhury, was turned away from meeting her. He considered it an insult to democracy (The Guardian, 2015). The sudden confinement of the opposition political leader without any acceptable explanation called down much criticism of the autocratic attitude of the ruling party. The media stated that the Government had resorted to tyrannical acts and had put democracy into a 'poisonous gas chamber'. The police carried out raids and arrested opposition leaders of BNP and, in January, 2015, the police arrested 7015 activists and leaders of opposition, and announced 100,000 taka ($1300) as a bounty on the heads of leaders who were protesting against the ruling party (BBC News, 2015). Similarly, many of the protesters of BNP destroyed vehicles and blocked roads, and 25 people died in the political unrest. The police also used pepper spray to disperse the party leaders and BNP activists waiting inside the gate of the office of Mrs Zia. Several BNP leaders and journalists were also injured in the police action. It was also claimed by the BNP officials that at least 400 party supporters were arrested and harassed, including two senior party figures for marking the 'Democracy Killing Day' (Hanif, 2015).

Nayeem borrows voices from the US President Abraham Lincoln – the closing words of his Gettysburg Address, delivered on 19 November 1863: 'We here highly resolve that these dead shall not have died in vain, that this nation, under God, shall have a new birth of freedom; and that government of the people, by the people, for the people, shall not perish from the earth' (Peters, 2001). Lincoln adapted his version from the abolitionist preacher Theodore Parker's sermon titled 'The Effect of Slavery on the American People', which Parker delivered at the Music Hall in Boston, Massachusetts on 4 July 1858. In that sermon, Parker said: 'Democracy is direct self-government over all the people, for all the people, by all the people'. Parker defined democracy as 'a government of all the people, by all the people, and for all the people' (Peatman, 2013: 28) Nayeem relocalizes these voices (even though he wrongly gives credit to the US President George Washington) and entextualizes it, referring to the absurdities observable in Bangladeshi political arena which impair the democratic rights of people. Thus, with the *intertextual reference* to the statement which historically epitomizes the spirit of democracy, he shows his frustration about the despotic political situations in Bangladesh.

Here the famous quotation gets resemiotized when he replaces the word 'people' with বালুর ট্রাক. With the replacement of the word, he wants to indicate that the presence of sand trucks in front of the office of Ms Khaleda Zia, in fact, has symbolically violated the human rights of the opposition political leader. The democracy of Bangladesh is no longer conducive for people in general, since it can be disrupted easily by placing sand-laden trucks. His friend also supports his contention, stating that Bangladesh is a 'so-called democratic country' and that it is natural that people's democracy and rights can be dishonored and trampled easily.

The entextualization of the closing words of the US President Abraham Lincoln in the Gettysburg Address, the photograph and link to the online news are laden with social, cultural, political and ideological meanings which help Nayeem to articulate his individual and affective condition and his experiences and opinions about the political situation and the contextual realities and collective opinions of people in Bangladesh. The statement of Lincoln is appropriated by Nayeem; it reflects its past history; and simultaneously, it is performed anew, since Nayeem uses it in a 'major radical act of semiotic reconstruction and reconstitution' (Kandiah, 1998: 100). The fluid movement from Bangla to English and English to Bangla, Nayeem's double-voicing, and intended meaning and sarcasm, the image of the sand-loaded truck, and the link to the news – all together contribute to the meaning of his status. Here, resemiotization occurs with the changes in mode, modality and location and the creation of new meanings.

Nayeem is involved in 'verbal art' using Bauman's (2005) term – making a conscious modification of linguistic forms. On the one hand, his language play indexes linguistic and pragmatic competences. On the other hand, as a young adult, he shows himself as a critically aware young Bangladeshi national reflecting on the current political situation in Bangladesh. In addition, his status is strengthened with the presence of other modes of meaning-making and as he selects, combines and moves between modes, he creates a transmodal ensemble.

Extract 2 refers to a series of catastrophic earthquakes that Bangladesh experienced in 2016. The trembles of earthquake were felt throughout the year and people were in a state of panic, since Dhaka city – an over-populated city with 140 million people living in poorly built houses – is prone to earthquakes. According to a research study done by a team of scientists led by Dr Michael Steckler from Columbia University, Dhaka is heading toward a catastrophic disaster (Miller, 2016).

Extract 2

Language guide: English – regular font; Bangla – *italic*

		Facebook status	**Translation**
1.	Ria:	'*ei bhumikompor jonno birodhi dol dayi … eishob* media'*r banano kotha … bangladesh'e kichhui hoi nai!!*	'The opposition party is liable for this earthquake … these are all fictitious propaganda initiated by the media … nothing happened to Bangladesh'.
2.	GFS:	hahahahah …	hahahahah …
3.	Ria:	*akhono hocche bhai*	A tremor is occurring now.
4.	FC:	damn it, u just stole my line, i was going to post this	Damn it, you just stole my line. I was going to post this.
5.	Ria:	share *koro*	Share it.
6.	SK:	Make it public. Needs due credit	Make it public. ((the status)) needs due credit.
7.	Ria:	done … go ahead and make me famous … apparently i am all about the drama … SK should work now ((grin emoticon))	Done … go ahead and make me famous … apparently I am all about the drama … SK should work now ((grin emoticon)).
8.	MI:	Mirpur, Gazipur, Mohammedpur … all reporting fallen buildings.	Mirpur, Gazipur, Mohammedpur … all reporting fallen buildings.
9.	Ria:	*ji* media *birodhi dol er hoye shob mittha chorachhe … apnara shobai nirbhoye bashai tala lagai ghumai thaken*	Yes, media is spreading lies on behalf of the opposition party … all of you lock the door of your house and peacefully sleep at home.
10.	TIK:	R *kom kom khan*	And eat less.
11.	Ria:	wait … *birodhi dol er neta ra shobai apnader* building *kapichhe, ami jante perechhi. oder jonno kothor bebostha newa hobe.*	Wait … the leaders of the opposition party are shaking your buildings. I came to know. Strict steps will be taken against them.
12.	TIK:	*Yea kintu shiri dhore nara chara korate eita hoise!*	Yea but it has happened because of the shaking of the staircases.
13.	Ria:	gate gate!	Gate gate!

14.	TIK:	Omg these statements were hilarious!	Omg these statements were hilarious!
15.	Ria:	oi mohila to aram kore nije bashai boshe achhe... gota desh akhon atongke...tar lojja howa uchit	That lady ((Ms Khaleda Zia)) is comfortably sitting at her home ... the whole nation is traumatized ... she should be ashamed.
16.	Ria:	^^^eita parliament house er speech theke inspired ... i am so proud of myself	^^^ This one is inspired by the parliamentary speech ... I am so proud of myself.
17.	AHS:	excellent!! hahahahahahahahahhhaahaha-hahahahhah!!	Excellent!! hahahahahahahahahhhaa-hahahahahhah!!
18.	THA:	Hahaahahahaha	Hahaahahahaha

In line 1, Ria refers to the earthquakes which have occurred in Bangladesh and mocks the political leaders of the ruling party by entextualizing their comment in her virtual conversation. The commonly uttered political statements recycled on FB by Ria and her friends *intertextually* refer to the blame-games that the political parties, both opposition and ruling, engage in for any sort of anarchy, political unrest, and safety and security issues in the country (Moniruzzaman, 2009). There is also a tendency of the political leaders to belittle the media in the name of yellow journalism if it reveals any loopholes in the government or identifies any misappropriation of power. Hence, expressions such as *ei jonno birodhi dol dayi* [the opposition party is liable for it] and *eishob media'r banano kotha* [these are fictitious propaganda initiated by the media] or *bangladesh'e kichhui hoi nai* [nothing has happened in Bangladesh] are very commonly known and repeatedly used by the political leaders and government key people. However, Ria is deliberately hyperbolic here, blaming political parties for natural calamity. In order to show the propensity of political parties to play the 'blame-game', Ria *subtextually* uses the quotations, resemeoticizing the dialogues of political leaders in Bangladesh.

Ria and her friends, students from the UOE, borrow voices from the political leaders in Bangladesh and resemiotize them with their own intentions and meaning. When Ria entextualizes the usual comments passed by political leaders of both the ruling and opposition parties in Bangladesh, she demonstrates the intense antagonism that both parties carry toward each other. Another widely accepted political practice is blaming each other whenever anything goes wrong in the state machinery. The vicious circle of hostility and bitterness between the ruling and opposition parties has also created public distrust about the competence and capacity of both parties (Moniruzzaman, 2009). Thus line 1 *intertextually* refers to the public acceptance of the two-party blame-game in Bangladesh between the ruling party, Awami League, and the opposition party, BNP.

In line 3, Ria makes fun of the situation, mentioning that the tremor is still going on. She also agrees with her friend to make the status shareable by her friends and she asks them to use it to make her popular. She claims herself as the drama queen. In other words, she is aware of the ludicrousness of the claims she has made. This is intentional since she wants to refer to the political leaders who exaggerate the political violence and unrest committed by followers of the opposition party. Ria and her friends *subtextually* refer to the practice of amplification of the range of violent activities committed by the opposition party. In order to take up the personae of a political leader, in line 8, her friend gives information that all the buildings in Mirpur, Gazipur and Mohammedpur (different localities in Dhaka) are reported to be falling down. In line 9, again Ria is 'double-voicing' (Bakhtin, 1981). She uses the dialogue of the political leaders and asks the Bangladeshi citizens to be peaceful, since nothing alarming has happened to the country. She even suggests that the people of Bangladesh should sleep, locking their doors – just the opposite of what people should do. Here, she takes the voice of the ruling party, which tends to minimize the intensity of any catastrophic events in Bangladesh.

Line 10 is a specific reference to the comment made by the Commerce Minister of Bangladesh, Faruq Khan, on 4 August 2011, in which he instructed the people of Bangladesh to eat less in order to avoid problems, like price hikes of food items and food adulteration (Jahan, 2011). He gave this specific piece of advice when he was questioned about the alarming price hike of food items and people's inability to buy daily necessities in Bangladesh. This comment of the Commerce Minister drew a lot of criticism for his insensitivity toward the pain and deprivation of ordinary people, which includes, in addition to lack of access to food, lack of pure drinking water, an electricity supply crisis, soaring prices of essentials, hot and sultry weather, floods, shortages of gas, power and water, and traffic jams. When the government is failing to provide the citizens the basic facilities, its sermon to 'eat less' is considered unsympathetic and insensitive (Sattar, 2011).

In line 11, Ria again goes back to 'double-voicing', restating what ministers usually claim during any tragedies – that is – that the leaders of the opposition party, in fact, shook the houses, causing the tremor. This statement triggers yet another comment from her friend which *intertextually* refers to the comment made by the country's home minister, Dr Mohiuddin

Khan Alamgir, when an eight-storey building housing several garment factories situated in Savar, Dhaka collapsed, killing over 1134 workers and injuring 2500 on 24 April 2013. The Rana Plaza disaster is considered the worst industrial accident in the history of Bangladesh and deadliest accidental structural failure in modern human history (Revolvy, 2013). While the owner of the building, Sohel Rana, claimed that the crack in the building had been identified as nothing alarming, the Home Minister passed the comment in an interview with BBC Bangla that the opposition party supporters might have shaken the building, leading it to collapse (Gomes, 2013). Eventually it was identified that Sohel Rana is a member of the local unit of 'jubo league' – the youth wing of the ruling party in power, Bangladesh Awami League, and had an affiliation with the ruling party. This accident was followed by two more fire accidents in garment factories in Dhaka that killed at least 117 people and injured at least 200 garment workers (Gomes, 2013). In line 11, Ria also adds that 'strict steps will be taken against them'. These words have two types of use: the government says them, on the one hand, when it intends to harass the leader of the opposition party; on the other hand, they are said as an empty threat when the government does not intend to take any action against the culprits, when these culprits belong to the ruling party. In both cases, their words of taking action against the political hooligans remain unsubstantiated.

In line 12, Ria's friend again *pretextually* refers to the comment made by Ria in line 11, in which she refers to the comment made by Dr Mohiuddin Khan Alamgir. He mentioned that Rapa Plaza collapsed because its columns were shaken by the opposition party leaders gathered in Savar to arrange demonstrations and *hartals*. The Home Minister was criticized for his illogical rationalization of the collapse of the building owned by a leader of the ruling party. To make the claim sound more preposterous, in line 13, Ria comments that it is the shaking of the gate that causes the fall of the building.

In line 15, Ria again takes up the voice of the Prime Minister Sheikh Hasina of Bangladesh. The frosty relationship between Hasina, the Prime Minister and the leader of the ruling party Awami League, and Khaleda Zia, the leader of BNP, is always an issue of public discussion. They have not been on speaking terms for more than a decade and they are constantly accusing each other. Since the ruling party considers the opposition party non-functional, the Prime Minister very often publicly criticizes the opposition leader. Here specific reference is made to the government property in Dhaka Cantonment that Khaleda Zia occupied by dint of her position as a wife of Major Zia, the Army General and the President of Bangladesh from 1977 to 1988, until he was assassinated on 30 May 1981. Former Prime Minister

Khaleda Zia was forced to vacate the upmarket residence in 2010 (The Indian Express, 2010), but she has repeatedly been reminded of her undue advantage and luxurious life. Ria thus mimics the common utterance made by the Prime Minister and the leaders of her political party, Awami league, 'that lady is comfortably sitting at her home ... the whole nation is traumatized ... she should be ashamed'. In the next line, Ria confirms that it is taken from the parliament discussions, showing the ludicrousness of Parliamentary discussions and activities in Bangladesh. Thus, the extract shows that Ria and her friends are engaged in mimicry and 'double-voicing' and by entextualization of these comments they ridicule the absurdity observable in the comments made by the political leaders in Bangladesh. They also satirize the petty politics in Bangladesh, which sustains the party agenda.

Ria and her friends are concerned about the continual earthquakes that have engulfed the lives of Bangladeshis with fear and anxiety. However, they reflect on the grave and volatile political order in Bangladesh with the lightness of mimicry. In the resemiotization process, they mock the nonchalance of the government and opposition parties, unhealthy political competition, political patronage and undemocratic practices and at the same time they emphasize the ludicrousness of how politics works in Bangladesh.

Here it should be mentioned that it is considered unsafe to comment openly about governmental issues since the number of extra-judicial killing has increased alarmingly in the last two decades. The harassment and jailing, torture to death in custody, extrajudicial killing and abuses of human rights have made people in Bangladesh more cautious about the comments they make about political issues in public spaces.

> Governments, past and present, have committed serious human rights abuses. The Special Powers Act, the Code of Criminal Procedure, and the so-called Public Safety Act are continually used to suppress political opposition. Extrajudicial killings, police atrocities, and prolonged detention of citizens without formally charging them are common. (Zafarullah, 2002: 1020)

Hence, it seems that virtual space, in both Extracts 1 and 2, works as a third space for these young adults. Bhabha (1994: 2) defines 'third space' with reference to postcolonial experiences. He identifies 'third space' as the 'in-between space which provides the terrain for elaborating strategies of selfhood, singular or communal – that initiate new signs of identity, and innovative sites of collaboration and contestation'. Here, as well, Nayeem (Extract 1) and Ria and her friends (Extract 2) prove themselves to be critically reflective and they contest the local politics in the third space of virtual space.

In addition, the extracts also draw our attention to the 'local-virtual' interface and demonstrate the permeability of the local to the virtual and the ways virtual works as the 'real' one for these participants in which they can share their opinions which they may not in the offline space (cf. also Sultana, 2016). Even though it may be considered as 'peripheral' in a broader sense, these participants use the virtual space as their 'third space'. They come to terms with issues that are ideological and value-laden and attempt to optimize the structural normativity in the social system by making self-deprecatory fun of their own country as well as of social, cultural and political practices. In other words, they demonstrate themselves as socially, culturally and politically sensitive citizens, who may not have power to change the society radically in 'real' life, but have a yearning to question and destabilize the norms through entextualization and resemiotization in the virtual space.

Conclusion

The chapter shows that Bangladeshi youths' virtual communication is enriched with quotations and images from both the local and global contexts. They decontextualize these linguistic and multimodal resources from dispersed contexts and entextualize and embed them within the layers of conversations in virtual space. They engage in resemiotization of these resources and endow them with new meaning and vitality with a varied range of intentions and purposes. In the process, Bangladeshi youths discursively claim their legitimacy in reusing these local and global multimodal semiotic resources.

Showing the intricate relationship among entextualization and resemiotization, voices and transglossia, the chapter demonstrates how young adults use the virtual space to give alternative views about the political, social and cultural norms in Bangladesh. While they may not have power to destabilize the existing practices in the society, they tend to voice their discomfort, frustration, and anxiety through the voices they borrow. These young adults also show their reservations about the political and social leaders when they engage in sarcasm, mimicry and mockery and express their alternative views of political practices in virtual space. The virtual space becomes a haven of resistance and a site of multidimensional experiences. Through their transglossic practices within the space and in their attempt to linguistically challenge the political, social and cultural practices in Bangladesh, they create their own sense of democratic and liberated self.

Compared with the pervasiveness and strong hold of political ideologies present in the society, the young adults' verbal protest in the virtual space may seem peripheral. However, it is a significant locus for their sense of being. Hence, a perceived dichotomous spatial relationship, such as center/periphery or top/bottom may be questioned. For their sense of being, virtual space does play a central role, even though it may be considered peripheral in the wider discourses. It creates an interface between the global and the local with these resources, engaging with locally relevant political, social and cultural issues. Young adults indicate themselves as politically and socially sensitive and critically aware of the local issues that contradict their individual rhetoric of civility.

Everyday acts of linguistic transgression in virtual space open windows for understanding young adults' denial, the affirmation of linguistic and social boundaries, and the subtle complexities involved in the process. Hence, the chapter concludes that virtual space in the era of globalization, with its immense multimodal potency, gives Bangladeshi youths opportunities for newer forms of communication and novel ways of expressing themselves. Most importantly, linguistic and multimodal semiotic resources, mediated within virtual space, create a fluid and democratic third space for these youths against the backdrop of the society, which is highly structured, normative and politically, socially, culturally and ideologically value-laden.

The chapter demonstrates that transglossic language practices in virtual space do not minimize the power struggle that young adults experience in the offline space. They in fact engage in extextualization and resemiotization within the broader ideological framework of a society. The subject positions negotiated by these participants occur in the nexus of structure and agency – very much lived and sustained in the moment of dialogic interaction, and hence momentary, performative and chaotic. The varied ranges of identity attributes that are unleashed in their language are not stable, but are shifting and transitory. We may develop an emerging feeling about these attributes and we may hear different voices if we listen to them closely, but these voices are continually changing in time and space. With these voices, they construct different facets of identity in different situations for different purposes which indicate the non-monolithic, contextually situated and unpredictable phenomenon of their identity. That is why identity is not something they have, but something they make of themselves with the available linguistic and multimodal resources and voices.

Note

(1) The name of the university and the participants are pseudonyms. The names in capital letters, such as XX and KK did not participate in the research, but agreed that their conversations could be used for research purposes.

References

Androutsopoulos, J. (2006) Introduction: Sociolinguistics and computer-mediated communication. *Journal of Sociolinguistics* 10 (4), 419–438.

Androutsopoulos, J. (2011) From variation to heteroglossia in the study of computer-mediated discourse. In C. Thurlow and K. Mroczek (ed.) *Digital Discourse: Language in the New Media* (pp. 277–298). Oxford: Oxford University Press.

Androutsopoulos, J. (2014) Moments of sharing: Entextualization and linguistic repertoires in social networking. *Journal of Pragmatics* 73, 4–18.

Bakhtin, M. (1981) *The Dialogic Imagination: Four Essays*, trans. C. Emerson and M. Holquist. Austin, TX: University of Texas Press.

Bauman, R. (2005) Indirect indexicality, identity, performance: Dialogic observation. *Journal of Linguistic Anthropolgy* 15 (1), 145–150.

Bauman, R. and Briggs, C.L. (1990) Poetics and performances as critical perspectives on language and social life. *Annual Review of Anthropology* 19 (1), 59–88.

BBC News. (21 January, 2015) Bangladesh arrests 7,000 opposition activists. BBC. See http://www.bbc.com/news/world-asia-30917345

bdnews24 (5 January 2015) Sand-laden trucks close off road to Khaleda's office. *bdnews24*. See https://bdnews24.com/politics/2015/01/05/sand-laden-trucks-close-off-road-to-khaledas-office

Bhabha, H. (1994) *The Location of Culture*. London: Routledge.

Blommaert, J. and Varis, P. (2015) Enoughness, accent and light communities: Essays on contemporary identities. *Tilburg Papers in Culture Studies* 139, 1–72.

Blommaert, J. and Varis, P. (2017) Conviviality and collectives on social media: Virality, memes, and new social structures. *Multilingual Margins: A Journal of Multilingualism from the Periphery* 2 (1), 31–31.

Dovchin, S., Sultana, S. and Pennycook, A. (2016) Unequal translingual Englishes in the Asian peripheries. *Asian Englishes* 18 (2), 92–108.

Dovchin, S., Pennycook, A. and Sultana, S. (2017) *A Popular Culture, Voice and Linguistic Diversity – Young Adults On- and Offline*. New York: Palgrave Macmillan.

Gomes, W. (9 May, 2013) The Rana Plaza tragedy was an outcome of a corrupt system that is rotten to the core. Who should – and can – be held accountable? *Open Democracy*. See https://www.opendemocracy.net/opensecurity/william-gomes/reason-and-responsibility-rana-plaza-collapse

Hanif, A. (5 January 2015) Khaleda Zia urges supporters to protest on 'Democracy Killing Day'. *Arynews*. See https://arynews.tv/en/khaleda-zia-urges-supporters-protest-democracy-killing-day

Huey, L. and Berndt, E. (2008) 'You've gotta learn how to play the game': Homeless women's use of gender performance as a tool for preventing victimization. *The Sociological Review* 56, 177–194.

Iedema, R. (2003) Multimodality, resemiotization: Extending the analysis of discourse as multi-semiotic practice. *Visual Communication* 2 (1), 29–57.

Jahan, N. (19 August, 2011) Commerce minister's advice. *The Daily Star*. See http://www.thedailystar.net/news-detail-199313

Kandiah, T. (1998) Epiphanies of the deathless native user's manifold avatars: A postcolonial perspective on the native speaker. In R. Singh (ed.) *The Native Speaker: Multilingual Perspectives* (pp. 79–110). New Delhi: Sage.

Karim, S. (2014) Erotic desires and practices in cyberspace: 'Virtual reality' of the nonheterosexual middle class in Bangladesh. *Gender, Technology, and Development* 18, 53–76.

Kee, J.S. (2011) *Erotics: Sex, Rights and the Internet*. APC, Ford Foundation.
Leppänen, S. and Piirainen-Marsh, A. (2009) Language policy in the making: An analysis of bilingual gaming activities. *Language Policy* 8 (3), 261–284.
Leppänen, S., Kytölä, S., Jousmäki, H., Peuronen, S. and Westinen, E. (2013) Entextualization and resemiotization as resources for (dis)identification in social media. *Tilburg Papers in Culture Studies* 57, 1–46.
Miller, B. (22 July, 2016) Bangladesh: Hidden fault could trigger major quake. *CNN*. See http://edition.cnn.com/2016/07/21/weather/bangladesh-earthquake-threat/index.html
Moniruzzaman, M. (2009) Party politics and political violence in Bangladesh: Issues, manifestation and consequences. *South Asian Survey* 16 (1), 81–99.
Peatman, J. (2013) *The Long Shadow of Lincoln's Gettysburg Address*. Illinois: SIU Press.
Peters, J.U. (2001) Lincoln's Gettysburg Address. *The Explicator* 60 (1), 22–24.
Pennycook, A. (2004) Critical applied linguistics. In A. Davies and C. Elder (eds) *Handbook of Applied Linguistics* (pp. 784–807). Oxford: Blackwell.
Pennycook, A. (2007) *Global Englishes and Transcultural Flows*. London: Routledge.
Ramany, S. (5 January 2015) 24 trucks parked as Khaleda's confinement continues. *Progressive Bangladesh*. See http://progressbangladesh.com/24-trucks-parked-as-khaledas-confinement-continues/
Revolvy. (2013) Savar building collapse. *Revolvy*. See https://www.revolvy.com/main/index.php?s=2013%20Savar%20building%20collapse&item_type=topic
Sattar, M.A. (19 August, 2011) Pinching words: Weird smiles. *The Daily Star*. See http://www.thedailystar.net/magazine/2011/08/03/impressions.htm
Sultana, S. (2014) Heteroglossia and identities of young adults in Bangladesh. *Linguistics and Education* 26, 40–56.
Sultana, S. (2015) Transglossic language practices: Young adults transgressing language and identity in Bangladesh. *Translation and Translanguaging in Multilingual Contexts* 1 (2), 202–232.
Sultana, S. (2016) Language and identity in virtual space. *Journal of Asian Pacific Communication* 26 (2), 216–237.
Sultana, S., Dovchin, S. and Pennycook, A. (2015) Transglossic language practices of young adults in Bangladesh and Mongolia. *International Journal of Multilingualism* 12 (1), 93–108.
The Indian Express. (29 November, 2010) Khaleda Zia loses posh Dhaka home. *The Indian Express*. See http://indianexpress.com/article/news-archive/print/khaleda-zia-loses-posh-dhaka-home/
The Guardian (5 January, 2015) Bangladesh rocked by violence on election anniversary. *The Guardian*. See https://www.theguardian.com/world/2015/jan/05/bangladesh-violence-election-anniversary-khaleda-zia
Theodoropoulou, I. (2016) Mediatized vernacularization: On the structure, entextualization and resemiotization of Varoufakiology. *Discourse, Context and Media* 14, 28–39.
Thurlow, C. and Mroczek, K. (eds) (2011) *Digital Discourse: Language in the New Media*. Oxford: Oxford University Press.
Varis, P. and Wang, X. (2011) Superdiversity on the Internet: A case from China. *Diversities* 13 (2), 71–82
Zafarullah, H. and Rahman, M. (2002) Human rights, civil society and nongovernmental organizations: The nexus in Bangladesh. *Human Rights Quarterly* 24 (4), 1011–1034. 10.1353/hrq.2002.0055.

2 Linguascaping the City: A Phenomenological Inquiry into Linguistic Place-making of Toronto's Chinatown and Kensington Market Neighborhoods

Dejan Ivković, Violetta Cupial, Jamie Arfin and Tiziana Ceccato

> A great city may be seen as a construction of words as well as stone
> Tuan, 1991: 686

Introduction

In urban spaces, language becomes a landmark. We orient others and ourselves in space with indexicals such as over there, before the Coca-Cola sign. Linguistic objects acquire the orientational function of landscape formations such as hills and rivers as well as human-made structures. Language presence and the use of visual modalities of representation (such as color schemes and special typefaces), coupled with the engagement of auditory, olfactory, haptic and gustatory senses, help us create our own, personal and unique places. This collaborative inquiry explores the agency in linguistic place-making, what we call *linguascaping*. With its emphasis on the process of meaning-making rather than on the materiality or presence of linguistic artifacts, the linguascaping view complements the traditional linguistic landscape approaches (e.g. Backhaus, 2007; Landry & Bourhis, 1997) and thus aims to bring newer insights to the existing sociolinguistics research on linguistic landscaping. It frames the extant discursive formations as contingent on the participants' phenomenologies (Thorne & Ivković, 2015), experiences and views, which wait to be conveyed.

The descriptor *linguascaping* conjures the meaning of *to shape* through and with language (cf. the hypothetical English cognate **to scape*), highlighting the role of human-made and human-experienced environments, including linguistic landscapes. By using the descriptor *linguascaping*, itself containing the Germanic suffix *-skap(e)* – which occurs as a free morpheme in Scandinavian phrases and compounds such as *å skape musikk* (make music) or *musikkskapelse* (music making) in Norwegian – we intend to convey the idea that, in the phenomenological sense, linguistic landscapes are *created* rather than *given a priori*, independent of experience. More specifically, our goal is to derive individual *linguascapes* of a vibrant, historically and culturally sedimented area of Toronto in the phenomenological act of linguascaping. To gather phenomenological data, we use the 'phenomenology walks' protocol (Vagle, 2014). We explore a predefined route in Toronto's neighborhoods of Chinatown and Kensington Market, bustling with businesses and population, that reflects both histories and more recent migratory trends. With a focus on personal meaning- and sense-making in a particular context, for people who share a particular experience of the linguistic landscape of the area examined, we are interested in how people derive their own sense of place-making through and with language. More specifically, the objective of the walk is to 'see (where, what, how, and why) given phenomena reside in various places' (Vagle, 2014: 85) and to identify the tokens of linguistic diversity, including language presence (or absence) and attendant semiotic artifacts, as they are situated in a given locale. The participants have a double role: that of a study participant as well as a researcher and co-author.

To this end, the participants–researchers first create their own phenomenologies of cityspace and then negotiate intersubjective readings. The main question, which serves to galvanize the phenomenological readings of the city, therefore, is: how do I experience and understand the (phenomena of) linguistic and cultural diversity/complexity of cosmopolitan Toronto as presented to me? More specifically, the following questions are addressed: what have I experienced in terms of the phenomena? What contexts or situations have influenced or affected my experiences of the phenomena? We end with the question: what is the potentiality of the concept and the term *linguascaping* to account for the linguo-semiotic place-making as an act of subjective and intersubjective experience of one's multilingual surroundings?

We situate these questions within the Tuanian paradigm of humanistic geography (Tuan, 1977, 1996) amenable to phenomenological inquiries. The phenomenological turn with its attention to the individual and their lifeworld (Cresswell, 2004: 29) complements a social constructivist view, which regards place, like space and time, as a social construct (Harvey, 1996: 261). This view is espoused primarily by sociologists who approach matters of space and place from the viewpoint of critical human geography and social and spatial justice (e.g. Lefebvre, 1991; Soja, 2010).

From Linguascape to Linguascaping

The terms linguascape and linguascaping are not entirely novel in the sociolinguistic literature. Hewitt (1995: 98) understands the global linguascape as the 'linguistic corollary of "ethnoscape"', which he views as a form of supracultural communicative processes, resulting, among other things, in 'the various creole languages and those where new urban forms were being generated through certain kinds of cultural contact within specific political dynamics'. Pennycook (2003) and Dovchin (2014, 2017) anchor *linguascape* within Appadurai's (1996) taxonomy of *scapes*[1] in the age of globalization as fluid, mobile and constantly changing global cultural flows. Pennycook (2003: 524) uses the term to 'capture the relationship between the way in which some languages are no longer tied to locality or community, but rather operate globally with the other scapes'. Dovchin (2017) elaborates further on this idea, focusing on the interactional flows within Mongolia's multilingual linguascapes, where the local meets the global, through English, in the sphere of popular music. By *linguascape*, Dovchin (2017: 16) means 'the transnational flows of linguistic resources circulating across the current world of scapes, creating local linguistic forms whilst intersecting and interjecting with other moving resources across these scapes'. According to Dovchin, the line between what constitutes local and global is not always clear, with English sometimes being perceived even as a local language in the context of Mongolian popular music.

Mufwene (2008: 258) uses the term metaphorically; he attributes changing of the African *linguascape* to the linguistic colonialism of the Western European nations and to new socioeconomic structuration, 'that favoured the emergence of new language varieties', bringing to the fore the changing nature of the phenomenon. Jaworski *et al.* (2003: 19) describe *linguascape* as a product of languages, domestic and host, and their associated referents, such as 'the shots of local people and scenery', ethnic music and even 'sampling and descriptions of local food and drinks' and *linguascaping* as a creative force.

Ivković (2012: 78) describes both linguistic landscape and virtual linguistic landscape as instances of linguascapes, whereby linguascape as a term in its own right, it is suggested, may serve as a common denominator for all of the instantiations of semantic spaces linguistically and semiotically created by human agency in the different embodiments of primarily public spaces, physical or digital. Focusing on the process and agency of the subject of experience, Thorne and Ivković (2015: 185) understand *linguascaping* as a dynamic process of formation of ontologies – discursive elements and practices that mediate social interactions. They explore multilingual communication and interaction on YouTube and conclude that the social media platform shares not only content alone: through postings in YouTube discussion fields, multilingual posters of comments also participate in the dissemination and propagation of beliefs, opinions and attitudes through monolingual and multilingual discussion threads, thus making 'everyday politics and lived ideologies visible as they are produced, transformed and contested', a process that they describe as 'linguascaping.'

Strolling the Cityscapes

Recently, research on the linguistic landscape of the city, amenable to discovery through walking, has garnered the attention of researchers, educators and students (Chern & Dooley, 2014; Chestnut *et al.*, 2013; Garvin, 2010; MacPherson, 2016; Malinowski, 2015; Trumper-Hecht, 2010). Chern and Dooley (2014) outline teaching and learning strategies for English language learners in an EFL context through 'English literacy walks' in which students explore multimodal and multilingual texts in the city of Taipei using digital cameras. With the elementary school student in mind, the teaching ideas that Chern and Dooley present are organized using the 'four resources model', which includes code-breaking, text participation, text use and text analysis to develop literacy skills for beginner to advanced language learners. Chestnut *et al.* (2013: 118) analyze three undergraduate students' experiences of the linguistic landscape of Seoul, focusing on the pedagogical aspects of publicly displayed language in the streets of Korea's capital city. They conclude that the narrative exercise, in which the students 'considered how culture and language shape language perception', contributed to raising awareness of the complex relationship between language and culture, showcasing the inherently idiosyncratic nature of interpretation.

The interpretation of the landscape can vary depending on various factors. According to MacPherson (2016), these linguistic landscape walking tours can be based on a relational approach that involves items such as the walk itself, the walker's physique and the walker's personal preferences and history, specifically, the terrain or length of walk, the pace at which people walk and personal characteristics and experience such as gender and ethnic and cultural background, as well as past experiences. When people complete these walking tours, Macpherson concludes, the above factors impact how they view, interact, and experience their environment.

During the completion of walking tours, different individuals experience different phenomena, perspectives and perceptions, even though they all walked the same route. Garvin (2010: 265) notes that, 'seeing the interpretation of text, images and icons [were] integrated with the [individual] viewer's background and experiences... [which triggered] strong emotions but had different, multiple meanings for each participant'. This is especially true when the perspectives of different ethnic backgrounds are analyzed within a particular linguistic landscape. In a study of the linguistic landscape of Upper Nazareth (Trumper-Hecht, 2010), a city that includes both Arab and Jewish individuals, Arab residents perceived that there was Arabic written on signs in their city, even though Arabic is not permitted, by law, on public signs, as Hebrew serves as the dominant language in this city. Hebrew was visible on 75% of business signs and on 100% of civic signs. Only 5.8% of the business signs included Arabic while there was no Arabic on civic signs.

Micallef (2010) explored the city of Toronto in a collection of psychogeographic walking tours using a combination of history, personal memory and observation in various neighborhoods as a guide for tourists and locals who wish to gain a richer understanding while navigating the city. The following quote from Micallef's narrative compilation of walking tours, in which he depicts his experience of navigating Toronto streets, epitomizes the idea of phenomenological inquiry, set in the context of the urban stroll:

> The old notion of the *flâneur* will be different for whoever engages in this activity, even in a diverse metropolis such as Toronto. But that doesn't mean that other *flâneurs* can't carve out ways to navigate the city comfortably, recording their own insights and noticing the ways their own particular bodies and histories interact with the cityscape. (Micallef, 2010: 11)

This kind of walking, termed *psychogeography* by Guy Debord and the Situationists in 1950s Paris, is concerned with 'the specific effects of the geographical environment, consciously organized or not, on the emotions and behaviour of individuals' (Coverley, 2018: 93).

Chinatown and Kensington Market Neighborhoods

Chinatown and Kensington Market are Toronto's two important historical landmarks frequented both by tourists and locals. The area includes several major streets stretching into Toronto's Downtown Core district, District C01 (Downtown, Little Italy and Little Portugal): Dundas Street West, Spadina Avenue, College Street and Bathurst Street. Kensington Market is an eclectic neighborhood consisting of Victorian-era homes with numerous businesses of various ethnic backgrounds, such as Spanish, Portuguese, Italian and Caribbean, with food specialty stores, restaurants and shops selling apparel. Chinatown, on the other hand, is home to shops, restaurants and businesses primarily from China, Vietnam, Thailand and other countries in the Far East.

In 1787, the British purchased the land – on which today's Kensington Market and Chinatown were built – from three Mississauga Native chiefs in a large sale treaty and settled the area. The population grew from fewer than 200 in the mid-1800s to 3000 in 1900 to 32,000 by 1913 (Cochrane, 2000). By 1931, the area became popular among the Eastern European Jews, who had emigrated as a result of persecution. After World War II, the Jewish population began to move out of Kensington Market toward the city's northwest. In 1947, the area surrounding Elizabeth Street between Queen Street West and Dundas Street West, originally known as Chinatown, was expropriated by the City to build a new city hall and private developers purchased land to build office complexes. As a result, Chinese immigrants and businesses moved west, to an area predominantly occupied by Irish, Jewish, Portuguese and Italian immigrants (Chan, 2013; Yee, 2005). This created the present Chinatown, centered between Spadina Avenue on the West, McCaul Street on the East, College Street to the North and Queen Street to the South (Thompson, 1989). This area was originally called Chinatown West or New Chinatown and was known to be one of the most overcrowded areas in all of Toronto (Thompson, 1989: 187). Thompson notes that residential houses in Chinatown West were in disrepair, although they were worth maintaining as residents desired to live there because it was a '"convenient location to Chinese businesses and their jobs" ... and the presence of other Chinese'. This neighborhood also included a center for social services (e.g. University Settlement House) where services were provided for Chinese immigrants who may not understand or be fluent in English (Thompson, 1989).

From 1950 to 1966, after the move west toward Spadina along Dundas Street, Chinese businesses gradually increased since the prices of buildings were much lower than in old Chinatown (Chan, 2013). Restaurants and groceries and market establishments grew by approximately 50%. In the 1970s, there was also an 'expansion of the Chinatown commercial area' with an influx of capital with new immigrants mostly from Hong Kong (Peng, 1994: 228). Peng (1994: 226) describes how Chinatown West on Dundas Street West between Beverly Street and Spadina Avenue changed from residential to commercial and the resulting atmosphere:

> The expansion of commercial activities in some cases took the form of conversion of existing stores to restaurants or grocery stores, but more often Chinese residents simply tore down old residential houses and constructed brash red brick, two- or three-storey buildings containing a mix of retail, office and restaurant facilities. By the late seventies, on both sides of the street, jumbled shop signs in both English and Chinese advertised everything.

It was in the 1960s and 1970s that, with the introduction of Pierre Trudeau's multiculturalism and changed immigration policies, the Chinese and also the Portuguese population in Toronto increased significantly (Cochrane, 2000; Peng, 1994). Cochrane (2000: 71) describes the influence that the Portuguese had on the Kensington Market neighborhood:

> By the '60s and '70s, Kensington was a major Canadian Portuguese centre. They became a new Kensington colony with a different style, but the same feeling of community ... They painted the old house fronts in bright, warm colours, and decorated front yards with religious icons. Kensington bloomed with the grapevines and vegetables and flowers they grew in their backyards. 'If there was a bit of soil', says Nick Da Silva, 'we grew collards, tomatoes, salsa, grapes.' They also lived the life of immigrants, working hard, learning English and the new ways, and making their home in the new world.

In the 1970s and 1980s, Kensington Market became a trendy tourist destination with the opening of stores such as *Courage My Love*, a vintage clothing store (Cochrane, 2000). In addition, Caribbean 'bakeries and food stores appeared on demand with patties and produce from Jamaica and Barbados ... there was never a concentration of West Indians living in Kensington, but they enjoyed shopping there, because like so many others, they could find familiar things to buy' (Cochrane, 2000: 108). On the other hand, Chinatown remained a cultural hub for the Chinese community. It is reasonable to expect that the demographic history of the area is still visible even though the population distribution has tended to shift in favor of one or the other ethnolinguistic group.

Interpretative Phenomenological Analysis

The philosophical underpinnings

Its Greek etymology – phainomenon ('that which appears') and logos ('study') – suggests that a phenomenological inquiry is interested in how things appear rather than in what things are. Therefore, a phenomenologist seeks to describe a phenomenon not to understand the 'thing' for its own sake but rather to reveal how the thing manifests itself to the subject of experience. With its focus on the subjective dimension of the phenomenological encounter within the life-world, this movement in philosophy challenges the central tenet of the positivist worldview according to which the world is out there to be described and measured independent of our experience. The philosophy of phenomenology recognizes at least three components central to the phenomenological doctrine espoused by Brentano (1838–1917) and Husserl (1859–1938): intentionality, natural attitude vs phenomenological attitude and phenomenological reduction (bracketing) (Sokolowski, 2000).

In the phenomenological sense, *intentionality* is not about intention in its ordinary meaning of purpose, but about directedness toward an object (another term for the technical notion of intentionality is 'aboutness'). Intentionality is 'consciousness of' and 'experience of' something or other (Sokolowski, 2000: 8), produced by the thinking, perceiving Subject in an act of intentional experience (Duranti, 1999: 34). Summarizing Husserl's view on intentionality, Duranti notes that, 'The focus on acts as opposed to entities provided the foundations for Husserl's phenomenology: meanings are constituted in our consciousness through the different ways in which we engage with the world. It is the ability to engage in such acts that makes us meaning-making individuals'.

According to Husserl, one of the obstacles to identifying essential qualities of our individual experience is our *natural attitude*, which is the state one is normally in and how one goes about in everyday life, as-a-matter-of-factly. To counter the natural attitude, Husserl advocates adopting a *phenomenological attitude* that involves stepping outside of the natural attitude and, 'requires a reflexive move, as we turn our gaze from, for example, objects in the world, and direct it inward, toward our perception of those objects' (Smith *et al.*, 2009: 12).

According to the phenomenological doctrine, in order to achieve the phenomenological attitude, we need to (a) develop awareness of the consequences of the natural attitude, (b) put them aside or 'bracket' them (what is also called *phenomenological reduction*) and (c) undertake a detailed examination of our perception of the world and the phenomena in question. The three-step approach is known as the 'phenomenological method'. Interpretative phenomenological analysis (IPA) is a popular approach to qualitative research that draws from the philosophy of phenomenology, in the traditions of Brentano, Heidegger and particularly Husserl (Smith *et al.*, 2009).

Method

Interpretative phenomenological analysis provides a set of guidelines for a systematic inquiry. The method complements as well as enhances more traditional ways of conducting ethnography by zeroing in on a smaller number of cases, which allows the researchers to explore them in greater detail. Rather than identifying and measuring phenomena, phenomenologists favor the human experience, perception, beliefs and what things mean in concrete terms, as a valuable source of data. IPA offers insights into how a specific person, in a specific context, makes sense of a specific phenomenon. The focus of a phenomenological study is 'on descriptions of what people experience and how it is that they experience what they experience' (Patton, 1990: 71).

For Rossman and Rallis (2003: 72), 'the purposes of phenomenological inquiry are description, interpretation, and critical self-reflection into the world'. However, van Mannen (2014: 36) notes that the open stance of phenomenology to the world and a wondering attentiveness does not make one a phenomenologist unless this exaltation is disciplined 'to become productive phenomenological reflection'. According to Smith *et al.* (2009: 33), 'IPA is concerned with human lived experience, and posits that experience can be understood via an examination of the meanings which people impress upon it'. The key orientation of IPA is on the commitment to in-depth analysis of particular experiential phenomena (such as the process of linguistic place-making) conceived from the viewpoint of particular people, in a particular context. On the other hand, experience is also relational and sharable, which allows the researcher to make comparisons and generalizations. The IPA researcher is therefore interested in the exploratory, open question, 'What is the individual experience of a phenomenon?', with the aim to capture variations between co-researchers. In the final stage of the analysis, detailed accounts of individual lived experiences are extracted, generating elaborate patterns as a result of shared phenomenological encounters (Smith *et al.*, 2009).

The present analysis begins with the examination of individual cases, moving forward to an examination of similarities and differences across the cases. More specifically, the investigation begins with an attempt to discern emerging themes in participants' individual phenomenological accounts, proceeding to the parsing of shared themes. Following this methodological trajectory, we approach this inquiry by adding an additional hermeneutic dimension, whereby participants step into the role of researchers and collaborators.

Participants as researchers

The project involves three former graduates of the MA program in Education at York University in Toronto (linguascapers), who partake in all key phases of the study led by their instructor: data collection, data analysis, text production and research dissemination at conferences (Ivković *et al.*, 2017) and in social media, such as Facebook (www.facebook.com/LinguascapingToronto). All three linguascapers are female, presently working as teachers. They previously took a graduate seminar in urban sociolinguistics and education at York University in Toronto with the project leader. The course provided training in the conceptualization and conduct of language-related research in urban contexts characterized by transnational migration, transience and flux. The thematic focus – within the broader topic of language in the cosmopolis – of the graduate seminar was on three interrelated areas of inquiry: superdiversity, linguistic landscape and language use in the digital realm. The course explored the following methodological approaches to analyzing language and multilingualism: autoethnography, surveys and interviews, phenomenology and psychogeography, discourse analysis, multimodal and semiotic analyses and corpus linguistics (Ivković, 2014).

For their final project, the students were asked to conduct a phenomenological investigation of a block or a neighborhood in Toronto, focusing on linguistic and cultural diversity. Moreover, the thematic and methodological preparation, as well as the final project, provided the students with the toolkit to conduct language-related research on urban conglomerations, but also equipped them with necessary theoretical and conceptual knowledge for conducting the phenomenological analysis at hand. While all seven students who completed the seminar were invited to participate, two years after, three students remained in the project: Jamie, Tiziana and Violetta. Each of them brings their unique experience and paints their own account of the area of Toronto around Chinatown and Kensington Market. Jamie's, Tiziana's and Violetta's life stories distinctly shape the context and thus situate their individual phenomenologies.

Jamie was born in a Montreal family which spoke English and French. While English is her dominant language, she studied French and Hebrew, the latter being utilized in synagogue and on her trips to Israel as a *Taglit Birthfight Israel* trip leader. Tiziana is a first-generation Italian-Canadian, who speaks both English and Italian fluently, having learned Italian at home. She grew up and still lives in a mid-size city, 100 kilometers east of Toronto. Violetta grew up in Poland and Germany, and migrated to Canada as an adolescent. While Polish and English are her dominant languages, she is fluent in German and studied French and Hebrew as additional languages. On two occasions, in 2015 and 2016, Jamie, Tiziana and Violetta, individually, embarked on a psychogeographic stroll following the same path, in the iconic neighborhoods of Chinatown and Kensington Market.

Data collection

According to Vagle (2014: 86), 'The phenomena do not exist in vacuums and intentionalities run all over the place – in systems, in discourses, in the ways objects are arranged, for example in a room, in a theater, in a home, in a classroom, in a hospital, on a street corner, in an art gallery, in a prison, and in practice'. To examine these cultural artifacts, we adopted the phenomenological walk protocol (Vagle, 2014: 85). Its purpose was to discern where, what, how and why the phenomena under investigation might exist. The total length of the route covered is 3.6 km. The walk originated at The Art Gallery of Ontario (AGO) and included the following streets, in the direction pointed by the arrow (see Figure 2.1): AGO → Dundas Street West → Spadina Avenue → College Street → Bathurst Street → Dundas Street West → Augusta Avenue → Baldwin Street → Kensington Avenue → Dundas Street West → AGO.

'Phenomenology walk' protocol

The protocol served as a data-gathering tool, but also 'as an opportunity to bridle and practice openness to the phenomenon and contextualize it' (Vagle, 2014: 86). The protocol provided the participants with a set of guidelines for constructing phenomenological narratives, the aim of which was to capture observations of unexpected, poignant and interesting objects, activities, settings and circumstances. To effectively observe the space and take detailed notes, the participants were asked to reflect on the following inquiry-guiding questions: what is happening here? What is the purpose of the place? What conversations and practices take place here? Furthermore, the participants were asked to draw upon their own understandings of phenomenological research and ecological aspects of the place, 'paying special attention to the cultures, discourses, systems and

Figure 2.1 The map of the walking route

everyday practices' (Vagle, 2014: 86). To gather phenomenological data, the participants used their cameras for stills as well as other gadgets to record videos and sound.

Narratives and Emerging Themes

> The act of walking is to the urban system what the speech act is to the language or to the statement uttered
> de Certeau, 1984: 97

Four dominant themes emerged from the narratives, further grouped into two distinct categories: *Environment* (Themes 1 and 2) and *Myself* (Themes 3 and 4). (a) The first theme elaborates on dynamics of human activity in city spaces. (b) The second theme addresses presence (or absence) of particular language(s) and associated cultural artifacts. (c) The third theme focuses on memories and associations. (d) Finally, the fourth theme centers on the feeling of inclusion/exclusion. To further illustrate the themes, the narrative excerpts – here described as *scenes* – are selected, as follows.

Environment

The themes of *human activity and interaction* and *language presence* are concerned with the external factors influencing perceptions and understanding of the space. The focus is on what I feel is out there in the space I am surrounded with (e.g. '*There is* [italicized for emphasis] a cluttered feeling', in Scene 1 below), rather than on how I feel (e.g. '*I* [italicized for emphasis] feel overwhelmed ...', in Scene 9). The latter, lingering in the background, is part of the phenomenological encounter with the 'intended object' (Brentano).

Theme 1: Human activity and interaction

Scene 1

> I pass by *Ten Ren's Green Tea* on the north side of the street. They display beautiful traditional teapots in the window. I notice they also sell bubble tea. Back on the sidewalk, I see many different trinkets spilling out of shops on to the street. It's very colorful. There is a cluttered feeling as the contents of merchant shops overflow onto the sidewalk forcing pedestrians to take notice. There is a great energy about this area. I hear various conversations in different languages and people hustle by on their way to wherever they're headed this sunny Wednesday afternoon during rush hour. Everyone seems to be out today. I pass by the bank, CIBC, which is written in English and Chinese script. (Jamie)

Scene 2

> So, I just crossed the street, heading north on Spadina. The audible tone of the crosswalk signal is in the background again. Reaching the other side of the street, I see a really cool dragon sculpture, two of them together where people are standing waiting for the streetcar. Again, looking at the signs here at this corner there are lots of Chinese and English signs to the left, to the right. Here's another one, Bank of Montreal with a Chinese/English sign. There are some exotic types of fruits such as fruit from Thailand and simpler items such as sweet oranges, all at reasonable prices. It is busy and there are people of both Chinese and English descent, more Chinese than English, mind you, although some girl just walked by me and she was speaking in French! I have someone behind me that is speaking in a European language, but I can't seem to decipher what it is. The signs continue to be written in English and Chinese, over and over again. *Kim Cuong Jewelers* doesn't seem to have any Chinese characters

on it, even though the store seems vacant. Maybe it's his last name? Across the street, again, Chinese stores are around and then right in between the Chinese stores is a mixture of Chinese and solely English signs. (Tiziana)

Scene 3

It strikes me that it is a lot quieter on College coming up to Bathurst. I think about how busy and loud Dundas east of Spadina was and in comparison, College Street is extremely calm and less populated. I expected a continuation of the business of Dundas on Spadina and College because they are major streets, but I just don't feel it here. The sidewalks are wide and the traffic seems to be moving better here. There are a lot of new restaurants and bars that have appeared over past few months and the past year ... I am walking south on Bathurst and there are a lot less people. The sun is shining. This area feels much more residential and I don't see businesses here. I look down the alleyway behind *Sneaky Dee*'s and the businesses on the south side of College and I see a wall filled with posters. It must be targeted at the smokers who stand outside of the club. The posters are all in English. (Jamie)

Human activity and interaction are more intense in certain stretches of the participants' walk than in other areas. The first two scenes give a sense of vibrant activity and human interaction that the participants experience on the first part of their walk. For example, Jamie and Tiziana describe Dundas Street West, from the Art Gallery of Ontario to Spadina Avenue, and north on Spadina Avenue, from Dundas Street West to College Street (see the map in Figure 2.1), as being bustling with people and activity. The stretch exhibits a variety of action and movement, including vehicular traffic, as well as people walking by and speaking in different languages, while moving throughout the space. The signage and the businesses in these areas are also plentiful, showcasing bilingual and monolingual inscriptions, mainly in English and Chinese.

Tiziana notices a display of exotic fruits from Thailand, and reacts with surprise (note an exclamation mark) on hearing one passerby speaking French, and others chatting in another European language that she cannot precisely identify. Later, when they both move westward, along College Street and eventually south on Bathurst Street, human activity is noticeably reduced. Jamie comments on how this drop in activity is contrary to what she had expected considering that this part of the route took place on major Toronto streets. She explains in Scene 1 that even the items for sale in the businesses demand the attention of the passerby, thus forcing interaction with the space. Violetta also experiences the decrease in human activity and interaction on College Street, hearing only English, as illustrated with the beginning line in Scene 4, when she discusses the theme of presence/absence of a particular language and associated referents.

Theme 2: Presence/absence of a particular language and associated referents

Scene 4

> Interestingly, on my walk on College Street, I do not hear any languages other than English. I decide to have a warm ramen bowl in the Japanese restaurant on College Street. As I enter and sit down, one of the waitresses brings me a menu. The menu is in Japanese and English. Most of the customers are Caucasian, except for a couple who seem to be Asian. As I sit down, I notice that all of the staff members are Asian in the restaurant. This piques my interest to determine what language they were speaking. After much attentive listening, I determined that all of the staff members are actually Japanese. I thought about the concept of authenticity. A friend once told me that it is difficult to find real Japanese restaurants in Toronto because most of them are businesses run by Chinese people. Well, here I was in an authentic Japanese restaurant run by Japanese people who made their signature dishes. (Violetta)

Scene 5

> I arrive at the intersection of Bathurst Street and College Street. Here I notice the sign *Italy Village*. I look around and do not hear any Italian language or see any Italian business in this neighborhood. I am surprised because the sign indicated to me that the specific area would have been taken over by the specific cultural group as it was in Chinatown. I am deliberating whether this area was ever as culturally vibrant as Chinatown is currently? Has the Italian community abandoned the area? (Violetta)

Scene 6

> Also a *Kooyi* Korean grill, unfortunately it looks like they're closed. There is also *Pizzeria via Mercanti* – another Italian pizza store with the Italian flag on it and the green, white and red painted below their logo. Some of the customers here on the patio were quite observant watching me talk and take pictures of the actual storefront. I also noticed a *Carlo's House of Spice* (Figure 2.2) and *Kings Café*, all signs in English that look like they are written in another language. There's *El buen precio Tienda Hispana*, which is Spanish and *Sweet Olenka's* definitely an Eastern-European name and *Hungary Thai* (Figure 2.3), which is an interesting name – combining a country name from Europe with a cuisine from the Pacific Ocean. Makes me wonder what kind of food they serve and/or what was the purpose to naming their restaurant that way. (Tiziana)

Figure 2.2 *Carlo's House of Spice*, 190 Augusta Avenue, Kensington Market henomenology Walk' Protocol

Participants noticed that some neighborhoods are more linguistically diverse than others. In Scene 4, Violetta comments that on College Street she only hears English, but then comes across a restaurant with Japanese food, which she visits. While ordering a meal, she observes that, in an Asian restaurant with the majority of customers of European descent, the menu is bilingual, in Japanese and English. After listening carefully to the conversation, she corrects herself in the previous assumption that the staff is not Chinese, but actually Japanese. Nevertheless, this leads her to think about the concept of authenticity. Further, along the way, she enters Little Italy, which is announced to her with the *Italy Village* sign (Scene 5). She now directs her attention not to the presence of English, but to the absence of spoken Italian, in an area called Little Italy. She wonders what has happened to the community once inhabiting the space. In Scene 6, Tiziana brings to our attention two examples of playful, hybridized use of writing systems. The Devanagari-like (a writing system used in Sanskrit and some other languages of India) inscription is fused with the Latin alphabet to represent the word 'spice' (Figure 2.2). A few meters further, she identifies another example of fusion, this time cultural and culinary (Figure 2.3). The restaurant offers menu items from the Hungarian and Thai

Figure 2.3 *Hungary Thai* Fusion Restaurant, 196 Augusta Avenue, Kensington Market

cuisines, announced by the flags of the Eastern European and Asian countries, and the inventive play with the noun Hungary and the adjective hungry, in symbiosis with the word Thai. Language presence (or absence) and the graphical representation of messages, such as typeface and lettering, is indexical of particular communities, ethnically marking a particular geopolitical location through symbolic means (Scollon & Scollon, 2003).

Myself

The themes of *memories and associations* and *feeling of inclusion/ exclusion* are concerned with the internal: where I fit in and how I perceive my place and myself in this space. Here the focus is not on what (I think) reality is like, but rather on my perceptions of, and reaction to, my surroundings.

Theme 3: Memories and associations

Scene 7

Across the street I see a building that says *Shaolin Lucky Food Mart*. There are businesses on every level – a tutoring center at the top with a sign featuring both Chinese characters and English words; pictures of dancers and some sort of food restaurant in the middle; and a moose (Figure 2.4), likely once part of Toronto's public art project featuring moose sculptures back in the 1990s/early 2000s. I remember the city-wide

Figure 2.4 *Shaolin Lucky Food Mart*, 393 Dundas Street West

art project when I was in grade school. Different places were given a big white moose, which could then be decorated. My high school was given a few because we had a visual arts program. I remember the moose stood in our lobby covered in whatever my peers had dreamed up. Here in Chinatown, almost twenty years later, stands a decorated moose. At street level, the building houses a fruit market with both Chinese and English writing on the signs. (Jamie)

Scene 8

I know *Scadding Court* has and continues to be an important place for the surrounding neighborhood. My husband used to play basketball there on Sundays. I've also heard stories from his *Bubby* (Grandmother) about the community center when she lived in Kensington as a young girl. At that time there was a strong Jewish presence. (Jamie)

Scene 9

Above the various fruits and vegetables, I notice a large yellow sign which reads the following text: *'Place all items from our store in shopping cart* and basket and not in your eco shopping bag until all items are paid for at the cashier. Please be advised that all shoplifting will be dealt by the law' (Figure 2.5). Next to the English text is, I believe, a Chinese version of the text in red letters. As I read the sign I think about its meaning. First, the phrase *eco shopping bag* stands out to me, as I have never heard that phrase being used in an English context by the people I know to be native English speakers. What comes to my mind is actually a German phrase where the speakers often use the words *Oko Tute/Tasche*, which is commonly used in German to indicate an environmentally friendly bag. Second, what is also visible to me here is that, perhaps, the sign is necessary so that individuals from different cultural backgrounds do not misunderstand their intentions during shopping and that there is no room for cultural and linguistic misunderstanding. Much of how the shop is set up and how the owner is interacting and bartering with the customers reminds me of the time I used to live and go grocery shopping in Korea. It seems that all of the people who are interacting with one another know each other well and are part of this community. (Violetta)

Perceptions of, and reactions to, the surroundings are often grounded in the participants' memories either in relation to the particular space or

Figure 2.5 'Eco-bag' sign on Spadina Avenue

as an association to people, other places or past events. In Scene 7, Jamie, who is a long-time resident of Toronto, recalls her grade school days evoked by the sight of the familiar moose sculpture that is still present (Figure 2.4). In Scene 8, she draws on the stories about Kensington Market that her husband's Jewish grandmother (*Bubby*) has told. She interprets the changes of the Jewish presence in the area, described by the grandmother, through the interwoven narratives of her family history as well as her own memories. In Scene 9, Violetta interprets the market in Chinatown through the lenses of her memories of a South Korean market. She uses her past experiences of traveling in East Asia and Germany to interpret the current space by making inferences as to the meaning and purpose of the prohibitive message (Figure 2.5).

Theme 4: Feeling of inclusion/exclusion

Scene 10

> I continue west on Dundas. I hear different languages as I walk, including Mandarin and Cantonese, although I'm not 100% sure. I see more multistory buildings with different restaurants displaying mini pictures of different types of food available. Perhaps these pictures are meant for those who cannot read Chinese and/or are not familiar with various regional cuisines. I pass by stores with wares spilling onto the street and again, I notice multiple-leveled buildings inhabited by different businesses. I see a number of spas and places where you can get a massage, as well as restaurants. It feels very densely populated here. There are so many signs. I can't read many of them. I feel overwhelmed by the sheer number of them. (Violetta)

Scene 11

> I'm at Huron and Dundas and streetcars zoom by. I look and see some dead ducks hanging in a restaurant window. A disturbing sight indeed. There are so many different smells as I stroll along walking by restaurants and markets. Seeing all the signs here remind me of being in certain areas of Beijing and Shanghai when I traveled there six or seven years ago. I notice a banner advertising space for rent and a realtor's contact. It is in Chinese characters. This banner is so intentionally targeting Chinese speakers or readers in Toronto. I think about how language really can include and exclude others. I also notice a sign in Chinese characters along with a Canadian flag. I have no idea what it says, but it makes me think about the multifaceted nature of identity. This sign is aimed at Chinese-Canadians. There is a duality of identities represented in this sign. It is not intended for me, an English-speaking Canadian, who

cannot speak or read Chinese characters. This sign is very specifically targeted. It prompts me to think of what it means to be Canadian in such a diverse city. It means so many different things to different people and in Chinatown it is one part of a much larger narrative of being Chinese or of Chinese descent in another country. (Jamie)

Scene 12

We're back to the *Tim Horton*'s that has only English characters on its sign and I have a sense of comfort and familiarity again, but as we're across the street, we're seeing a lot of Chinese and/or Korean only signs that are protruding off the sides of the buildings, that is those that are sticking out of the building – not those that are flush. I've just counted two that are fully Chinese. The other ones are both bilingual with English. Even the signs advertising the restaurant food, which is nice to see – a mixture of both but some are all in Chinese, except for how much it costs! It is still very overwhelming to see – all these unfamiliar characters coming at you when you don't understand what they mean, especially since further down, many of these signs are solely in other languages. It's funny because while my husband keeps harping about being hungry, I'm feeling overwhelmed about what I see around me. […] I saw fluorescent signs that are entirely written in Chinese. This time I'm feeling more overwhelmed walking along this side of the street due to the number of signs that are solely written in a language I don't know. I'm shocked because how are the people who walk by supposed to know what is being said on the sign? Is this neighborhood solely geared toward a single linguistic community – what about the rest of the individuals in the city who want to come to visit? Won't they feel left out if they can't understand what is being said? These are some of the thoughts that went through my mind as I was walking back to the AGO. (Tiziana)

Entering space where one's language or culture is not represented may make one feel alienated and excluded. In Scene 10, Jamie describes feeling overwhelmed by seeing and hearing multiple languages that she does not understand. In Scene 11, she describes the street signage as targeting a single group, namely, Chinese-Canadians, revealing the multifaceted nature of Canadian identity. She is aware that there is an intention to communicate but not to her. Similarly, in Scene 12, Tiziana questions the intentions of having the messages geared exclusively toward specific groups and the impact that this may have on others (Figure 2.6). She notes that the linguistic profile of a given area may make it more inclusive to one group, while excluding those who do not comprehend the language. On the other hand, one of the salient moments in all three of the narratives, exemplified in Scene 12, is the presence of the Tim Horton's – Canada's

Figure 2.6 Hand-written messages in Simplified Chinese

famous chain with coffee and donut shops spread throughout the country – alcoved in Chinatown, with signage exclusively in English. The presence of a shared language serves as a code and also has an emblematic function. It may serve to flag an Anglophone Canadian area, while creating an inclusive space for those English speakers who are not bilingual with Chinese, without excluding those who are.

Discussion

> Place is security, space if freedom
> Tuan, 1977

Towards a phenomenology of linguascaping

Mediated through language and personal narratives, among other semiotic conduits, phenomenological experience, as evidenced, is constituted in numerous episodes, large and small, imprinted on our minds that may or may not resurface in our conscious awareness. Once the experience becomes explicit, it becomes a word, corroborating in evoking a sense of place: a more concrete, stable and secure incarnate of space (Tuan, 1977: 7). Tuan

(1991) notes that physical spaces are imbued with meanings as a result of large and small events, while the former, he goes on to say, are often passed on orally and recorded in people's lore. The latter, seemingly inconsequential, 'will quickly fade from memory if their unique flavor and poignancy were not recreated in words, preferably written words that endure and have a certain public visibility' (1991: 693). The narrative transformation of supposedly unattended happenings renders the invisible visible once told and shared, as exemplified in this quote from Scene 2, 'some girl just walked by me and she was speaking in French!' Words thus become part of the places they depict, just like a label or a tag. It is the traces of a constant flow of people and their actions in public spaces that constitute the fleeting reality of everyday life. Unrecorded, these voices remain flickering moments of a conversation and vestige of images that, perhaps, no one has ever *intended* (heard, seen or otherwise brought attention to), except for those involved. '[W]ritten signs are always traces of human activity' (Blommaert, 2010: 31). They disclose the underlying motivations in the process of production of semiotic artifacts. Once some worker puts signs up (Figure 2.5, Scene 9), now situated, they become 'ordinance in place', as well as 'biding law when and where the signs are posted, when and where the signs become discourses in place' (Scollon & Scollon, 2003: 1).

Although simulacra of events, things or people, recorded traces of human activity reveal their stable nature before us more readily because we may return to them and experience them anew. On their own or coupled with the physical landscape forms they latch on, the moments of human activity become places each time someone engages with the text or image. Once told or signed or written down, painted or composed, they extend the physical space: crossing a street, entering a building and window-shopping are some of the activities for which we are likely to need language to navigate through in urban spaces. We perform these sequences of steps quite routinely even if we are not particularly familiar with the space, drawing from previous experiences in similar environments.

One's sense of wonder is lost in the encounter with the expected. A first-time Toronto visitor who lives in New York, perhaps, wouldn't need much effort to find their way around Toronto's Chinatown, thus missing an opportunity to experience the surroundings to the fullest. In contrast, by abandoning the *natural attitude*, which shapes our everyday life and also ensures that we function productively in the society otherwise constrained by time and space, we privilege certain phenomena over others by purposefully bestowing them with attention and thus examining the phenomena in more detail. Then, while navigating busy metropolitan areas, we direct our attention to the choice of language presented to us on a billboard and in window displays. In a moment of heightened awareness, we recall our memories (Scene 8) to create new and recreate old assumptions (Scene 9), to form a chain of associations (Scene 4) and experience emotions (Scene 11). Recalling the city-wide art project and reminiscing on time spent in grade school, evoked by the image and inscription *Shaolin Lucky Food Mart* and the image of a moose right in front (Scene 7, Figure 2.4), indexical of Chinese and mainstream Canadian cultures, respectively, may serve as an example of all those mental states mentioned above.

This move is the first step leading to the phenomenological attitude, still restricted to the subjective side of experience. In this phase, we already go beyond the everyday encounter with a word or an image in our surroundings, yet stay in the realm of the Self. It is only when we are capable of taking a step back from the subjective experience by bracketing it that we are closer to seeing the phenomenon in its essence. Once we distance ourselves from the things observed, examine them, and thematize them in a theoretical manner, we are completing a full phenomenological circle.

Through this turn toward *phenomenological reduction* (bracketing, epoche), which guides us back to the objective world and the source of meaning, what initially appeared to us as 'a cluttered feeling' and 'a great energy' (Scene 1) in some parts of the city but not in other parts, now becomes a distinctive marker of the effects of mobility resting in the new tapestry of migratory patterns of globalization and a pointer of urban cities in transition (Garvin, 2010). A surprise effect, expressed in writing by an exclamation mark, of overhearing a French conversation (Scene 2) in 'unexpected places' (Pennycook, 2012), is now a testimony to the corollaries of the rapid changes (Scene 5). We now reveal authenticity and hybridity (Blommaert & Varis, 2011), in which 'language plays a role in the management of shifting relations between commodity' (Heller, 2003: 474), in Scene 4 identified as the dialectical triad of the Japanese food as a consumer product, people of European descent as consumers and Chinese managers as business owners. What initially appeared as 'signs in English that look like they are written in another language' (Scene 6; see Blommaert, 2010: 29; Ivković, 2015: 90) emerges as an index of cultural and linguistic blending and inclusion (Scene 10), whereby, playfully merging the resources from different writing systems, the sign-owners skillfully expand their client base.

The concept and its name

Linguascaping is introduced as a construct, a metaphor and a heuristic. As a construct, *linguascaping* highlights the transformative power of language and its capacity to create and recreate personal 'places' endowed with human meaning. It emphasizes the intrinsically idiosyncratic nature of the experience as a result of the encounter of the Self with a given space and one's surroundings, as well as the capacity of language to co-construct and co-create intersubjective meanings through shared experiences. As a metaphor, *linguascaping* stands for place-making, as its name and the morpheme *-skape* (to make, to create) suggest. It brings to the fore the process of discursive formations of ontologies (Thorne & Ivković, 2015) here and now, empowered by language, in contrast to and in concert with the objective reality that exists regardless of our grasp of it. As a heuristic, *linguascaping* presents a set of steps, with the purpose to lead an inquirer through a systematic discovery of intimate as well as shared exploits of space with language as a focal point and using IPA to execute these steps.

Conclusion

Focusing on Toronto's urban spaces, the collaborative initiative explores the agency of language and other semiotic means in the process of linguistic place-making, what we are terming *linguascaping*. The aim of this chapter is two-fold: first, it has introduced IPA as an approach to qualitative inquiry in the linguistic landscapes studies framed as *linguascaping* or linguistic place-making. Second, the chapter has shown the theoretical and methodological promise of the framework, seen as the agentive process of creating and co-creating personal and shared readings of urban spaces, to uncover negotiated and intersubjective, but also idiosyncratic, interpretation of linguistically and culturally complex discourses. As the narrative excerpts (scenes) and the analysis of emerging themes have shown, the interpretation of space is subjective and contextual. Interpretations are highly contingent on participants' life-world – histories, backgrounds, linguistic repertoires, memories – which is in constant flux, but which still displays stability allowing accounts of life experiences to be shared and reified. The study reveals the following emergent themes: human activity and interaction, the presence/absence of a particular language and associated referents, memories and associations, and a feeling of inclusion/exclusion. Exemplifying the role of subjectivity and intersubjectivity in linguistic profile of urban spaces, this study may serve as a blueprint for a collaborative project, involving not only an instructor and students, but also professional ethnographers in uncovering impressions of globalization in cosmopolitan cityspaces on individuals.

Note

(1) Appadurai (1996) identifies the following 'scapes': ethnoscape (transnational flows of people), technoscape, mediascape, fianancescape (flows of money, goods and capital) and ideoscape (ideas and ideologies).

References

Appadurai, A. (1996) *Modernity at Large: Cultural Dimensions of Globalization* (Vol. 1). Minneapolis, MN: University of Minnesota Press.
Backhaus, P. (2007) *Linguistic Landscapes: A Comparative Study of Urban Multilingualism in Tokyo.* Clevedon: Multilingual Matters.
Blommaert, J. (2010) *The Sociolinguistics of Globalization.* Cambridge: Cambridge University Press.
Blommaert, J. and Varis, P. (2011) Enough is enough: The heuristics of authenticity in superdiversity. *Tilburg Papers in Culture Studies* 2, 1–13.
Chan, A. (2013) *The Chinese Community in Toronto: Then and Now.* Toronto, ON: Dundurn.
Chern, C.I. and Dooley, K. (2014) Learning English by walking down the street. *ELT Journal* 68 (2), 113–123. See http://eprints.qut.edu.au/63299
Chestnut, M., Lee, V. and Schulte, J. (2013) The language lessons around us: Undergraduate English pedagogy and linguistic landscape research. *English Teaching* 12 (2), 102.
Cochrane, J. (2000) *Kensington.* Erin, Ontario: Boston Mills Press.
Coverley, M. (2018) *Psychogeography.* Oldcastle Books Ltd.
Cresswell, T. (2004) *Defining Place. Place: A Short Introduction.* Malden, MA: Blackwell Ltd, 12.
de Certeau, M. (1984) *The Practice of Everyday Life*, trans. Steven Rendall. Berkeley: University of California Press.
Dovchin, S. (2014) The linguascape of urban youth culture in Mongolia (Doctoral dissertation).
Dovchin, S. (2017) Translocal English in the linguascape of Mongolian popular music. *World Englishes* 36 (1), 2–19.
Duranti, A. (1999) Intentionality. *Journal of Linguistic Anthropology* 9 (1/2), 134–136.
Garvin, R. (2010) Postmodern walking tour. In E. Shohamy, E. Ben-Rafael and M. Barni (eds) *Linguistic Landscape in the City* (pp. 254–276). Bristol: Multilingual Matters.
Harvey, D. (1996) *Justice, Nature and the Geography of Difference.* Oxford: Blackwell.
Heller, M. (2003) Globalization, the new economy, and the commodification of language and identity. *Journal of Sociolinguistics* 7 (4), 473–492.
Hewitt, R. (1995) The umbrella and the sewing machine: Transculturalism and the definition of Surrealism. In A. Aalund and R. Granqvist (eds) *Negotiating Identities* (pp. 91–104). Amsterdam: Rpdopi.
Ivković, D. (2012) Virtual linguistic landscape: A perspective on multilingualism in cyberspace. Unpublished doctoral dissertation, York University.
Ivković, D. (2014) *Language in the Cosmopolis: Theory and Method* [Syllabus]. Toronto, Ontario: Faculty of Education, York University.
Ivković, D. (2015) Towards a semiotics of multilingualism. *Semiotica* 207, 89–126.
Ivković D., Cupial V., Arfin J. and Seccato T. (2017, July) A phenomenological Inquiry into Linguo-semiotic placemaking of Toronto's Chinatown and Kensington Market neighbourhoods. Paper presented at *Semiofest*, Toronto.

Jaworski, A., Thurlow, C., Lawson, S. and Ylänne-McEwen, V. (2003) The uses and representations of local languages in tourist destinations: A view from British TV holiday programmes. *Language Awareness* 12 (1), 5–29.

Landry, R. and Bourhis, R.Y. (1997) Linguistic landscape and ethnolinguistic vitality: An empirical study. *Journal of Language and Social Psychology* 16 (1), 23–49.

Lefebvre, H. (1991) *The Production of Space* (Vol. 142). Blackwell: Oxford.

MacPherson, H. (2016) Walking methods in landscape research: Moving bodies, spaces of disclosure and rapport. *Landscape Research* 41 (4), 425–432.

Malinowski, D. (2015) Opening spaces of learning in the linguistic landscape. *Linguistic Landscape* 1 (1), 95–113.

Micallef, S. (2010) *Stroll: Psychogeographic Walking Tours of Toronto.* Coach House Books.

Mufwene, S.S. (2008) *Language Evolution: Contact, Competition and Change.* London: Continuum International Publishing Group.

Patton, M.Q. (1990) *Qualitative Evaluation and Research Methods.* London: Sage.

Peng, J. (1994) A community in motion: The development of Toronto's Chinatown and Chinese Community, 1947–1981. Unpublished doctoral dissertation. The University of Guelph, Guelph, Ontario.

Pennycook, A. (2003) Global Englishes, rip slyme, and performativity. *Journal of Sociolinguistics* 7 (4), 513–533.

Pennycook, A. (2012) *Language and Mobility: Unexpected Places.* Bristol: Multilingual Matters.

Rossman, G.B. and Rallis, S.F. (2003) *Learning in the Field: An Introduction to Qualitative Research* (2nd edn). Thousand Oaks, CA: Sage.

Scollon, R. and Scollon, S.W. (2003) *Discourses in Place: Language in the Material World.* Routledge.

Soja, E.W. (2010) *Seeking Spatial Justice* (Vol. 16). Minneapolis, MN: University of Minnesota Press.

Sokolowski, R. (2000) *Introduction to Phenomenology.* Cambridge: Cambridge University Press.

Smith, J.A., Flowers, P. and Larkin, M. (2009) *Interpretative Phenomenological Analysis: Theory, Method, Research.* London: Sage.

Thompson, R.H. (1989) *Toronto's Chinatown: The Changing Social Organization of an Ethnic Community.* New York: AMS Press.

Thorne, S.L. and Ivković, D. (2015) Multilingual Eurovision meets plurilingual YouTube. *Dialogue in Multilingual and Multimodal Communities* 27, 167.

Trumper-Hecht, N. (2010) Linguistic landscape in mixed cities in Israel from the perspective of 'walkers': The case of Arabic. In E. Shohamy, E. Ben-Rafael and M. Barni (eds) *Linguistic Landscape in the City* (pp. 235–251). Bristol: Multilingual Matters.

Tuan, Y.F. (1977) *Space and Place: The Perspective of Experience.* Minneapolis, MN: University of Minnesota Press.

Tuan, Y.F. (1991) Language and the making of place: A narrative-descriptive approach. *Annals of the Association of American Geographers* 81 (4), 684–696.

Vagle, M.D. (2014) *Crafting Phenomenological Research.* Routledge.

Yee, P. (2005) *Chinatown: An Illustrated History of the Chinese Communities of Victoria, Vancouver, Calgary, Winnipeg, Toronto, Ottawa, Montréal, and Halifax.* Toronto: James Lorimer & Co. See http://books.scholarsportal.info/viewdoc.html?id=37794

3 'That's my Husband's sees the Smoke on this Card Bill he Doesn't like me Smoking': Service Interactions in Persian Shops in Sydney

Dariush Izadi

Introduction

Service encounters are by nature goal-and-task-oriented. Goffman (1963) claims that a service encounter is a 'face engagement' in which participants with specific goals conduct a mutual activity through the use of various communicative means. However, many studies of service encounters have shown that goals are not simply limited to achieving business transactions (Bailey, 2000; Félix-Brasdefer, 2015; Zhu Hua et al., 2017). These studies have reported that talk in service encounters is quite intricate and strategic with opportunities for interactants to participate in interpersonal and interactional relationships during their encounters.

At first glance, service encounters seem to be viewed as relatively rudimentary social practices. Turning to Merritt's (1976) definition of service encounter, one can assume that such interactions are predetermined by a limited set of actions with participants engaged in their institutional roles (i.e. shopkeeper and customer). However, there are occasions where interpersonal and relational concerns are inextricably implied and have consequences in the talk and alignments between the participants in such settings (Aston, 1988), and thus are far more complex and unpredictable than they are often imagined to be. The position of a service provider, for instance, requires an ability to advise customers, to facilitate their choices and to coordinate with other colleagues. In such settings, joint actions are not taken exclusively through language use, but frequently incorporate non-verbal conduct and references toward material objects available in the physical environment (Filliettaz, 2004, 2005). As long convincingly argued by scholars such as Goffman (1981) and Scollon (2001), social practices occurring in transactional settings are inextricably intertwined with material objects or various semiotic practices (Pennycook & Otsuji, 2014), including graphic acts or inscriptions.

Traditional discourse analysis in the domain of service encounters, particularly in ethnic shops, is limited to the logo-centric approaches of conversation analysis and interactional sociolinguistics without taking into account the importance of mediational means other than language, the sociocultural setting and the historical trajectories of the participants involved. These studies have documented the minimal forms of social interactions taking place in the site of engagement of such encounters. In other words, in such studies, it seems as though the findings were seen as a product of text rather than as a social phenomenon. To get a sense of what is going on in Persian ethnic shops and of how the social actors use their linguistic repertoires as meaningful resources to take actions in the shop under scrutiny, we need a theory that allows us to examine both discourse and its linkages to workplace practice. Pennycook (2010), for instance, emphasizes that '[T]o think in terms of practices is to make social activities central, to ask how it is we do things as we do, how activities are established, regulated and changed'. However, a practice view of language does not only advocate a focus on the locally organized activities (Garfinkel, 1967) of social actions, but also a particular attention to the discourses these actions are embedded in, convincingly argued by Pennycook (2010: 6): 'we need to appreciate that language cannot be dealt with separately from speakers, histories, cultures, places, ideologies'.

Mediated discourse analysis (MDA) (Scollon, 2001) and nexus analysis (Scollon & Scollon, 2003, 2004) are such practice-based approaches, which seek to establish concrete links between different discourse analytical traditions. MDA provides the researcher with a different entry point. The aim of the analysis is 'to understand the relationship between "what's going on" and the discourse that is available in the situation to perform these "goings on"' (Jones, 2012: 33), in lieu of specifically focusing on language or on action alone. Furthermore, MDA research is committed to gaining an understanding of how our mundane daily activities interact with broad social issues. In other words, it explains how discourse (with a small d: any instance of language in use) with the help of other mediational means (cultural tools), of which language is only a part, reproduces and transforms Discourses (with a capital D: language with other 'stuff') (Gee, 2011: 28) and how Discourses create, reproduce and transform the actions the social actors can individually take at given moments (Norris & Jones, 2005: 10).

The unit of analysis in MDA is the mediated action by which the social actor takes action in a site of engagement. If we take shopping in a Persian shop as a mediated action, then there are multiple mediational/ semiotic tools available in the shop. In the broadest sense, these comprise the built-in environments, the layout, the design, the backstage, the front-stage (see Izadi, 2015), the cash register, the space where the queue is formed, the methods of payment (cash/credit cards) used for the transaction, the shelves where the products are positioned, the products themselves, as well as the background Persian music. Thus, MDA and in particular mediated action investigates how, at the nexus of practice, discourse becomes a tool for 'claims and imputations of social identity' (Norris & Jones, 2005: 4). In this way, MDA does not view buying the authentic Persian products from a Persian ethnic shop, for instance, as 'context'. Rather, it shifts its focus to the actions which the participants take with the (cultural) tools (Wertsch, 1998) available in such settings. The concept of nexus of practice refers to a regular repetition of a site of engagement and a linkage of multiple practices, 'never perfectly, never in any finalized matrix ... but as a network which itself is the basis of the identities we produce and claim through our social actions' (Scollon, 2001: 142).

A service encounter in a Persian shop might be analyzed as a nexus of practice in that it consists of the mediated actions of shopping and perhaps having a conversation (relational and transactional goals). To this extent, the notion of the nexus of practice indicates 'a genre of activity' (Scollon, 2001) and the group of people who engage in that activity. From this point of view, paying by credit card or chatting with the shop-owner while shopping makes sense as an action within the higher-level action (see also Norris, 2004) of service encounters in the Persian ethnic shop. This sensemaking aspect of social action, or 'semiosis' involves taking the credit card out of one's wallet at the time of paying, hence viewed as 'paradigmatically located in these levels of social action' (Scollon, 2001: 163).

Additionally, in MDA, a mediational means or a cultural tool (the two constructs are interchangeably used) refers to '[a]nything an individual uses to take action in the world' (Jones, 2012: 84). This concept of mediational means is adopted from Wertsch's (1998) development of Vygotsky's (1981) notion of the psychological tool. An example to explain the construct of mediational means is the action of 'purchasing an authentic item from a Persian shop'. To leverage this social practice, the customer uses multiple mediational means, e.g. the counter, the layout, the frontstage and backstage in the shop, his/her familiarity with the products and with the locally organized activities (Garfinkel, 1967; ways of doing things in the Persian shop in question). This example illustrates that there are always multiple mediational means involved in carrying out an action, and that these mediational means can be more material (the credit card) or symbolic (the discourse used to ask for the availability of an authentic item). Together they account for the multimodal aspect of any action. As not all of these means are used simultaneously, an MDA analysis is interested in finding out which ones are actually used at which moment and therefore become salient in the process, in order to understand the mechanisms of the social action.

In the same vein, the essence of superdiversity is an attempt to integrate languages, language groups and speakers and communication with 'situated action' (Blommaert & Rampton, 2011). This integration has been proposed as an alternative to approaches to discourse that view social action as secondary and approaches to social analysis taking discourse as secondary (Scollon, 2001). Superdiversity, not very different from MDA or nexus analysis, tries to focus on and identify the complexity of the social action by viewing discourse and its wording as one of many tools available for participants upon which they draw to take action, make meanings and make sense of meanings in various social fields. In this way, to refer to interactions in ethnic shops similar to the one in question as 'service encounters' somehow misses the point that 'what's going on here' involves a complex range of claims and imputations of identity that go far beyond the provision of service. Of importance here are the relationships between linguistic resources, shop multitasking and the complex and intricate patterning of activity and semiotic supplies. My interest in this chapter is the ways in which linguistic and semiotic resources (mediational/cultural tools) are deployed through interactions in the shop and how this is linked to an understanding of an ethnic shop in a multicultural and multilingual city, Sydney.

Goffman (1974) also argues that in order to get a sense of what is actually going on in an interaction, participants must arrive at the definition of the situation, known as the 'frame'. Goffman (1959) regards this definition as a 'working consensus', which involves 'not so much a real agreement as to what exists but rather a real agreement as to whose claims concerning what issues will be temporarily honoured'. This process involves negotiation about the situation concerning the power relation, the status and social distance between the participants, thus in line with Bourdieu's concept of habitus (1977). This negotiation is an ongoing process in all types of interaction, be it institutional or relational/interpersonal. Accordingly, an understanding of framing can be useful in the analysis of how an issue is defined and problematized in service encounters.

Persian Ethnic Shops

In multicultural cities like Sydney, many retail businesses can be viewed as 'ethnic'. These shops often have a location pattern different from the major supermarkets. Immigrants may perceive shopping opportunities as having distinct characteristics not only by the cultural meaning of these shopping spaces but also by their size and location. Spatially, Persian ethnic retail markets, like many others, are located in places where ethnic populations are concentrated. These cultural shopping places are readily distinguishable by the employees, the ethnicity of the owners, and customers as well as service languages provided, background music, merchandise mix, signage and indoor decor. This is of major significance for the immigrants as the first generation shoppers want goods or services that are reminiscent of home.

In addition, such businesses sometimes serve as a gathering place where immigrants obtain information and reinforce their social connections. Many of these businesses provide opportunities for employment for migrants unable to find jobs within their pre-migration fields. These stores serve not only as a shopping space where purchases are made, but additionally as social spaces where individuals negotiate and renegotiate their identities through browsing, consuming the goods and interacting with other co-ethnics. Customers' accounts of their shopping experience reveal that Persian ethnic shops provide a social and cultural space where self-identity can be promoted through browsing imported products.

Generally, most of the Persian ethnic shops are run by Persian husband–wife teams, sometimes with the help of siblings or children, or a few hired unrelated migrant Persians as employees, with a few of the shops run by Afghans. The shops are open seven days a week, typically from 70 to 100 hours a week. Proprietors will often spend all of these hours in their shops, especially when it is a small store or there are no children or siblings to assist. These Persian ethnic shops sell a variety of food products that are not available in mainstream Australian supermarkets (such as Coles or Woolworths) and which are imported from Iran. Additionally, the shops also assist their customers with other business, including the provision of the most recent Persian TV series and movies on DVDs, currency exchange and international money transfer, and telephone cards and tickets for Persian concerts. Furthermore, the store serves as a convenience store and offers a wide range of non-ethnic items for general consumption such as milk, cigarettes and tobacco.

As I have argued elsewhere (Izadi, 2015, 2017; Izadi & Parvaresh, 2016), within the shop, which itself is a semiotic aggregate, defined as 'very complex systems of the interaction of multiple semiotic systems' (Scollon & Scollon, 2003: xii), many discourses intersect, among them shop signage, ethnic food distribution and service, payment options (i.e. credit cards, cash), interior design, telephone ordering, money exchanges, ethnic music, bulletin news (such as job advertisements) and business cards. Discourse in the shop is therefore formed by the arrangements of the shelves and the (narrow or long) passages within the space as well as the position of the shop owner.

Methods and Data Collection

The data for the study were selected and analyzed drawing on the multiperspectival approach to discourse analysis (Candlin & Crichton, 2013). They stem from the 'situated context' of a Persian ethnic shop in Sydney and were collected over a two-year period. A multiperspectival approach involves the collection and triangulation of discourse data generated from a variety of overlapping and mutually informing analytical perspectives within a specific discursive context. These typically involve texts, spoken discourse and other semiotic artifacts (the semiotic resource perspective), interpretative accounts of participants (the participants' perspective), recordings and observations from ethnographic sites of engagement (the social action perspective), as well as wider contextual resources (the socioinstitutional perspective). Dependent on the particular interests, theoretical concerns or research orientations of the analyst (the analysts' perspective), each of the different data sets collected – relative to the perspective it represents – is examined using different analytical traditions.

Key to such a research agenda is the call for 'ecological validity' (Cicourel, 1992, 2007) in research practice. The multiperspectival approach is a research agenda that holds the researcher accountable for his/her data and that views Cicourel's construct of ecological validity as its integral part from the beginning of the research process to the dissemination of the data to the reader. Cicourel (2007) argues that the researcher needs to draw from a wide range of methodological resources so as to accommodate real-world interactions by allowing for the contingencies of participants, the localized and interpersonal mechanisms, all of which display and shape the institutional and social practices that are being investigated.

For a research study to be valid the researcher needs to implement ecological validity (Cicourel, 2007), which refers to the ways in which the research methodology adopted and what is counted as data are shaped by the tacit or unstated knowledge of the materials, the researcher and their participants. That is, what we take at face value is the hidden knowledge, which impacts all aspects of the research process. In the context of *Persia*, for instance, casual conversations between the shop-owner and the customers are replete with 'normative institutionalized features' (Cicourel, 1992: 295), which are associated with encounters in public places. These encounters carry with them considerable cultural and personal 'baggage' (p. 295) for the shop-owners and their customers since they might have had long-term relationships, which are unknown to or overlooked by the researcher. A multimodal perspective allows for the possibility of such encounters to be accounted for by the researcher.

Site of Engagement in *Persia*

To gain a better understanding of the effect of spoken utterances in an ethnic shop, one needs to explore how they are negotiated and taken up in situated activities and moments of social practice through which the social actors are performing. Scollon (2001) refers to such situated moments as sites of engagement as the real-time 'window' that is opened through an intersection of social practices and mediational means (cultural tools) that make that action the focal point of attention of the relevant participants (Scollon, 2001: 4). Drawing on conversation analysis and Gumperz's interactional sociolinguistics, the site of engagement focuses on 'practice/activity theory, the insistence on the real-time, irreversible, and unfinalizable nature of social action' (2001: 4). According to this definition, action is situated in a unique historical moment and material space when separate practices (i.e. in a service encounter context) such as greeting staff, asking for the availability of an item or handing the credit card to the shop-owner, come together in real time to construct an action (shopping in an ethnic shop). Each of these sites of engagement is a combination of the patterns of orientation toward space and time that participants bring with them to these moments and locations of social settings, which are mediated through what Jones refers to as 'attention structures' (Jones & Norris, 2005: 141), which themselves are 'cultural tools' (2005: 152).

In fact, one of the most significant characteristics of sites of engagement in which social action and the practice of service encounters take place in the Persian shop under scrutiny is that they accommodate customers who are members of different communities of practice (including

Persian migrants, along with second-generation Persians and members of other ethnic or national groups such as Anglos, Greeks, Turkish, etc.). Crucial to those sites of engagements is not only the experience (perhaps knowledge about shopping in (Persian) ethnic shops), but more importantly the different (socially acceptable) norms of communication in the shop as a small community of practice among Persian-speaking customers and understandings of the intricacies of the culturally related interactions in the shop and of the role of communicative challenges in coping with service interactions and the mediational tools available in the shop (see Extract 2, for instance).

Thus, different notions hinge upon what communicative competence (Hymes, 1972) in shopping in the shop means. In other words, half of the interactions occurring in the shop (according to the shop-owners, half of their customers being non-Persian speaking) are under the banner of 'intercultural communication', that is, interaction between non-Persian speaking customers and the shop-owners who have different language backgrounds, who are following different tools about how language and non-language elements should be interpreted. Perhaps, owing to the habitus of the regular non-Persian speaking customers, they have instilled in them some sort of possible understanding of 'competence', which in the shop may refer to knowing how to act as a customer in this particular community of practice in its particular sites of engagement. Through implementing such knowledge, those customers have developed and combined the various cultural tools that those sites of engagement have made readily available for them to take actions.

Any social interaction that takes place in a site of engagement is closely linked to not only an understanding of the interaction order (Goffman, 1983) and the structure of the physical space, but also the social understandings of the space in which it occurs. In this sense, Scollon and Scollon (2003) have reminded us that it is crucially important to perceive interaction order as semiotic signs in that it 'gives off' (Goffman, 1959) social insights into social actors. The interaction order (Goffman, 1983) is defined as the way in which individuals organize their social interactions in a social setting. Additionally, it includes any analytical tools associated with 'the current, ongoing, ratified (but also contested and denied) set of social relationships we take up and try to maintain with the other people who are in our presence' (Scollon & Scollon, 2003: 16). The interaction order of the shop is formed from four main types of interaction units (see Figure 3.1) conceptualized by Goffman (1971), namely 'singles', 'withs', 'conversational encounters' and 'platform events' (see Izadi, 2015 for detailed discussion).

Figure 3.1 Conversational encounters in the shop

Mediational Means (Cultural Tools) as an Identity Construction

Owing to the space limitations of the present chapter, I have selected two different interactions to demonstrate what can be captured when attention is directed to the concepts of MDA and in particular to the mediational means (cultural tools). The extracts I present here are two scenes out of the 80 hours of audio-recordings of interactions between the shop-owners and customers (also customers–customers) that I observed during the fieldwork period. Extract 1 comes from an interaction between the shop-owner (the wife) and a customer in her late 30s. According to the shop-owner, she is a regular customer who visits the shop three times a week and the only item she purchases is tobacco. The initial part of this conversation, which is not displayed here, consists of a routine business transaction between the participants.

Extract 1

C: The customer
SW: shop-owner (the wife)

((I'm talking to SW about a customer who has just left the shop. Suddenly, a new customer comes in and we stop talking. English music is on and it's loud enough. SW is cleaning the counter and takes a short look at the entrance and suddenly sees C.))

1. C: you know what if I give you this card <u>rather</u> (.)
   that's my husband's sees the smoke on this card bill hhh
   he doesn't like me smoking ...
2. SW: it's a [credit
3. C: [yeah
4. SW: and signature (.) or pin (.) or]
5. C: yeah (.)sign (1.0) he says I smoke t<u>oo</u> <u>much</u>
6. SW: (2 sec)((**looking down no eye contact**))

Extract 1 takes place at the entrance near the cash register where the tobacco is positioned. SW is standing behind the cash register. The interaction order is in small 'withs' (Scollon & Scollon, 2004), an event in which two or more people are seen as being together with one another and have their focus on their own interaction (see also Izadi, 2015, 2017), on the border of formal and informal whose participants have relatively equal status in their right to hold the floor and the topic of conversation is 'tobacco'. However, their historical bodies (Scollon & Scollon, 2004) (their habitus) may be significantly different as the shop-owner is perhaps viewed as the connoisseur of the items of the shop and of the Persian values whose knowledge about a particular product (mediational means) requires knowledge of the standard variety. The participants in this interaction speak English.

While paying at the counter, the customer has already given the shop-owner her husband's credit card and suddenly changes her mind and asks the shop-owner whether she could use hers in place of her husband's in line 1 'that's my husband's sees the smoke on this card bill hhh' followed by a laugh. Here, from an MDA point of view, the husband's credit card has become an important mediational means, even though the husband is not present during this interaction, where he is brought into play (i.e. the credit card replaces the husband). The customer provides an account of why she cannot use her husband's credit card 'he doesn't like me smoking' (line 1).

In Extract 1, we can observe a prime example of the use of a mediational means. It is mainly this mediational means, with its various interpretations for different social actors owing to their differences in the historical body that links the multiple practices incorporated in the present nexus. In other words, the participants at this site of engagement have different perceptions on the mediational means (i.e. the credit card), which has led to a critical moment, 'those moments within the processes and practices of a crucial site of engagement in which the participants identify and orient to the occurrence (or the potential occurrence) of contradictions arising among conflicting orders of discourse' (Candlin, 2001: 188). Credit cards, as a mediational means, carry with them a sociocultural history. While they do not in themselves define this Persian shop as a place where a unique use of credit cards is practiced, they are, in essence, a mediational means that are inherent in the practice of the customer's shopping experience in the shop as it materially embodies and reproduces a social structure embedded in that practice of the participants. Taken together with the cardholder's name, the card number, the signature bar, the card verification value,[1] the issue and expiration dates, and the customer service number engraved on the card, credit cards materially reproduce and embody a social structure.

Additionally, it seems that on account of the credit card as a mediational means in this interaction the backstage activities may have become frontstage ones. Originating from Goffman (1959), the twin notions of 'frontstage' and 'backstage' suggest that individuals in their daily dealings have two different modes of presenting themselves to others, namely one when they are 'on the stage' (frontstage) and the other one when they let down their guard (backstage), which is 'out of bounds to members of the audience' (1959: 79) and where they can dispose of their role or identity which they play when they are in front of others.

The frontstage activities now necessitate different rules of the game (see Blommaert & De Fina, 2017) that change completely while the new rule of the game simultaneously displays different identities of the participants present in the discourse at hand and more importantly those who are not present (the husband, for instance) that arise from the mediational means and the linguistic utterances produced by the participants. For instance, at the start of the sequence (line 1), the customer accomplishes the action of displaying concern that she does not wish her husband to find out that she is smoking. After the customer has stated her problem and entered the frontstage (i.e. not allowed to smoke), it would be expected to be followed by compliance on the part of the shop-owner. Nonetheless, in line 2, after a pause of two seconds, her account is not taken up by the shop-owner. The shop-owner then directly goes to the business and asks whether it is a credit card, a signature[2] or pin in line 4. It seems that the shop-owner is fulfilling the category-bound 'duties' of expressing concern here as a (responsible) 'mother' of two children (her habitus).

An interesting formulation of what might be interpreted as 'intertextuality in interaction' may be implied through the exploitation of the mediational means (the credit card). In Tannen (2007), this could be categorized as an instance of 'intertextuality in interaction' in that the words and topics that have been previously exchanged between the couple, perhaps in the backstage, are privileged in a public domain. Intertextuality is then defined as 'the insight that meaning in language results from a complex of relationships linking items within a discourse and linking current to prior instances of language' (Tannen, 2007: 9). In the example analyzed above, the topic of the tension about whether or not to use her husband's credit card is recycled, reframed and rekeyed across time both between the couple and in conversation with others: in this case with the shop-owner in a Persian shop.

Owing to the routine nature of the service interactions, at least in the shop in question, expectations about the roles and identities are rather fixed in that the roles of the game are similar for the shop-owner (accommodating customers' needs) and the customer (making purchases). Accordingly, deviation from the pre-established roles may give rise to potential imputations of identities that produce negative consequences for the deviant customer, for example, a disobedient wife. It should be noted that after the customer left the shop, the shop-owner confided to me that she herself smokes cigarettes but not tobacco. She stressed she was worried about the customer because the customer breastfeeds her two-year old child, thus smoking tobacco is detrimental not only to her health but also to her child. She concluded that smoking tobacco is about 9 or 10 times as harmful as smoking cigarettes.

Mediational Means and Participation Framework

As discussed above, an MD analysis centers its attention on the social actors as they are acting in a site of engagement. For any action to take place in a social setting, the social actor (in any culture) should be well equipped at least with some mediational tools, which he/she should use in order to perform that action. These mediational tools have a history that is embedded and understood through the social actor's practice, which otherwise leads to confusion, dissimilarity and misunderstanding. Extract 2 is an example of this.

Extract 2

SW: shop-owner's wife
C: an Anglo-Australian customer (in her early 30s)
CD: customer's daughter

1. C: hey (0.3) who was that ↑
2. SW: (0.6) uh (.) to<u>ma</u>to <u>p</u>aste ((no eye contact trying to tidy things up at the counter))
3. C: Oh O<u>K</u>
4. SW: = yeah (0.3)
5. C: that's a <u>lot</u> of tomato <u>p</u>aste

6. SW: = Yeah
7. C: hhh
8. SW: because the Iranian people using a lot ((eye contact and gazing at the customer))
9. CD: making noises
10. C: o:::h right ((having a cursory look at her daughter))
11. CD: ((making loud noises))
12. SW: = food
13. C: = yeah
14. SW: for (.) uh Persian food
15. C: = yeah
16. SW: = y:::eah

In this extract, the interaction is taking place between the shop-owner (the wife) and a customer, a lady in her early 30s, Anglo-Australian. According to the shop-owners, they have known her for about three years and the customer often visits the shop but is regarded as more of a window-shopper. The customer usually comments on the product items and on customers' purchases or makes inquiries regarding their shopping experiences. During my fieldwork, I had the opportunity to talk to the customer about various issues, and she provided me with some accounts of her regular visits to the shop. She informed me that her shopping experiences in Australian stores including Coles, Woolworths or IGA exclude interpersonal interactions with the shop assistants: 'All you can do is to put the items you have purchased in the trolley and leave the shop as nobody wants to talk to you. Here, (she means the shop), although they are busy, they have a word with you, ask about your daily activities etc.' The customer revealed that the shop-owner (the wife) often provides her with Persian cuisine. The customer has an eight-month-old daughter, with whom the shop-owners play, and they teach her some Persian. For instance, in one of my observations, the shop-owners were teaching the daughter to clap while speaking Persian with her. Interestingly, the daughter was imitating the shop-owners' instructions (i.e. clapping).

Going back to the interaction in Extract 2, one can notice that there was no uptake by the shop-owner in relation to the customer's question in line 2. As can be shown, because the shop-owner knows that the customer is a 'busybody' and that the customer is curious to know about the things going on in the shop, the shop-owner may not have wanted to reveal the person's identity and change the 'who' question to a 'what' question. This is evidenced by a pause and a repair (uh) in line 2, where the shop-owner provides an irrelevant response. This moment of 'trouble' may suggest that the shop-owner is either reluctant to provide a response to the customer's request as evidenced in her non-verbal actions (i.e. maintaining no eye-contact) or she might have misheard the question.

In the foregoing scene, the deconstruction of the speaker suggested by Goffman (1981) in footing illustrates the power of an analytical framework that places its attention on the 'dialogic interplay of separate voices with reported speech' (Goodwin, 2007: 18). In Extract 2, the shop-owner provided an account in which she quoted something that the *Iranian people* frequently do. Thus, the interaction is about five cans of 'tomato paste' that a Persian, male-speaking customer had purchased, while the female customer was observing. After the male customer had left the shop, the female customer commented on the amount of tomato paste the customer had purchased (lines 2–8). However, in response to the customer's surprise in line 5, 'that's a lot of tomato paste', the shop-owner offers an account that gives an impression that the amount of tomato paste the Iranian people use is taken as typical in line 8. Now, who is speaking in line 8? Arguably and intuitively, the voice that is heard is the shop-owner's. However, she is referring to something that the Iranian people consume within their cultural practice. The shop-owner is both quoting the talk of other Iranian people and taking up a stance toward the customer's comment. To some extent, the shop-owner (the current account-provider) and the Iranian people are both 'speakers' of what is earlier referred to in line 8, even though in a different cultural perspective and understanding. The theoretical framework underpinned in footing for what Goffman called the 'Production Format' (Goffman, 1981: 18) of an utterance offers a powerful lens not only for decomposing the 'speaker', but also for investigating how speakers position themselves vis-à-vis each other in interaction.

In terms of the categories identified by Goffman, the shop-owner is the *Animator*, the party who uses her voice in order to utter this strip of talk. Nonetheless, the *Author* of this speech, the party who actually produced the phrase (who used 'a lot of tomato paste') in line 8, is the Iranian people who are not present at the moment during this interaction. Here, it is safe to say that the Iranian people are held responsible both as the author and as the principal, the people who are socially and culturally accountable for carrying out that action (i.e. 'buying a lot of tomato paste') performed by the utterance and perhaps the main source of that speech.

Goffman sees the speaker's talk in interaction as an entire theater, where they are put on stage. The shop-owner, in informing the customer that the Persian-speaking customer did not buy 'a lot of tomato paste' and that it is not a laughing matter, as evident in line 7, is actually putting the Iranian People on stage and animating them as a Figure (Goodwin,

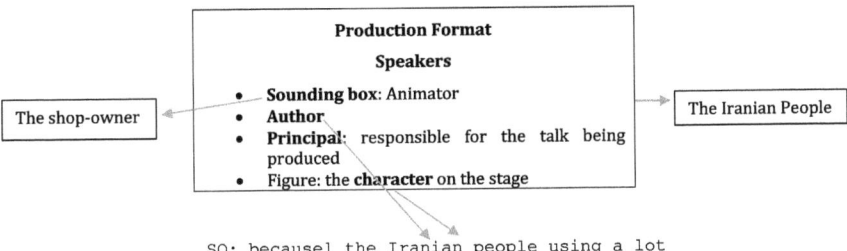

Figure 3.2 Production format

2007: 20) (see Figure 3.2). Furthermore, through her phrase in line 8, the shop-owner displays her own position, constructing her talk as something to be taken seriously through her eye contact and her gaze.

Additionally, after the shop-owner's account of why the previous customer had purchased 'a lot of tomato paste', the customer provides a narrative outside of the recording situation in which she refers to a TV show on an Australian national channel called 'Food Safari'. Perhaps this change of footing in the customer's account is due to her lack of knowledge of Persian culture with its complex network of expectations regarding the use of tomato paste and the activities (i.e. how much is 'a lot of?'). The examination of the larger food discussion taking place demonstrates that particular competence in the domain of discourse. This involves not only knowledge about the food (the mediational/cultural tool) being discussed, but also the ability to recognize the food type, as well as specific practices for making expertise in this subject matter, which is evident moment by moment in the talk the participants produce.

As can be observed, the utterance 'a lot of tomato paste' has a history in both the shop-owner's and the customer's habitus (historical body) as both are progressively understood in terms of the when, how and how much to use in their food along with the other meditational means, amounting to structures of expectations or knowledge structure (Tannen, 1985) concerned with a particular item in the shop. Much of what can be understood from mediational tools, therefore, does not actually need to be unpacked but rather is embedded in the knowledge of the participants engaged in interaction.

Conclusion

At the inception of this chapter, the approach to discourse analysis that has been set out in this article has been informed by MDA (Norris & Jones, 2005; Scollon, 2001). MDA is an approach that heavily relies on how actions are mediated through discourse and other cultural tools that are available at the site of engagement in which an action is taking place. As demonstrated, key to the application of such an approach is how these cultural tools afford and constrain the types of social actions that the customers, for instance, in Persian shops can carry out and the kinds of social identities with which they can be affiliated.

The notion of 'cultural tools', one of the constructs that has broadened the scope of the current study, incorporates three important considerations, namely *ways of saying*, *ways of doing* and *ways of being* (Gee, 2011). 'Ways of saying', to some extent connoting Goffman's 'framing', help participants organize their social interaction and make sense of the world in which they live and make up 'much of our [their] everyday, common-sense knowledge of social reality' (Rampton, 1995: 31). 'Ways of doing', which provide the social actors with some sets of methods through which they perform a social action, draw on Garfinkel's 'ethnomethodology' in the sense that the participants, who carry out the social practices in a social setting, have mastered them in their communities in which these tools have shaped their perception and come to be considered typical of participation because of their habitus. Finally, 'ways of being' focus on the various social identities which the Persian shops, for instance, allow the members to claim (through interaction). As observed in the extracts above, many mediated actions (along with the use of mediational means) that the customers in the shop have conducted have in part given rise to the identity construction of them, both implicitly and explicitly.

Such intricacies encourage us to re-evaluate our understanding of the sociolinguistics of globalization (Blommaert, 2010) and of the critical complexity of the language practices of late-modern urban groups who employ and exploit features from a wide range of cultural and semiotic resources. For MDA, the answer lies in how, in the historical body of the customer, for instance, service interaction discourse is constructed and interacts with overlapping other discourses and practices, and how, when it emerges in a moment of a service interaction it is connected with other discourses and practices that are brought back to the historical body and to the interaction order.

Transcription Conventions

(.)	pause of less than one second
↑	marked rising intonation
↓	marked falling intonation
(1.0)	pause timed to nearest second

:::	each colon indicates further lengthening of a sound
ones	underlining indicates a stressed word or syllable
[	Squares brackets aligned across adjacent lines denote the start of overlapping talks
]	the point at which overlap stops is marked by right-hand square brackets
(( ))	A description enclosed in a double bracket indicates a non-verbal activity Alternatively double brackets may enclose the researcher's comments on contextual features
yeah =	Equals signs indicate no break or gap
hhh	Laughter syllables
( )	Unclear speech or noise to which no approximation is made

Notes

(1) The card verification value, or CVV, is a three- or four-digit code on a credit card that is used as an extra security measure to prevent fraudulent transactions.
(2) The option of signature and pin here predates August 2014, when signatures were phased out in Australia for security reasons.

References

Aston, G. (ed.) (1988) *Negotiating Service: Studies in the Discourse of Bookshop Encounters*. Bologna: Cooperativa Libraria Universitaria Editrice.

Bailey, B. (2000) Communicative behavior and conflict between African-American customers and Korean immigrant retailers in Los Angeles. *Discourse and Society* 11 (1), 86–108.

Blommaert, J. (2010) *The Sociolinguistics of Globalization*. Cambridge: Cambridge University Press.

Blommaert, J. and De Fina, A. (2017) Chronotopic identities: On the timespace organization of who we are. In A. De Fina, J. Wegner and D. Ikizoglu (eds) *Diversity and Super-diversity. Sociocultural Linguistic Perspectives*. Washington, DC: Georgetown University Press.

Blommaert, J. and Rampton, B. (2011) Language and superdiversity. *Diversities* 13 (2), 1–22.

Bourdieu, P. (1977) *Outline of a Theory of Practice*. Cambridge: Cambridge University Press.

Candlin, C.N. (2001) Medical discourse as professional and institutional action: Challenges to teaching and researching languages for special purposes. In M. Bax and J.W. Zwart (eds) *Reflections on Language and Language Learning: In Honour of Arthur van Essen*. Amsterdam: John Benjamins.

Candlin, C.N. and Crichton, J. (eds) (2013) *Discourses of Trust*. Basingstoke: Palgrave Macmillan.

Cicourel, A. (1992) The interpenetration of communicative contexts: Examples from medical encounters. In A. Duranti and C. Goodwin (eds) *Rethinking Context: Language as an Interactive Phenomenon*. Cambridge: Cambridge University Press.

Cicourel, A.V. (2007) A personal, retrospective view of ecological validity. *Text and Talk* 27 (5–6), 735–752.
Félix-Brasdefer, J.C. (2015) *The Language of Service Encounters*. Cambridge: Cambridge University Press.
Filliettaz, L. (2004) The multimodal negotiation of service encounters. In P. LeVine and R. Scollon (eds) *Discourse and Technology: Multimodal Discourse Analysis*. Washington, DC: Georgetown University Press.
Filliettaz, L. (2005) Mediated actions, social practices, and contextualization: A case study from service encounters. In S. Norris and R.H. Jones (eds) *Discourse in Action: Introducing Mediated Discourse Analysis*. New York: Routledge.
Garfinkel, H. (1967) *Studies in Ethnomethodology*. Englewood Cliffs, NJ: Prentice Hall.
Gee, J.P. (2011) *How to Do Discourse Analysis: A Toolkit*. London: Routledge.
Goffman, E. (1959) *The Presentation of Self in Everyday Life*. New York: Doubleday, Anchor Books.
Goffman, E. (1963) *Behavior in Public Spaces: Notes on the Social Organization of Gatherings*. New York: The Free Press.
Goffman, E. (1971) *Relations in Public: Microstudies of the Public Order*. New York: Basic Books.
Goffman, E. (1974) *Frame Analysis: An Essay on the Organisation of Experience*. New York: Harper & Row.
Goffman, E. (1981) *Forms of Talk. Philadelphia:* University of Pennsylvania Press.
Goffman, E. (1983) The Interaction order: American Sociological Association, 1982 Presidential Address. *American Sociological Review* 48 (1), 1–17.
Goodwin, C. (2007) Interactive footing. In E. Holt and R. Clift (eds) *Reporting Talk: Reported Speech in Interaction*. Cambridge: Cambridge University Press.
Hymes, D. (1972) On communicative competence. In J. Holmes and J. Pride (eds) *Sociolinguistics*. Harmondsworth: Penguin.
Izadi, D. (2015) Spatial engagement in Persian ethnic shops in Sydney. *Multimodal Communication* 4 (1), 61–78.
Izadi, D. (2017) Semiotic resources and mediational tools in Merrylands, Sydney, Australia: The case of Persian and Afghan shops. *Social Semiotics* 27 (4), 495–512.
Izadi, D. and Parvaresh, V. (2016) The framing of the linguistic landscapes of Persian shop signs in Sydney. *Journal of Linguistic Landscape* 2 (2), 182–205.
Jones, R. (2012) *Discourse Analysis: A Resource Book for Students*. London: Routledge.
Jones, R. and Norris, S. (2005) Discourse as action/discourse in action. In S. Norris and R. Jones (eds) *Discourse in Action: Introducing Mediated Discourse Analysis*. London: Routledge.
Merritt, M. (1976) On questions following questions in service encounters. *Language in Society 5* (3), 315–357.
Norris, S. (2004) *Analyzing Multimodal Interaction: A Methodological Framework*. London: Routledge.
Norris, S. and Jones, R. (eds) (2005a) *Discourse in Action: Introducing Mediated Discourse Analysis*. London: Routledge.
Pennycook, A. (2010) *Language as a Local Practice*. London: Routledge.
Pennycook, A. and Otsuji, E. (2014) Metrolingual multitasking and spatial repertoires: Pizza mo two minutes coming. *Journal of Sociolinguistics* 18 (2), 161–184.
Scollon, R. (2001) *Mediated Discourse: The Nexus of Practice*. New York: Routledge.
Scollon, R. and Scollon, S. (2003) *Discourses in Place: Language in the Material World*. London: Routledge.

Scollon, R. and Scollon, S. (2004) *Nexus Analysis: Discourse and the Emerging Internet.* London: Routledge.

Rampton, B. (1995) *Crossing: Language and Ethnicity among Adolescents.* London: Longman.

Tannen, D. (1985) Frames and schemas in interaction. *Quaderni Di Semantica* 6 (2), 326–335.

Tannen, D. (2007) *Talking Voices: Repetition, Dialogue, and Imagery in Conversational Discourse* (2nd edn). Cambridge: Cambridge University Press.

Vygotsky, L.S. (1981) The instrumental method in psychology. In J.V. Wertsch (ed.) *The Concept of Activity in Soviet Psychology.* Armonk: M.E. Sharpe.

Wertsch, J.V. (1998) *Mind as Action.* New York: Oxford University Press.

Zhu Hua, Otsuji, E. and Pennycook, A. (2017) Multilingual, multisensory and multimodal repertoires in corner shops, streets and markets: introduction. *Social Semiotics* 27 (4), 383–393.

4 Language, Scale and Ideologies of the National in Kazakhstan[1]

Kara Fleming

Introduction

The supposed opposition between 'global' and 'local' is an oversimplified ideological binary, which nevertheless has important consequences at many levels. Research in sociolinguistics has been closely engaged with the construction of the 'global' and 'local' and the flows of linguistic and other semiotic material across different scales of reference (Blommaert, 2010; Pennycook, 2007; Hill, 1999). Many of these works emphasize that 'global' and 'local' categories should not be taken for granted. In this chapter I want to consider the 'global' and 'local' as scales and categories which are discursively constructed and contested, and how they then make different language ideologies expressible. In other words, how are different scales made relevant in particular discourses, and what kinds of ideological moves does this allow?

Although it has received little sociolinguistic attention, Kazakhstan is a particularly fascinating and productive context in which to examine these processes. After the breakup of the Soviet Union in 1991, Kazakhstan was faced with establishing a new national identity along with new civic institutions and new relationships to other nation-states. A key component of this process has been defining the composition and orientations of the new state. Within these debates, the role of language has taken on key symbolic roles, particularly regarding the status, domains of use and appropriate speakers of Kazakh, Russian and English. Accordingly, this chapter will consider the role of language in competing discourses about 'authentic' national identity, and how these discourses construct and use 'global' or 'local' frames to give their ideologies meaning.

Although Kazakhstan's trajectory toward nationhood has often been presented as one of liberation, emancipation and sovereignty for a previously oppressed minority, the situation is not necessarily so clear cut. Debates on national identity in Kazakhstan are frequently set up as a choice between an ethnically defined 'Kazakh' identity primarily incorporating ethnic Kazakhs, and a civically defined 'Kazakhstani' identity that at least potentially includes other ethnic groups. However, both sides share key assumptions about what it means to be a state and an ethnic group, and about the relationship between nations, ethnicities and language. At the same time, ideologies about the 'global' and 'local' are used in complex and competing ways by different parties in these negotiations. 'Global' and 'local' frames are called upon to justify particular stances and moves with regard to the nation and its symbols, especially language. Orientations to particular types of scale play a significant role in making sense of many of these ideologies.

Thus, although scales are implicated in a wide range of discursive projects, this chapter focuses on how they are invoked in relation to language and nation-building. In seeking to understand different scales of reference and their consequences, it is important to keep in mind that 'scale-making practices are ideological, hence semiotic, activities reliant on perspective and meaning' (Irvine, 2016: 214).

This chapter will examine some of the competing perspectives from which the global and local are framed, and the many ways these categories intertwine. Kazakhstan is a clear example that scale-making plays a significant part in establishing dominant ideologies, and the policy moves that follow from them.

Scale and Language Ideology – Creating the 'Global' and 'Local'

The concept of scale in sociolinguistics has roots in metaphorical borrowings from geography and political science (Blommaert *et al.*, 2015; Canagarajah & De Costa, 2016). Although scale is sometimes taken to be an *a priori*, straightforwardly hierarchical category, researchers have increasingly argued for an understanding of scale as socially constructed. Thus, 'the questions that are important are how people and institutions engage in scaling their practices' (Gal, 2016: 3).

Although scales may include and reinforce hierarchical relations, particular hierarchies should not be assumed; it is not necessarily the case, for instance, that the 'global' is always of a higher order than the 'local'. The idea that higher-level scales are always deterministic and abstract and local scales are fluid and hybrid is sometimes taken as common sense; yet 'the higher level scales can be redefined by how policies are taken up [at] the local level. Furthermore, we cannot rigidly separate the local and global if we consider how they constitute each other. There is considerable fluidity and scope for renegotiation at all scale levels' (Canagarajah & De Costa, 2016: 3). Instead of a strictly linear model wherein one scale level encloses another, Gal argues that researchers must consider the possibilities of scales as 'rhizomatic relations where the influences are non-linear, unpredictable, layered, and multidirectional' (Canagarajah & De Costa, 2016: 3), which operate in different ways in different social domains. Thus, scales are not necessarily 'flat', but particular sets of hierarchical relations that should not be assumed without investigation.

Gal proposes a recursive understanding of scale, using the semiotic concept of 'fractal recursivity' she developed with Irvine (Gal, 2016; Irvine & Gal, 2000). Fractal recursivity, or recursion, describes a situation in which a particular binary distinction is highlighted and used to explain a host of other social characteristics and perceived distinctions – i.e. 'men' vs 'women', 'east' vs 'west'. The binary can be scaled upward or downward indefinitely, although it always means something slightly different at each new level of invocation. This process of distinction and scaling involves the other two semiotic processes that Irvine and Gal (2000) outline, namely iconization, as a particular feature associated with a group, sign or situation comes to be seen as representing something about its inherent nature, and erasure, whereby anything that does not fit into the prevailing model is ignored or explained away. The 'global'/'local' distinction is one such binary which, as the following will demonstrate, can be scaled up or down in far-reaching and sometimes unpredictable ways. As Gal points out and as the case of Kazakhstan demonstrates, the distinctions are not fixed but always depend on a particular perspective and interpretation.

Of course, as many scholars have pointed out (Blommaert, 2010; Dovchin *et al.*, 2018; Pennycook, 2010), 'global' and 'local' (and similar binaries like 'center vs periphery') are oversimplified categories which are not easily identifiable in reality and are fundamentally matters of context and perspective. These descriptors are being used here not to suggest that simplistic binaries should be the primary analytical framework for questions of globalization, but because these categories are ideologically important to many people. Many speakers use 'global' and 'local' as oppositional frames to explain their own identities, choices and beliefs, but it is of course not the case that the world is somehow inherently divided into 'global' and 'local' spheres – indeed, I hope this chapter will contribute to the problematization of those categories.

Context in a broad sense is an important construct for sociolinguistics, and similar questions of perspective, spatiotemporal framing and participants have been engaged with by sociolinguists working on center–periphery dynamics and the relationship between language and space, among many others (Jaworski & Thurlow, 2010; Pietikäinen & Kelly-Holmes, 2013). As Blommaert *et al*. (2015: 121) write, 'Scale ... might be a way of pointing toward the complex distinctions people make within "context", between things that are widely presupposable and things that are not, widely available meanings and others, normative meanings and others'. Thus, it is a concept with potentially wide relevance for work on language and the social construction of meaning.

It has sometimes been suggested that the world is moving toward a post-national phase, in which the nation-state is becoming increasingly irrelevant (Heller, 2011; Muehlmann & Duchêne, 2007; Pujolar, 2007). Yet the power of nationalist movements around the world, and the particular case examined here, demonstrates the enduring strength of the concept of 'nation'. Thus, it is important to examine how exactly this concept is built up, maintained and operationalized. Language is one of the tools and terrains on which the process of nation building and scaling takes place, as participants draw on particular linguistic resources to construct particular senses of scale. At the same time language serves as a symbol whose scalar reach is part of the contested process of nation building (Brubaker, 2011).

Kazakhstan has experienced a re-scaling of a very dramatic and obvious kind, with its sudden transition to independent statehood following the collapse of the Soviet Union in 1991. This change has been accompanied by a host of correlated re-scaling processes, which are still ongoing as Kazakhstan's identity and positioning are continually negotiated.

Methodology

This chapter draws on semi-structured interviews conducted in 2016 with participants in both Astana, Kazakhstan's capital since 1997, and Almaty, the former capital and the largest city. Participants were largely urban professionals, who responded to the researcher's request for people who might be interested in talking about language and identity or were recruited through the 'friend-of-a-friend' method. There were in total 15 hours of audio data from interviews lasting on average 30–45 minutes. Interviews included questions about the relationship between Kazakh identity and language, in relation to the interviewee and to other groups in Kazakhstan, Kazakhstan's relationship with other states, and specific language policies, particularly trilingualism and latinization (described below). Interviews were subsequently transcribed and coded for dominant themes,[2] drawing on theoretical frames from language ideology (Irvine & Gal, 2000; Kroskrity, 2000, 2010) and language policy research (Spolsky, 2004).

Thus, the responses included here are not claimed to necessarily be representative of the broader population in Kazakhstan. Instead, this chapter examines how, in both policy moves and individuals' responses to questions about Kazakhstan and the role of language in the country, a variety of scales are invoked, shifted between and contested. These responses make it clear that the 'local' and the 'global' are categories that are in a continual process of creation, which are applied in complex, recursive ways, and ones whose taken-for-granted definitions mask particular non-neutral viewpoints on language and the meaning of the nation.

'Local' Negotiations – who does the Nation Include?

The post-Soviet states have had to negotiate their newfound national status while in many cases creating new senses of 'authenticity' and new criteria through which that authenticity can be signaled and evaluated. Thus, drawing borders around the nation has involved debates on what exactly it means to be part of Kazakhstan, and who gets to make these judgments.

The territory that now composes Kazakhstan came under Russian imperial control gradually, starting from the 1700s. After the Bolshevik Revolution in 1917 and the formation of the Soviet Union in 1922, Kazakhstan was incorporated into the USSR and eventually declared the Kazakh Soviet Socialist Republic in 1936 in its present-day borders. Soviet authorities used the Kazakh SSR, whose population suffered large-scale deaths from famine and forced settlement, as a destination for other ethnic groups being deported from other parts of the Soviet Union. Such policies are the reason for the presence in Kazakhstan of, for instance, ethnic Germans, largely deported from the Volga river region, and ethnic Koreans deported from far eastern Siberia, among other groups. These policies and other migration patterns meant that ethnic Kazakhs were only 40.2% of the population at the time of the 1989 census. Many ethnic Kazakhs, especially those living in urban areas, had shifted to the use of Russian as their primary language (Dave, 2003, 2007), with 64.2% of Kazakhs claiming fluency in Russian in 1989, and up to 77.8% in urban areas (Fierman, 2006: 101), although as Pavlenko (2013) notes, Kazakhs may have overstated their Russian abilities owing to the status of Russian at the time. By the time of the Soviet Union's collapse in 1991, Kazakhstan was one of the most heavily russified republics, where, unlike in the Baltic states, there was little well-defined drive toward statehood; instead, independence came as somewhat of a surprise (Ó Beacháin & Kevlihan, 2013).

Today, post-independence Kazakhstan is officially a constitutional republic with strong presidential power – Nursultan Nazarbayev has been president since 1991 (and was leader of the Kazakh SSR's communist party from 1989 to 1991). Schatz (2008) describes the Kazakh system of government as 'soft authoritarianism' – political dissent is tightly repressed and there are no genuine elections, but the regime, promoting an image of Nazarbayev as a benevolent leader and of Kazakhstan as an open and modernizing state, has generally not made use of the kind of heavy-handed, violent suppression that has characterized regimes in some of its Central Asian neighbors (although there have been exceptions). Nazarbayev's government has justified its centralized power as necessary to avoid political instability and violence, and to move Kazakhstan into a more prosperous economic reality.

The Kazakh population had grown to approximately 18.2 million in 2017 (United Nations Department of Economic and Social Affairs, 2017); the majority of the population are now ethnic Kazakhs, representing 63.1% of the population in 2009 (Smailov, 2011). Besides the still large presence of ethnic Russians (23.7% of the population in 2009), there are also significant minorities of ethnic Uzbeks (2.9%), Ukrainians (2.1%), Uyghurs (1.4%), Tatars (1.3%), Germans (1.1%), Koreans (0.6%) and others (Smailov, 2011).

After independence Kazakhstan's elite set about building up a new state apparatus and promoting new national ideologies to match it. Brubaker describes Kazakhstan as a 'nationalizing' state; the key characteristic of such states is an ideology that the state contains a 'core nation', an ethnic group which takes primacy over others living in the state's territory, and that 'state action is needed to strengthen the core nation, to promote its language, cultural flourishing, demographic robustness, economic welfare or political hegemony; and … that such action is remedial or compensatory, needed to redress previous discrimination or oppression suffered by the core nation' (Smailov, 2011: 1786). Part of that nationalizing process has been to determine what and who exactly the core nation includes and excludes, a matter of both elite policy- and image-making and wider public debate. The next section will consider some of the arguments made on this subject, and how scales are invoked in this process.

Building and Being an Authentic 'Local'

Nationalist ideologies of unity as national homogeneity centered around the titular (Kazakh) ethnic group have played a significant role in Kazakhstan's post-independence identity negotiations. Yet there is also a widely promoted image of Kazakhstan as a multicultural, multiethnic state, whose citizens are 'Kazakhstanis' of many backgrounds, not just ethnic Kazakhs. These two images of Kazakhstan are not as contradictory as they might initially appear. There are sharp divisions constructed between ethnic groups, such that ethnic Kazakhs are tasked with being 'pure' and 'authentic', especially linguistically; yet non-ethnic Kazakhs are under less serious pressure to learn Kazakh, perhaps because it is clear that they will never be able to move fully into the 'Kazakh' category. In the view of many respondents it was important that ethnic Kazakhs already know or are learning Kazakh, but this was not a requirement for other groups – although a number of interview participants did say that they knew of increasing numbers of people from other ethnic groups who spoke or were learning Kazakh. The strengthening and revival of the Kazakh language is overwhelmingly on the shoulders of the ethnic Kazakhs.

Thus recursive ideologies of national purity and authenticity scale downwards to the individual level. Such ideologies put pressure on ethnic Kazakhs to be idealized representatives of the Kazakh people instead of 'mankurts' or 'shala-Kazakhs' – 'cultureless person' or 'half-Kazakh', respectively (Dave, 2007). Hints of hybridity are taken as signs of inauthenticity; this creates a sense of anxiety around authentic 'Kazakhness'. Many urban and russified Kazakh participants expressed regret that they did not speak better Kazakh, and told stories of being chastized by Kazakh speakers for not using Kazakh. Potential effects of this heightened tension around Kazakh are illustrated in the following excerpt, from a blog post written as part of a university course by a student using the name 'aidana17':

Excerpt 1

> As for me, I am sick and tired of hearing that Kazakh people must speak Kazakh, unless they are not patriotic. With the help of our Media I get the sense that Kazakh language is a language of an 'ideal' person, who is a highly-moral and well-mannered. It creates the feeling that Kazakh language is something sacral and sometimes you are even afraid to speak it because of the possibility to make a mistake. Maybe it is the reason why people are not minded to start speaking Kazakh? ('aidana17')

Because Kazakh is framed as a threatened, vital symbol of Kazakh identity, any hint of inauthenticity is taken as a sign the speaker is not really on the right side of the cultural binary. Similar anxieties about authenticity, ownership and morality have been found by other researchers working in contexts of language revival (Duchêne & Heller, 2007; Jaffe, 1999; Pujolar, 2001; Schmidt, 1985). This very pressure to be pure can, somewhat ironically from the perspective of the revivalists, situate speakers who might otherwise use the language outside the boundaries of the authentic. Interestingly, one pair of ethnic Kazakh participants said that they had both experienced pressure to use more or better Kazakh within Kazakhstan, but when they traveled abroad they sometimes found themselves adding a bit of Kazakh to their speech even (or especially) when around non-Kazakh former Soviets. Ethnic signaling can be more attractive when one is sure of where the boundary lines will be constructed.

The tension between authentic and inauthentic 'locals' plays out on both a national and an individual level and a whole host of scales and contexts in between. Although the construction of Kazakhstan as a multiethnic state seems to be an alternative to a restrictive vision of 'Kazakhstan for Kazakhs', it is still based in classic framings of nationalism; each ethnic group is envisioned as a self-contained 'nation' with its own symbols and homogenous characteristics (Dave, 2007). Given the restrictive nature of these definitions, it is not too surprising that some individuals are seeking alternatives. A few (especially younger) interview participants said that, rather than call themselves 'Kazakhs' or 'Kazakhstanis', they preferred to think of themselves as 'global citizens'. So, then, what does 'global' mean?

Global Forces

The ongoing construction of Kazakhstan's new national identity is one with significant ramifications across many spheres within Kazakhstan. Yet the 'national' or 'regional' are not the only levels at which policy is conceptualized, decided, implemented and framed. A 'global' or 'international' frame is also invoked by many participants and by the government and policy-makers as Kazakhstan seeks to increase its prominence outside its own borders. The desire for global prestige and recognition as a legitimate regime (Fauve, 2015) has surely influenced a number of actions that the Nazarbayev government has (or has not) taken, including hosting the 2017 World Expo in Astana and hiring international PR firms to improve Kazakhstan's image abroad (Lewis, 2016). Kazakhstan's government and residents are well aware that it sits between powerful neighbors, and orientations to or away from those neighbors, as well as toward a more vaguely defined global scale, have played a significant role in 'international' policies, as well as in establishing the justification for policies that might otherwise be said to apply largely to nation-internal processes.

The International as Opportunity

Two major language policy moves, which have been framed at least partially as efforts to increase Kazakhstan's engagement with a 'global' stage are the new trilingualism in education policy and moves toward the latinization of written Kazakh. The following section will examine them each in turn.

Kazakhstan's policy of trilingualism was announced in 2015, to be implemented in the 2020–2021 school year. The trilingual policy stipulates that in place of the previous system of sorting students into either Kazakh or Russian language schools, or into distinct Russian and Kazakh language streams in 'mixed' schools (as well as some minority language schools; see Fierman, 2006; Smagulova, 2008, 2016 for more details of previous language in education policy), schools should implement instruction in Kazakh, Russian and English, organized by subject (Ministry of Education and Science, Republic of Kazakhstan, 2015). This policy has been promoted as a necessary step toward embracing modernity and globalization, and many interview participants said they felt this policy was a positive way for Kazakhstan to increase its international engagement (although many also expressed reservations, as in Excerpt 4 below). The following excerpt discusses some of the competing orientations within that international gaze.

Excerpt 2

> Kara: What do you think of this new policy of trilingualism overall?
>
> K11 (F, 30s, working in higher education, Almaty): … hmm … well, well I think it's a natural move for Kazakhstan. Kazakhstan is moving towards – nowhere. hhh It's been looking for its ways and policies for a while, it wanted to be part of Eurasian, it has this Eurasianism idea, then back in 90s there was Turkish way and then Iran way and then we wanted to take the path of Singapore and Malaysia so so many different models mixed in Kazakhstan's path um but the tendency is that a lot of young people, they went to Western countries by Bolashak program and other programs, this westernization and globalization, it's here. Cause certain amount of, certain percentage of young people are English

speaking. And I think this is a really good mix and maybe this trilingualism policy is good to change the mindset or mentality of people. Through language. I think it's a good move.

From this excerpt we see the potential competition in international orientations, and the equivalency that is drawn between trilingualism (here meaning English), Westernization and globalization. Language is presented as a tool to support the kind of 'Western'-facing mobility already in place with the Bolashak scholarship, an initiative by the Kazakh government to send Kazakh students to prestigious universities abroad.

Similar justifications were suggested by many participants in relation to another major language policy move, which is tied up with debates about globalization and international orientations – namely, the issue of changing the script for Kazakh from Cyrillic to Latin. The Kazakh government has debated introducing a Latin script for many years, but recently it has taken on a new urgency and reality. The government has announced that latinization will take effect by 2025, and a new alphabet has been presented to the public, the reception of which has not been particularly positive. The government has emphasized pragmatism and modernism as the reasons for this change, but many observers perceive it as primarily a move away from the influence of Russian (Rysaliev, 2017).

Participants in this study, who were interviewed before a specific Latin script was announced, also displayed mixed views toward the overall concept of latinization, but international scales of various types were invoked in many of the responses. Particularly, several respondents suggested that moving to a Latin script would make Kazakhstan more accessible to foreign visitors. The following excerpt is one example of such a justification:

Excerpt 3a

K20 (F, 20s, working in nonprofit sector, Astana): If it would be, if it would be written in uh Latin I believe there would be more possibility for those who are coming to Kazakhstan to read something and to learn language again. Yeah again it's a freedom and whatever is I don't know majority, we can say majority of countries in the world they – they have the percentage of having a Latin alphabet and it would be really how to say an opportunity again for Kazakhstan to, to let other people be able to read what's written on the ... [taps table] on anything.

Just after this the participant imagines the effect latinization would have on a hypothetical visitor, describing it as an opportunity for greater international engagement with Kazakhstan:

Excerpt 3b

> K20: So what it means – she takes a photo, she put it on Facebook, use a hashtag, I don't know, Kazakhstan, slash Shymkent I don't know what it is and it would also grow the territory, […] it would – it would how to say bring someone's attention?

So latinization here is being cast as a way for Kazakhstan and the Kazakh language to engage with a broader community beyond its borders. Of course, it must be highlighted that this discourse targets a specific version of imagined visitor – one who is presumably a native speaker of a language which already uses a Latin alphabet and who is able to create a valued kind of engagement with Kazakhstan.

In fact, in both cases the positive portrayal of 'international' engagement subtly targets a particular type of international audience – primarily one that is Western and presumably English-speaking, not Russian. Engagement with this imagined audience is intended to both increase the number of desirable visitors who come to and experience Kazakhstan and accordingly increase its visibility among the desired audience, and to improve the chances for Kazakhs to engage with the international through work, education or travel abroad – where, once again, 'abroad' primarily means those countries in which it is seen as prestigious to work or study (e.g. the UK, Western Europe, and the USA). From these examples it is clear that the 'international' is not a neutral and homogenous field, but, like the 'local', it is differentiated in complex ways. This becomes perhaps even more evident when we examine the more negative ways that international scales are invoked.

Threats from Abroad

The sorting of the 'international' space is particularly interesting when we consider that the 'international' is not just a place of opportunity – it is also potentially the source of threat. This threat is one of the fundamental features of Kazakhstan's nationalizing discourses – which, as noted above, emphasize that it is a new, 'weak' state that requires consolidating and remedial state action to safeguard its stability and existence (Brubaker, 2011; Dave, 2007).

In 2016, the Kazakh government implemented a land reform measure that would allow foreign stakeholders to lease land for longer periods of time – an increase from a maximum of 10 years to 25. This move triggered protests in several cities across Kazakhstan, including Atyrau in the west and Aktobe in the north. These were some of the largest protests in independent Kazakhstan, where protests are very rare, and were largely seen to be driven by a fear of Chinese encroachment and control. As one Aktobe protestor quoted by the BBC put it, 'After 25 years, they will stay for 65. After 65 their descendants will take Kazakhstan's citizenship and our descendants will be their slaves' (BBC Staff, 2016). China seems to be the most frequently and explicitly invoked foreign 'threat', particularly in relation to anxieties over investment in natural resources and land. These anxieties have not lessened with the announcement of China's One Belt One Road policy, which involves potentially a great deal of investment in and opportunities for Kazakhstan but also fears that China will be the only beneficiary. Many interview participants said either that they themselves distrusted the Chinese or that such attitudes were fairly common in Kazakhstan, although some suggested things were changing as more Kazakhstanis spend time in China for study or work.

Given its size, power, long border with Kazakhstan and shared Soviet history, Russia is obviously another nation whose presence and real or predicted intentions have had a significant impact on Kazakh foreign and domestic policy. Namely, fears about Russian expansionism and – especially in the early days of independence – ethnic Russian separatism from within Kazakhstan have been one of the key justifications for an emphasis on achieving an ethnic Kazakh demographic majority, especially in north Kazakhstan where Russian speakers had been the majority. These concerns justified Kazakhstan's *oralman* policy of encouraging ethnic Kazakhs living outside Kazakhstan to 'return' (which will be discussed further below). While it was not an explicit government policy, large-scale emigration of non-Kazakhs was also not discouraged. This additionally lead to the reconstruction or 'ethno-territorial gerrymandering' (Dave, 2007: 122) of the northern *oblasts* (districts), such that ethnic Kazakhs became a majority in all of the restructured regions, and was a key if unspoken reason for the decision to move the capital from Almaty in the predominantly Kazakh south to the Russified north. Interestingly, however, in interviews Russia and Russians did not seem to inspire the same kind of anxiety that the Chinese did – clearly there are historical, demographic and linguistic factors at play, but it seems that it is typically only on a national scale that Russia plays a threatening role.

The policy moves and discourses outlined here are not all immediately about language, but again, these discourses of contrast, affiliation and scaling have implications for what is happening within Kazakhstan's own borders and for the position of language in the Kazakh state. This section and the next demonstrate the role of supranational constructions in state-level policy, but also how these international sites of contrast are used to bolster particular nation-internal and nationalist ideologies. Nations have proven to be durable, and the fact that Kazakhstan is increasingly in contact with and concerned about its image in other nations does not necessarily mean that the state apparatus is weakening – it can in fact mean the opposite.

The Global in the Local: Complex Scaling Processes

The examples above have already demonstrated some of the complex ways that 'global' and 'local' forces interact. Fears about Russian occupation led to the redrawing of internal borders; the perceived need to bolster the nation against threats of linguistic and cultural loss manifests in anxieties about whether individuals are sufficiently Kazakh. So while on one scale of reference the homogenized nation of Kazakhstan is imagined to be enacting certain positions on a 'world' stage, the 'global' and 'local' are recursively constructed as divisions within Kazakhstani society itself. Even in describing itself as a multiethnic state, Kazakhstan has kept the Soviet 'nationalities' system, which 'regards nationality as a homogenous and bounded entity, which can (and should) be represented by a single official national-cultural centre and leadership' (Dave, 2007: 130) – in other words, the nation is composed of smaller, mutually exclusive nations. 'Global' positionings have effects on 'local' policies, but the 'local' can also recursively be framed as, to various extents and from particular perspectives, 'international'.

Although nationalist ideologies often seek to portray the 'nation' as a homogenized whole, this is clearly an oversimplification. International forces are also seen to have greatly different impacts on 'centres' and 'peripheries' within Kazakhstan. For example, 'urban' vs 'rural' is a significant division onto which other types of categories – like 'local' vs 'global' – are mapped. Urban/rural distinctions have played a meaningful role in nationalist ideologies in many contexts, and Kazakhstan in particular is a vast nation with low population density outside a few major urban centers, primarily Astana and Almaty, making this contrast especially acute. The kind of 'globalizing' opportunities envisioned in the trilingual policy are sometimes framed as potentially inappropriate for the 'less global' peripheries of Kazakhstan, as one participant, an English teacher, argued:

Excerpt 4

> K16 (F, 50s, working in higher education, Astana): Maybe trilingual policy will be good only for Astana or Almaty. But uh for south

Kazakhstan or west Kazakhstan, what for they need uh animal doctor with English language education? Or what for they need cleaner with English language education? hhh yeah you know? Maybe it will be good only for city people. And government I'm sure will spend huge money I think uselessly over that policy, yeah.

In this excerpt, English seems to be understood as a way to connect with international forces – but that connection is more appropriate and available to particular segments of the population.

Another example, which illustrates these conflicting invocations of scale and authenticity, is the 'oralmans'. As mentioned above, ethnic Kazakhs were a minority in Kazakhstan at the time of independence in 1991. One of the measures taken by the Kazakh government to redress what they felt was a serious issue for Kazakhstan's territorial integrity and claims to statehood was inviting ethnic Kazakhs living elsewhere (many in China, Mongolia and various parts of the former Soviet Union) to 'return' to Kazakhstan, where they would be provided with either some land or financial help in buying a home, and other financial benefits.

The oralmans now occupy a complex position in Kazakhstan's public discourse (Zardykhan, 2016), which illustrate how layered 'global' and 'local' scales can become. On the one hand, the consolidation of an ethnic Kazakh demographic majority was a major reason for the oralman policy, and the oralmans are sometimes suggested to be more authentic Kazakhs than people already resident in Kazakhstan, especially russified urban Kazakhs. At the same time, many oralmans do not speak Russian, leaving them without a resource that is still important to accessing many spheres in Kazakhstan. Oralmans may also face resentment from 'local' populations in places they move to, who may express anger at the benefits accorded to oralmans and at the way they introduce a new frame of reference for the places they arrive in, as seen in Excerpt 5 below.

Excerpt 5

K25 (F, 20s, working in higher education, Astana): I talked with one woman from Pavlodar, from the northern part and she was like from the Russian I think, ethnic group and she was like I lived in Pavlodar for so many years, my parents lived there, now my children and now now when oralmans create the like hostile environment? They say to us it's not your like, it's not your motherland? Just go away and so on, and she was very um was very how to say angry for the oralmans? Cause she said that before that we didn't have any problems, we just were living together despite any ethnicity identity. But now when oralmans came we feel ourselves like not in our place.

This participant outlines an example of how simply introducing new participants and new perspectives creates fraught new debates and sites of contrast in defining authentic local belonging. The participant describes how an ethnic Russian woman from Pavlodar draws on her personal and familial history to stake her claim to being local, yet these claims are called into question by oralmans. Despite being newcomers in a temporal sense, they are, to some extent at least, able to draw on ethnicized qualities of language and culture to position themselves as the true locals. The oralmans thus redefine the social space and its social divisions just by entering it. The issue of who is really 'local' is a matter of where particular boundaries are drawn, and the perspective from which you draw them.

Conclusion: Re-scaling the National

This chapter has provided a broad overview of language policy and ideologies in Kazakhstan in order to illustrate how scale is drawn upon to constitute and make sense of the 'global' and 'local', and how language is deployed to negotiate scales. The process is recursive, shifting and continually in a process of redefinition. Scales are often taken for granted in ways that mask particular vested interests, in which sense they share key features of language ideologies (Kroskrity, 2000, 2010). Scales are at once multiple, complex, continually renegotiated and fundamentally located within particular non-neutral viewpoints; yet we can still see that scales have power, to define and make possible particular types of meanings (cf. Pietikäinen & Kelly-Holmes, 2013: 5 on center–periphery negotiations). Scales are clearly not objective systems of reference; instead we must see 'scale as a qualitative feature of meaning making' (Blommaert *et al.*, 2015: 126).

These arguments have implications for the overall process of revival, national definition and nationalist consolidation that Kazakhstan is undertaking. Different policy moves become justifiable at different scales of reference – so it is useful to examine how these scales are invoked, contrasted or erased. All of the issues and policies above deserve a fuller discussion than space in this chapter allows, but their inclusion here is meant to show how different scales of reference are highlighted to justify various claims of being 'threatened', 'authentic' or 'legitimate'.

Discursive and political projects within Kazakhstan since independence to consolidate national identity, particularly many which concern language, can in certain ways be seen as a re-scaling and recreation of traditional nationalist models and structures. Revival is in this sense achieved through the realization of the nationalist ideal on a different scale of reference, as a previous minority becomes the new nation-building majority, creating new minorities in turn. Yet it would be tempting but far too simplistic to describe the pre- and post-independence situations as a simple role reversal for Kazakhs and other ethnic groups. There are much more complex forces at work, which, even when simplified into other kinds of binaries, can reveal some of the tensions and complexities inherent in trying to pin down matters of scale.

These examples also suggest that neither rescaling nor resisting rescaling necessarily implies greater democracy or equality of access (Canagarajah & de Costa, 2016: 7; Haarstad & Fløysand, 2007). Power moves in complex ways, and attempts to strengthen the core nation that are bound up in nationalist movements cannot uncritically be seen as positive just because they are framed as revival – instead, it is important to ask who specifically benefits and how, and from what perspective those benefits are assessed.

These processes of constructing the 'local' and orienting to the 'global' are of course not unique to Kazakhstan; they are just potentially more visible in a society that has had to undertake such an explicit process of self-construction since its independence. Yet all nations are continually resting on a wide range of unspoken shared assumptions even as they continually redefine themselves. The nation-state is a discursive project with complex meanings, and its importance does not seem likely to fade. Such issues are not new, but perhaps increased attention to 'globalization' has heightened our awareness and interest in how ideologies circulate on a global scale and what 'global' even means. Examining the construction and invocation of scales is crucial to our understanding of these processes: it provides a lens with which to view the complicated interaction of global and local meaning, and its consequences.

Note

(1) This chapter originates in research being conducted in collaboration with Umberto Ansaldo, and I would like to thank him for many useful comments, discussions and insights; any remaining errors are of course my own. I thank the University of Hong Kong as well for providing the funding for this fieldwork.
(2) As noted above, this research is part of a broader project; additional data was collected in Ulaanbaatar, Mongolia, comprising interviews on similar themes with 32 participants, which is not reported on here.

References

BBC Staff (2016, April 28) Why Kazakhstan's protests are unusual. *BBC News*. See http://www.bbc.com/news/world-asia-36163103
Blommaert, J. (2010) *The Sociolinguistics of Globalization*. Cambridge: Cambridge University Press.

Blommaert, J., Westinen, E. and Leppänen, S. (2015) Further notes on sociolinguistic scales. *Intercultural Pragmatics* 12 (1), 119–127.

Brubaker, R. (2011) Nationalizing states revisited: Projects and processes of nationalization in post-Soviet states. *Ethnic and Racial Studies* 34 (11), 1785–1814.

Canagarajah, S. and De Costa, P. (2016) Scales analysis, and its uses and prospects in educational linguistics. *Linguistics and Education* 34, 1–10.

Dave, B. (2003) *Minorities and Participation in Public Life: Kazakhstan*. UN Commission on Human Rights: Sub-commission on Promotion and Protection of Human Rights, Working Group on Minorities.

Dave, B. (2007) *Kazakhstan: Ethnicity, Language and Power*. London: Routledge.

Dovchin, S., Pennycook, A. and Sultana, S. (2018) *Popular Culture, Voice, and Linguistic Diversity*. Cham, Switzerland: Palgrave Macmillan.

Duchêne, A. and Heller, M. (2007) *Discourses of Endangerment*. London: Continuum.

Fauve, A. (2015) Global Astana: Nation branding as a legitimization tool for authoritarian regimes. *Central Asian Survey* 34 (1), 110–124.

Fierman, W. (2006) Language and education in post-Soviet Kazakhstan: Kazakh-medium instruction in urban schools. *Russian Review* 65 (1), 98–116.

Gal, S. (2016) Scale-making: Comparison and perspective as ideological projects. In E.S. Carr and M. Lempert (eds) *Scale: Discourse and Dimension in Social Life* (pp. 91–111). Berkeley, CA: University of California.

Haarstad, H. and Fløysand, A. (2007) Globalization and the power of rescaled narratives: A case of opposition to mining in Tambogrande, Peru. *Political Geography* 26, 289–308.

Heller, M. (2011) *Paths to Post-nationalism*. Oxford: Oxford University Press.

Hill, J.H. (1999) Styling locally, styling globally: What does it mean? *Journal of Sociolinguistics* 3 (4), 542–556.

Irvine, J.T. (2016) Going upscale: Scales and scale-climbing as ideological projects. In E.S. Carr and M. Lempert (eds) *Scale: Discourse and Dimension in Social Life* (pp. 213–231). Berkeley, CA: University of California.

Irvine, J.T. and Gal, S. (2000) Language ideology and linguistic differentiation. In P.V. Kroskrity (ed.) *Regimes of Language: Ideologies, Polities, and Identities* (pp. 35–83). Santa Fe, NM: School of American Research Press.

Jaffe, A. (1999) *Ideologies in Action: Language Politics in Corsica*. Berlin: Mouton De Gruyter.

Jaworski, A. and Thurlow, C. (eds) (2010) *Semiotic Landscapes: Language, Image, Space*. London: Continuum.

Kroskrity, P.V. (2000) Regimenting languages: Language ideological perspectives. In P.V. Kroskrity (ed.) *Regimes of Language: Ideologies, Polities, and Identities* (pp. 1–34). Santa Fe, NM: School of American Research Press.

Kroskrity, P.V. (2010) Language ideologies--evolving perspectives. In J. Jaspers (ed.) *Language Use and Society (Handbook of Pragmatics Highlights)*. Amsterdam: John Benjamins.

Lewis, D. (2016) Blogging Zhanaozen: Hegemonic discourse and authoritarian resilience in Kazakhstan. *Central Asian Survey* 35 (3), 421–438.

Ministry of Education and Science, Republic of Kazakhstan (2015) *Дорожная карта развития трехъязычного образования на 2015–2020 годы (Road Map for the Development of Trilingual Education for 2015–2020)*. Kazakhstan.

Muehlmann, S. and Duchêne, A. (2007) Beyond the nation-state: International agencies as new sites of discourses on Bilingualism. In M. Heller (ed.) *Bilingualism: A Social Approach* (pp. 96–110). Basingstoke: Palgrave Macmillan.

Ó Beacháin, D. and Kevlihan, R. (2013) Threading a needle: Kazakhstan between civic and ethno-nationalist state-building. *Nations and Nationalism* 19 (2), 337–356.

Pavlenko, A. (2013) Multilingualism in post-Soviet successor states. *Language and Linguistics Compass* 7 (4), 262–271.

Pennycook, A. (2007) *Global Englishes and Transcultural Flows*. London: Routledge.

Pennycook, A. (2010) *Language as a Local Practice*. Abingdon: Taylor & Francis.

Pietikäinen, S. and Kelly-Holmes, H. (2013) Multilingualism and the periphery. In S. Pietikäinen and H. Kelly-Holmes (eds) *Multilingualism and the Periphery* (pp. 1–16). Oxford: Oxford University Press.

Pujolar, J. (2001) *Gender, Heteroglossia and Power: A Sociolinguistic Study of Youth Culture*. Berlin: Walter de Gruyter.

Pujolar, J. (2007) Bilingualism and the nation-state in the post-national era. In M. Heller (ed.) *Bilingualism: A Social Approach* (pp. 96–110). Basingstoke: Palgrave Macmillan.

Rysaliev, A. (2017, April 12) Kazakhstan: President calls for switch to Latin Alphabet by 2025. *EurasiaNet*. See http://www.eurasianet.org/node/83206

Schatz, E. (2008) Transnational image making and soft authoritarian Kazakhstan. *Slavic Review* 67 (1), 50–62.

Schmidt, A. (1985) *Young People's Dyirbal: A Case of Language Death from Australia*. Cambridge: Cambridge University Press.

Smagulova, J. (2008) Language policies of Kazakhization and their influence on language attitudes and use. *International Journal of Bilingual Education and Bilingualism* 11 (3), 440–475.

Smagulova, J. (2016) The re-acquistion of Kazakh in Kazakhstan: Achievements and challenges. In E.S. Ahn and J. Smagulova (eds) *Language Change in Central Asia* (pp. 89–108). Berlin: Walter de Gruyter.

Smailov, A.A. (2011) *Results of the 2009 National Population Census of the Republic of Kazakhstan: Analytical Report*. Astana, Kazakhstan: The Agency on Statistics of the Republic of Kazakhstan.

Spolsky, B. (2004) *Language Policy*. Cambridge: Cambridge University Press.

United Nations Department of Economic and Social Affairs, Population Division. (2017) *World Population Prospects: The 2017 Revision. Key Findings and Advance Tables*. New York: United Nations.

Zardykhan, Z. (2016) Ethnic Kazakh repatriation and Kazakh nation-building: The awaited savior or the prodigal son? *Region: Regional Studies of Russia, Eastern Europe, and Central Asia* 5 (1), 17–34.

5 The Politics of Injustice in Translingualism: Linguistic Discrimination

Sender Dovchin

Introduction

The phenomenon of discrimination based on one's linguistic background directed to non-standard English speakers is growing around the globe (TT, 2016). For example, a young Polish man was beaten to death by a gang of teenage boys after they heard him speak Polish in Harlow, Essex, UK (MN, 2016). In the USA, more than 10,000 educators who responded to an online survey sponsored by a project of the Southern Poverty Law Center said that they had heard derogatory language or racist hate speeches used against students of color, Muslims and immigrants in 2016 (CNN, 2016). A French woman, for instance, was abused for singing the 'Marseillaise' on public transport in Melbourne; a young girl made a racially derogatory verbal attack against Adam Goodes in a match to start the National Indigenous week in AFL football.

ABC's investigative program *Four Corners* showed footage filmed largely at a youth detention center in the Northern Territory between 2010 and 2015 in which young Indigenous Australians were seen being tear-gassed, stripped naked and shackled to a chair. Although clearly the abuse of these young people was based on far broader issues, teen inmate Dylan Voller read a personal statement to the Northern Territories youth detention royal commission later, highlighting the fact that linguistic discrimination was indeed one of the crucial factors of abuse, 'On a number of occasions, I have witnessed officers abusing young Aboriginal men in here and putting them down *because they can't speak English properly*' (ABC, 2016).

In the face of today's globalization, there is a distinct lack of public understanding and large gaps in academic knowledge concerning what 'linguistic discrimination' means in contrast to other more established 'discriminations' based on one's skin color, ethnicity, religion and gender (Piller, 2012). There is a pressing need to investigate what 'linguistic discrimination' may actually mean or cause for modern speakers worldwide (Major et al., 2014). The proposed research thus addresses this critical need by advancing knowledge in contemporary studies of sociolinguistics of globalization.

In particular, this study aims to critique a current prominent strand in sociolinguistics studies on translingualism, which tend to celebrate the linguistic hybridity, fluidity and creativity aspects of translingual speakers, missing out on critical dimmer issues that come up with the actual speakers. It is clear that translingual speakers are creatively involved with different types of 'languaging' since they are involved in the sophisticated transcendence of lingua-cultural boundaries to create multiple and hybrid expressions, identifications and meanings (Leppänen et al., 2015; Nørreby & Møller, 2015). Yet it is not at all clear to what extent, how and why particular local constraints such as discrimination, racism and injustice either limit or expand one's translingual practices (Dovchin et al., 2018). Translingual speakers can be linguistically productive and inventive but they are also deeply embedded in local politics of disparity and discrepancy (Dovchin et al., 2016).

Based on an ethnographic study conducted among young Mongolians, this chapter thus aims to fill this critical research gap in existing translingual theories, urging a stronger need to acknowledge one of its most overlooked characteristics – linguistic discrimination and prejudice experienced by translingual speakers. The proposed study thereby points to the critical issues between language and inequality, innovating the analytical potential of sociolinguistics theories by taking the concept of 'linguistic discrimination' (cf. Alim et al., 2016; Piller, 2016) seriously.

Translingualism

Recent youth studies in the field of sociolinguistics of globalization have found that many young speakers in late modernity are creatively, playfully and resourcefully involved with different types of translingual practices (Creese & Blackledge, 2010; Higgins, 2009a, 2009b; Pennycook & Otsuji, 2015). Sultana et al. (2015) note that not only is it difficult, and at times pointless, to demarcate linguistic features according to specific languages, but it is also clear that the smooth movement between languages that is often observed requires different ways of thinking. In a similar vein, Creese and Blackledge (2010: 106) note that languages are not 'hermetically sealed units', urging us to consider the possibility that we cannot fully understand the usual and normal practice of bilingualism by separating its 'diglossic function'. It is therefore important to describe 'the use of vernaculars that leak into one another to understand the social realities of their users' (Creese & Blackledge, 2010: 106).

Translingual speakers are thus engaged with complex linguistic practices that move beyond their cultural boundaries to form manifold communicative aims, agencies, identities, desires and lexes (Jørgensen et al., 2011; Pennycook, 2007). The translinguistics tradition sees the creative linguistic practices of speakers as members of transnational groups, whose linguistic practices are activated by 'the co-presence of multilingual talk (exercised by de/reterritorialized speakers) and electronic media, in contexts heavily structured by social indexicalities and semiotic codes' (Jacquemet, 2005: 265–266). Central to translingual vision is the ways in which cultural forms move, change and are reused to fashion new identities in diverse contexts. Pennycook (2007: 47) defines translingualism as 'the communicative practices of people interacting across different linguistic and communicative codes, borrowing, bending and blending languages into new modes of expression'. Translingual practices are thus mainly characterized by the type of unconventional use of language in which particular language moves beyond linguistic, cultural, ethnic and racial boundaries, whilst being taken up, transformed and remade into new hybrid kinds of local forms (Li Wei, 2017). Speakers integrate all available codes and resources as a repertoire in their everyday communication (Blommaert, 2010).

From a translingual perspective, as soon as the standardized form of language comes into contact with other semiotic and linguistic resources, the standard system of language makes different and alternative sense (Dovchin, 2015). Language is understood not so much through the fixed grammar anymore, but rather focuses on how individuals resourcefully mobilize and transcend through different linguistic resources at their disposal and adopt different negotiation strategies to make meanings (Canagarajah, 2013). Objecting to 'a monolingual orientation to communication', Canagarajah (2013: 1–2) argues that translingual speakers participate within transnational contacts, while adopting 'creative strategies to engage with each other and represent their voices'. In this framework, Canagarajah (2013: 68–70) treats 'practices as primary and grammatical norms as emergent', while recognizing the significance of the 'complexity to processes like pidgins, creoles, and interlanguage'. The translinguistics tradition therefore is used to help legitimize the language practices of individuals who naturally blend named languages that often include low and other under-represented varieties of linguistic practices, including different accents, parodies, dialects, voices (Bailey, 2007, 2012; Rampton, 2005), jargons, taboos, verbiages and terminologies from mediascapes and technoscapes (Dovchin *et al.*, 2018; Sultana *et al.*, 2013, 2015).

The language practices of young speakers, such as those who were involved in this study, are thus not seen as the standard form of certain language grammar systems, but rather from its transgressive nature, where the speakers are actively yet smoothly involved with the mixed fusion of linguistic codes and resources.

Linguistic Discrimination

Meanwhile, this study also aims to expand knowledge in the theories of translingualism, proposing a stronger focus on its underexplored area – 'linguistic racism' in understanding late-modern speakers worldwide. Recent studies have found that a majority of current youth sociolinguistic studies tend to celebrate the linguistic fluidity and creativity aspects of translingual users, missing out on critical issues that come up with translingual speakers (Kubota, 2015). Dovchin *et al.* (2016) caution that the tradition of translingualism does not seem to sufficiently interrogate inequality experienced by its actual speakers. In fact, it is not very clear to what extent, how and why particular local constrictions such as discrimination and racism either limit or expand one's translingual practice.

In fact, there are many studies that have shown how translingual English speakers, i.e. non-standard English speakers, are discriminated against and socially excluded on a daily basis (Dixon & Angelo, 2014; Poynting & Noble, 2004). For example, Asian students are often ridiculed by local students in the USA for speaking 'broken' (Lindemann, 2005) and 'Ching-Chong English' (Chun, 2016), or writing weak and illogical essays in the Australian higher education system (Mahboob & Szenes, 2010). Job applicants with non-English-sounding names are instantly denied job interviews, as the employers only give consideration to English-sounding names (Piller, 2012, 2016). From this view, the theorization of contemporary translingual studies does not seem to sufficiently interrogate the inequality and injustice experienced by speakers, romanticizing the resourcefulness and originality of language without sufficiently interrogating injustices involving race, ethnicity and socioeconomic realities (Kubota, 2015). Tupas and Rubdy (2015) conclude that contemporary approaches toward hybrid English brush aside inequalities that mediate relations between English users since they have been seduced into celebrating hybrid English, but forget the massive inequities sustained by the different usage of English today. Translingual speakers can be linguistically creative but they are also deeply embedded in local economies of inequality, disparity and discrimination (Dovchin et al., 2016).

This study thus aims to fill this critical research gap in contemporary theories of translingualism, urging a stronger need to acknowledge one of its most overlooked characteristics – 'linguistic discrimination' experienced by translingual speakers. This article thereby points to the critical issues between language and inequality, innovating the analytical potential of translingual theories through taking the concepts such as 'linguicism' (Skutnabb-Kangas, 2015), 'linguistic injustice' (Piller, 2016), and 'raciolinguistics' seriously (Alim et al., 2016).

'Linguistic discrimination' here refers to the ideologies and practices that are used to legitimate, regulate and reproduce an unequal division of power between people, which are defined on the basis of an individual's use of language (Skutnabb-Kangas, 2015). Linguistic discrimination is categorized as: (1) all types of indirect institutional or interpersonal discrimination based on how or what languages one speaks/writes (Piller, 2016; Mahboob & Szenes, 2010); and (2) all kinds of direct institutional/interpersonal (verbal/written) abuse (race-hate talks/written discourses, racial slurs or name-calling, etc.) against others based on one's race and ethnicity (Chun, 2016). As Rastas puts it in terms of youth in Finland:

> For those, who are subordinated in racialized social relations, the meanings of racism are not limited to experiences of open, intentional racism they may face. They have to be prepared to be seen and treated differently wherever they go. They have to learn to live with other people's color-blindness and everyday language peppered with racist slurs and expressions. They also have to learn to deal with various racist representations in media and other cultural products that remind them of how 'people who look like me' are seen and valued in our society. Although many Finns would claim that such things 'have nothing to do with racism', these experiences nevertheless continue to make my informants' everyday lives different and more complicated compared with their peers who are positioned differently in racialized relations. (Rastas, 2009: 40)

From this view, the theory of 'linguistic discrimination' thus examines how one's basic human rights are violated, and how one is deprived of education, employment, health and social opportunities based on an individual's use of language (Musgrave & Bradshaw, 2014). It focuses on the central role that language plays in the enduring relevance of race/racism and institutional/interpersonal discrimination in the lives of people of color, ethnic minorities and Indigenous people, who experience disparity as an everyday lived reality (Alim *et al*., 2016). In particular, the main ethos of this concept seeks to understand what it means to speak as a racialized subject in the highly linguistically and culturally diverse societies of the 21st century. It raises critical questions about the co-relation between language, race, ethnicity and unequal power across diverse ethno-racial contexts, rather than seeing them as discrete and unconnected social processes (Piller, 2016). The article thereby focuses on the central role that language plays on the enduring relevance of race/racism, discrimination and institutional/interpersonal inequality in the lives of people of color, ethnic minorities and Indigenous people, who experience disparity as an everyday lived reality (Chun, 2016).

Linguistic Ethnography

The data used in this article builds on my ethnographic study on young translingual speakers with Mongolian backgrounds (cf. Dovchin, 2017a–d). Recent studies in the debate of translingual speakers have found that the methodological framework of 'linguistic ethnography' may constitute seeds of profound understanding about the sociolinguistic realities of language users (Blommaert & Dong, 2010a; Dovchin *et al*., 2018). Linguistic ethnography is specifically characterized by the appropriation of both 'ethnographic' and 'linguistic' perspectives, where researchers are interested in understanding one's sociolinguistic experiences through ethnography (Copland & Creese, 2015). Linguistic ethnography allows an improved explanatory warrant for statements about language and its actual connection with a real sociocultural context (Rampton *et al*., 2004). It pays a good deal of attention to people's daily social activities so as to derive their rationality from the local perspectives, focusing on how speakers' linguistic actions at particular moments and in spaces are connected (Maybin & Tusting, 2011). The study thus adopted a 'linguistic ethnographic' qualitative design in understanding young people's everyday sociolinguistic experiences and realities.

The project looked into the translingual practices of young adults living in Ulaanbaatar, Mongolia, conducted between 2010 and 2016. First, around 40 students from various social backgrounds aged between 17 and 29 years from the National University of Mongolia volunteered to participate in the research. Their socioeconomic and regional backgrounds were diverse, varying from affluent to poor and from rural to urban, before they gained admission to university and came to live in Ulaanbaatar. One of the most common methods in linguistic ethnography – 'open ethnographic observation', which often involves some kind of shadowing of participants, was applied. The research participants were thereby shadowed by me, while they went on with their daily lives. 'Open ethnographic observation' is open in the sense that the ethnographer has a flexibility to write down what he/she sees, hears, smells, feels and senses in the field. It involves taking as many notes as possible about the people, social spaces and practices in the site under investigation, mainly documented through field notes (Copland & Creese, 2015). Under this method, casual face-to-face conversations among students were audio-recorded during classroom breaks, libraries, lecture halls and university coffee shops. In the process, I monitored what everyday translingualism would look like to young Mongolian speakers. Later, the participants were interviewed on a one-to-one basis in terms of their metalinguistic practices. Their direct voices and their first-person perspectives were captured in relation to their translingual practices and their everyday linguistic struggles and resistances. These participants were interviewed face-to-face or through Skype in order to understand what everyday linguistic discrimination would look like to them, documenting the events they deemed critical, including issues such as what exactly led to the incident and why it was significant or critical (Dovchin, 2018).

Linguistic Discrimination in Translingual Speakers

Russian-sounding English

Bolor is a Mongolian girl, a student at the National University of Mongolia, who briefly lived in Sydney, Australia in 2006 to study English, with a vision of starting her postgraduate degree in Australia upon her completion of undergraduate degree in Mongolia. She returned to Mongolia in 2007. As part of an open ethnographic observation, I shadowed Bolor for 18 hours in Ulaanbaatar, Mongolia and interviewed her afterwards. In the process, I extensively observed and took field notes in terms of how she communicated with people on a daily basis. Bolor's use of English illustrates some classic examples of translingual English, in which the speaker seems to mobilize a range of stylistic resources such as accents for their communicative purposes (Dovchin *et al.*, 2018). When Bolor asks her friend 'Hi, where were you?', it sounds like a Russian English. She uses a heavy Russian-sounding English accent – 'Hi, vair ver you?' In fact, the standard phonetic form of English is heavily Russian-accented by Bolor as if she is speaking English through Russian. For example, when Bolor pronounces the fricative consonant /h/ in words such as 'how' and 'happy', it seems to sound in the mouth /x/ rather than in the throat /h/. English dental fricatives /θ/ and /ð/ are also often replaced with /s/ and /z/ by the speaker. For example, Bolor pronounces words such as 'mother' [/ˈmʌðərˠ/] as '/ˈmʌzərˠ/' or 'thunder' [ˈ/ˈθʌndə(r)/'] as '/-ˈsʌndə(r)/'. In addition, she integrates a lot of Russian and Mongolian expressions, terminologies and words when she speaks English. For example, she seems to excessively use the Russian personal pronouns such as 'я' ['I'], 'мы' ['we'] and 'она́' ['she'] instead of English. As Bolor says, 'Она́ my best friend' ['She is my best friend'].

From a translingual perspective, as soon as the standardized form of English comes into contact with other linguistic resources, the standard system of English makes no clearer sense (Dovchin, 2015). Bolor would often ask friends, 'cocktaildehuu?' ['Shall we go out and have some cocktails?'], combining English and Mongolian linguistic resources. The English stem 'cocktail' is mixed with the Mongolian question suffix '-dehuu?' ['Shall we do something?'], creating the unconventional question phrase 'cocktaildehuu?' (cf. Dovchin, 2017b).

Overall, despite her Russian-sounding English accent, Bolor's English is quite good. She is able to communicate in English without major obstacles. Nevertheless, she encountered a lot of problems in terms of how she speaks English when she was in Australia. Bolor was born in Mongolia in 1983. She first started learning Russian in a Russian elementary school in Mongolia. This was in the early 1990s when Mongolia transformed itself from a communist to a democratic society. Before 1990, Mongolia was a socialist country and a satellite of the USSR. Clearly, Russian language was the most popular foreign language in the country, while other Western languages such as English were deemed 'capitalists' languages', carrying the wrong ideological messages. During the Soviet era, there were many Russian elementary and high schools in Mongolia run by Russian expats and professionals. After 1990, when Mongolia became a democratic nation, a majority of the Russian educational institutions were closed down. The popularity of Russian was replaced by that of English, followed by other languages such as French, Japanese, Chinese and Korean. Nevertheless, some of the most prestigious Russian schools in Ulaanbaatar still remain open today. In fact, these Russian schools are still considered some of the elite educational institutions in the country. It is highly competitive to enter these schools and children with elite backgrounds or wealthy parents tend to attend these Russian schools.

When Bolor was a student at one of these Russian high schools, she also started learning English. Her first English teachers were all Russian native speakers and her first ever English textbook was a Russian two-volume edition textbook called 'English Step by Step' by Natalya Bonk. The book was very popular among Russian native speakers, with its descriptions and explanations all in Russian. It is thus natural for Bolor to possess a Russian accent when she speaks English, since her very first contact with English was achieved through Russian teachers and Russian textbooks.

Meanwhile, Bolor started experiencing 'linguistic discrimination' based on how she speaks English when she moved to Australia. According to Bolor, owing to her strong Russian-accented English, she was labeled by some 'guys' and 'men' in Australia for speaking 'sexy sounding English'. As Bolor describes, 'I didn't know how to take it when men said that my English sounded "sexy". As a compliment or disgrace? I was confused. I didn't know how to respond but I was not feeling good about it. I couldn't figure out why I was speaking "sexy" English and started becoming quite self-conscious when I started speaking English with my males, for example. I definitely didn't want to feel sexualized the way how I spoke English' (Facebook Interview, 21 September 2015). Clearly, Bolor did not realize why her way of speaking English was viewed 'sexy' and 'hot' by some men in Australia, and found it intimidating and embarrassing when the opposite sex openly declared their affection for her speech style. As a young girl from Mongolia, she did not fully understand the stigmas and stereotypes in relation to the Russian-accented English in the Western world.

Moreover, Bolor also recalls one specific event when she felt absolutely helpless because of how she speaks English. One of her female flat mates at her dormitory once mocked her English as making her sound like a 'hooker'. As Bolor describes, 'One day she started yelling at me for no reason because I did not know how to operate the gas stove and I asked her how to make it work. She told me that I sounded a bit like "naughty Russian hookers" from the movies. She also copied my accent and tried to speak English like me. She said she was annoyed because I could not even speak proper English. Then, she slammed the kitchen door and left me in the kitchen. Since then, I did not want to make friends with Australian girls because I just felt so out of place. They just seemed so bossy and mean to me. I was bullied a lot by these confident, beautiful and blonde Australian girls. They never made friends with us Asians anyway. They seem to have their own circle' (Facebook Interview, 21 September 2015).

This incident also reminds us about the public evaluation of the 'accent' of Melania Trump, wife of Donald Trump and a native of Slovenia, who does not speak English as her first language. For many people, as Lee (2018: 48) acknowledges, her 'accent' was pathologized through xenophobic and sexist rhetoric by online users for sounding like a 'hooker', 'bitch' and 'prostitute' and so on (Lee, 2018).

Overall, because of these types of linguistic discriminations that she has experienced in Australia, Bolor's initial positive imagery and vision about Australia being multilingual and multicultural nation were shattered. She decided to leave Australia shortly afterwards with a lot of confusion, self-doubt and low self-esteem.

Wrong Russian, wrong place

Bujin is a student at the National University of Mongolia. I shadowed Bujin for approximately three days while she was going on with her daily life in Ulaanbaatar. In the process, I found out that Bujin is a 'straight A' student, who is very responsible and hardworking. She can speak fluent Russian and English on top of her first language, Mongolian. However, I noticed her dominant tendency to integrate heavy Russian resources in her daily linguistic repertoire, especially when she hung out with her best friends. Occasionally, she would exclusively use long and complicated Russian sentences and paragraphs while interacting, joking and messing around with her close friends. However, in her best friends' circle, integrating heavy Russian resources seemed to be the linguistic norm. All of her friends seemed to show great familiarity with Russian resources while interacting with one another. A majority of Bujin's best friends either went to the same Russian high school in Mongolia or had extensively traveled to Russia. Bujin believes that her interaction with her best friends is her own private and liberal space where she can freely hang out, talk and behave the way she wants to without any external judgments.

Meanwhile, achieving a fluent level of Russian has not been straightforward for Bujin. She attended one of most reputable Russian elementary schools in Mongolia when she was 7 and started learning Russian. When she reached 12, her family moved to Russia. Her father had to pursue his postgraduate degree at one of the universities in Moscow, Russia. Consequently, Bujin started attending Russian high school in Moscow. This is, according to Bujin, when she started experiencing 'major bullying' from local people, mainly based on how she spoke Russian. Back in Mongolia, Bujin was considered a top student in the classroom, and her level of Russian was never questioned or ridiculed. She was accustomed to receiving praise and compliments in terms of her academic achievements and high level of Russian when she was a student in Mongolia. In contrast, when she moved to Russia and started living with local Russians, she started feeling different and uneasy.

Bujin specifically recalls one of the events that has affected her mental health for a long time, 'One day in my classroom, my teacher asked me a question. I responded to her question using the wrong word choice in Russian. I was supposed to say, "Moya mama skazala" ['My mom said that']. Instead, I wrongfully said, "Moya mama govorila" ["my mom talked that"]. Everyone in the classroom burst into laugh because they thought I sounded funny. I cried straight away because I was so ashamed of myself. My teacher took me to her office and told me that I should not cry and take it easy. She told me that my classmates who laughed at me could not even speak any foreign language, yet alone Mongolian. By contrast, I was speaking Russian when I was not even a Russian person. Since that event, I started becoming really shy and self-conscious when I spoke Russian to my classmates. I did not even want to speak Russian in the classroom. I did not want to go to school' (interview, Ulaanbaatar, Mongolia, 3 September 2010).

This example shows how one's translingual speech can be mocked and ridiculed by the native speakers (e.g. by local Russians), while it can also be accepted and acclaimed in other contexts (e.g. widely praised by Mongolians in her home country). Bujin notes that she felt specifically heartbroken and distraught because she had always thought that her Russian was fluent. She always assumed that she was a top student when she was in her home country. Her self-esteem, however, crashed for the first time in her life when she felt discriminated against based on how she speaks Russian. This type of external migration or mobility thereby tends to reshuffle one's translingual practice use in certain domestic and foreign contexts, in which certain translingual repertoires may indicate an identity of high-achiever in particular domestic settings, while simultaneously also marking low levels of literacy and marginal or peripheral sociocultural status in certain other foreign contexts. This puts into question of what counts as high and low varieties of translingualism or greater and lower mobilities that may have multiple facets since, for example, standard language may also not be equivalent to higher scale. Translingual practices that are 'low scale' may also become powerful or prestigious because of their recontextualization or because of the importance of local over global identities, affiliations and articulations (Blommaert, 2010; Blommaert & Backus, 2013).

Rural Mongolian is not cool

Language guide: Mongolian – regular font; English – **bold**; Russian – *italics*.

Transcription guide: (:) – elongated pronunciation.

Transcript
Line 1: Bi yostoi bugdengi:kh ni ulaan peenshdee kho!
Line 2: Bugdeeree Mongol *pilsoop* aguulsan, Mongol duuchid bolokhooor yamar kheleer duulakh ni yamar khamaa bainaa?
Line 3: Yamar bid nar shig demii balai yum chalchisa:n zavtai **stu-dent**uud baigaa bishdee?
Line 4: Uursdiin gesen yanz buriin shaltgaanaar duu bichij, **bidoo khiikhdee** yanz buriin khel kheregledeg bailguidee.

Translation
Line 1: I'm like the hugest fan of all of them.
Line 2: They are all Mongolians, so they all produce Mongolian philosophy. Why does it matter what languages they use?
Line 3: I mean they are not like us, a bunch of laid-back students just chit-chatting, are they?
Line 4: They use those different languages for their own particular reasons for writing songs and making videos.

The example above is an extract retrieved from the casual conversation of one of my research participants, Uurtsaikh (18, Ulaanbaatar born) – a first-year student at the National University of Mongolia. In this context, Uurtsaikh is talking to his classmates about the authenticity of popular music artists in Mongolia. He believes that all popular music artists in Mongolia are authentic no matter what languages they use because they sing and write about the Mongolian philosophy anyway.

While engaging in the conversation, Uurtsaikh is involved with translingual practice. For example, he illustrates a strong regional dialect from Uvurkhangai province in Mongolia. The locals from Uvurkhangai province are well known for speaking with a distinctive regional dialect, in which they extensively use the expression '*kho*' (line 1), something like 'dear' or 'mate' in English, positioned specifically at the end of the sentences. When Uurtsaikh says, '*Bi yostoi bugdengikh ni ulaan peenshdee kho!*' (line 1), it basically means 'I'm like the hugest fan of all of them, dear!' or 'I'm like the hugest fan of all of them, mate!' Uurtsaikh further shows his Uvurkhangai dialect through prolonging the vowel [i:] in '*bugdengi:kh ni*' ['all of them'] (line 1) and the vowel [a:] in '*chalchisa:n*' ['to chitchat'] (line 3), which is a very popular Uvurkhangai way of pronouncing words by greatly prolonging the last syllables.

Moreover, English and Russian semiotic resources embedded within the Mongolian lexical system are observed: 'Student' for example is pluralized by the addition of the Mongolian suffix '*-uud*', creating an Anglicized

Mongolian plural term 'studentuud' (meaning 'students') in line 3. Referring directly to 'student' as English is problematic here, since 'student' has been transformed into a Mongolian phrase now, with its direct contact with the Mongolian suffix '-*uud*'. Without this suffix, it would not make a proper meaning in the context. It is also similar to German root words with regional dialects, blended with English, in the context of online activities of German teenagers (Fetscher, 2009: 37). In addition, certain English root words such as 'fan' (line 1) and 'video' (line 4) are pronounced through Uvurkhangai-style talking: '*peenshuudee*' ['[I'm] a fan'] basically stands for the combination of English and Mongolian resources, 'fan + *shuudee = fanshuudee*'. It has been constructed around the English stem word 'fan', which has been relocalized in accordance with the Mongolian pronunciation, with the initial consonant 'f' replaced by the Mongolian stop consonant 'П' '[p]', and the middle consonant 'a' replaced by the Mongolian prolonged vowel 'ee' (line 1). In a similar vein, in line 4, English 'v' for 'video' has been replaced by the Mongolian stop consonant 'Б' '[b]', with the last English morpheme '-deo' pronounced through the Mongolian regional accent, '-doo', creating, '*bidoo*', sounding similar to the Uvurkhangai regional dialect. Urban people would often pronounce these words as '[*feenshüüdee*]' and '[*vidyoo*]', using the consonants 'f' and 'v', with the vowel 'yo' instead of 'oo' in 'video'. The Russian word 'философи' (line 2) is also pronounced as '*pilsoop*' ['philosophy'], in which it has been transformed into Mongolian with the Russian consonant digraph 'ф' '[ph]' replaced by the Mongolian stop consonant 'П' '[p]', and the Russian morpheme '-лософи [-losophy] is simply replaced by the regional Mongolian dialect '-*lsoop*'.

Overall, this style of speaking is generally referred to as 'rural-style speaking' by young urbanites in Mongolia. Translingual Mongolian users with strong regional or rural dialects and accents are often teased, parodied and discriminated against by urban Mongolians. Uurtsaikh is one of those post-Soviet era, rural-to-city migrants who moved to Ulaanbaatar back in the late 1990s. He previously resided in Taragt, Uvurkhangai, a small rural town situated in the southern region of the country. Uvurkhangai dialect is thus very common in his household since his parents and grandparents are all from this region.

When Uurtsaikh arrived in Ulaanbaatar, he started to feel outdated because of the general negative attitudes of urban people toward rural people. There is often a sharp tension between the urban and rural populations in Mongolia. Multigenerational city dwellers tend to blame rural people for many of Ulaanbaatar's current social and environmental problems such as the chronic overcrowding created by the expansion of the 'ger districts' in the city, causing both severe traffic congestion, and also magnifying problems with air pollution, particularly during the winter months. Almost half of the total Ulaanbaatar population lives in the 'ger districts', which are situated in the outskirts of Ulaanbaatar, lacking basic access to water, sanitation and infrastructure. Most of the families live in the ger (traditional Mongolian felt dwelling) or small houses. Many urbanites also accuse the rural migrants of harming the city image with their antisocial behavior (spitting, littering, urinating in the street) and also mock them for popularizing '*zokhioliin duu*' ['country songs'], a distinctive country-style musical genre that is quite popular among the rural population, with monolingual lyrics often written in Mongolian, glorifying the love for homeland, mother's love or the love for great horses, often performed by singers originating from rural areas. Many urban Mongolians believe that urban people are 'cool', and rural people are '*khuduunii khuusun mantuu*', a derogatory reference to a rural person, literally meaning 'a stupid rural bun'. This discrimination negatively affected Uurtsaikh when he first moved to the city. His rural dialect had become a problem, as Uurtsaikh describes, 'People would often laugh at me when I talk. They tell me I have a strong rural accent. So I felt urban people did not want to hang out with me. I wanted to change my speaking style but it was not happening as quickly as I imagined. I try to take it easy nowadays because I don't want to change myself. I think urban people are just plain rude and arrogant' (interview, Ulaanbaatar, Mongolia, 1 October 2010).

A similar account was also noted by another research participant, who moved to Ulaanbaatar from a rural town of Mongolia, located in the Gobi Desert. As Naran describes, 'When I opened my mouth, I started feeling the tension because I had this heavy rural dialect. I didn't want to sound like a "stupid rural bun". I wanted to be one of the proper modern members of the city'. This for example included changing her appearance and how she dresses – 'I wanted to get rid of my tacky looking "Made in China" platforms, as I was advised to wear Converse trainers instead because they were considered cool within my urban classmates' – and what music she listens to – 'I needed to go to cool pop concerts instead of going to cheesy comedy shows. They would often laugh at me when I listen to "*zokhioliin duu*"' (interview, Ulaanbaatar, Mongolia, 22 September 2010).

These examples remind us of Blommaert and Dong's (2010b: 377) discussion on the growing internal migration from rural areas to the cities in the context of China owing to the country's economic boom. This internal migration tends to reorder the language use in the city, in which 'certain accents mark a metropolitan, sophisticated identity, while others mark rural origins, low levels of education, and marginal social-economic status'. Here, translingual varieties, by and large, are associated with lesser privilege, since rural speakers who engage in translingual practices are in lower socioeconomic classes than city people whose linguistic practices come closer to what is assumed to be standard. As Blommaert and Dong (2010b: 368) further note, 'The spaces are always someone's space, and they are filled with norms, expectations, conceptions of what counts as proper and normal (indexical) language use and what does not.' The speakers never move across empty spaces, because mobility is a trajectory through different spaces – 'stratified, controlled, and monitored ones', where language 'gives you away' (Blommaert & Dong, 2010b: 368). Large and small disparities in language use may locate the speaker at specific levels of social indexicality. There are 'multiple layers of normativity in the form of self-, peer- and state-imposed norms' (Varis & Wang, 2011: 71), in which diversity is coordinated and regimented.

Conclusion

In this chapter, I aimed to expand the current discussions on the notion of translingualism by integrating the knowledge of 'linguistic discrimination' as a way of understanding the discrimination and injustice of one's translingual repertoire. There is little doubt that translingual speakers are involved with varied creative and sophisticated linguistic practices that integrate multiple resources, repertoires, styles, dialects, accents and features that may go beyond one's national and ethnic boundaries. Youth translingual practices are fundamentally diverse and produced by varied forms and styles, which are often relocalized, for example, in the forms of Russian-accented English, fluent Russian, rural-dialected Mongolian, Anglicized and Russianized Mongolian terminologies and so on.

Yet there are also particular local restraints that limit their translingual practices. Translingual speakers do not necessarily represent a clear-cut and straightforward picture. Clearly, they are linguistically innovative and dynamic but they are also embedded in deeper politics of discrimination racism, and injustice. The particular translingual repertoire of the particular speaker may signal certain social, cultural and linguistic differences by specific features, accents, dialects, word choices and frequencies of their language practices in defiance of their sociolinguistic background and history. This varied sociolinguistic locatedness of speakers further leads to negative responses, mockeries and bullying from their fellow discussants. For example, an international female student from Mongolia in Australia, who possesses a heavy Russian-accented English, was teased by some local men for speaking 'sexy' and 'hot' English, while being mocked by some local females for speaking like a 'hooker'. A young girl from Mongolia who moved to Russia was laughed at by the entire class for choosing a wrong word in Russian. A young male student from the countryside, who moved to the capital city in Mongolia, was discriminated against by urban people for speaking 'rural' and 'unacceptable' Mongolian. All of these research participants revealed that the subjective feeling of being discriminated caused a deterioration in their sense of belonging to the community.

Following these lines of thought, this chapter seeks to show that it is not always appropriate to celebrate youth translingual creativity and fluidity without fully acknowledging the local disparities and constraints. It is almost impossible to develop a thorough analysis of people's apparent linguistic choices and practices without acknowledging how ongoing communication is always associated with the existing social realities/experiences of those making these choices (Butorac, 2014). Translingualism might be a universal feature of youth language in today's globalization, but it is neither optimistic nor neutral, since it comes with its own gloomy sociolinguistic ostracism and marginalization.

References

ABC (2016) Dylan Voller reads a statement to the royal commission. See http://www.abc.net.au/news/201612-12/dylan-voller-reads-a-statement-to-the-royal-commission/8113868 (see 11 January 2017).

Alim, H.S., Rickford, J.R. and Ball, A.F. (eds) (2016) *Raciolinguistics: How Language Shapes our Ideas About Race*. Oxford: Oxford University Press.

Bailey, B. (2007) Heteroglossia and boundaries. In M. Heller (ed.) *Bilingualism: A Social Approach* (pp. 257–274). New York: Palgrave Macmillan.

Bailey, B. (2012) Heteroglossia. In M. Martin-Jones and A. Blackledge (eds) *The Routledge Handbook of Multilingualism* (pp. 499–507). Abingdon: Routledge.

Blommaert, J. (2010) *The Sociolinguistics of Globalization*. Cambridge: Cambridge University Press.

Blommaert, J. and Dong, J. (2010a) *Ethnographic Fieldwork: A Beginner's Guide*. Bristol: Multilingual Matters.

Blommaert, J. and Dong, J. (2010b) Language and movement in space. In N. Coupland (ed.) *The Handbook of Language and Globalisation* (pp. 366–385). Chichester: Wiley-Blackwell.

Blommaert, J. and Backus, A. (2013) Superdiverse repertoires and the individual. In I. de Saint-Georges and J.J. Weber (eds) *Multilingualism and Multimodality: Current Challenges for Educational Studies* (pp. 11–32). Rotterdam: Sense.

Butorac, D. (2014) Like the fish not in water. *Australian Review of Applied Linguistics* 37 (3), 234–248.

Canagarajah, S. (2013) *Translingual Practice: Global Englishes and Cosmopolitan Relations*. London: Routledge.

Chun, E. (2016) The meaning of Ching-Chong: Language, racism, and response in new media. In H.S. Alim, J.R. Rickford and A.F. Ball (eds) *Raciolinguistics: How Language Shapes our Ideas about Race* (pp. 81–97). Oxford: Oxford University Press.

Copland, F. and Creese, A. (2015) *Linguistic Ethnography: Collecting, Analysing and Presenting Data*. London: Sage.

CNN (2016) Harassment in schools skyrockets after election, teachers report. See at http://edition.cnn.com/2016/11/29/health/school-survey-post-election-negative-incidents/ (accessed 4 February 2017).

Creese, A. and Blackledge, A. (2010) Translanguaging in the bilingual classroom: A pedagogy for learning and teaching? *The Modern Language Journal* 94 (1), 103–115.

Dixon, S. and Angelo, D. (2014) Dodgy data, language invisibility and the implications for social inclusion. *Australian Review of Applied Linguistics* 37 (3), 213–233.

Dovchin, S. (2015) Language, multiple authenticities and social media: The online language practices of university students in Mongolia. *Journal of Sociolinguistics* 19 (4), 437–459.

Dovchin, S. (2017a) The role of English in the language practices of Mongolian Facebook users: English meets Mongolian on social media. *English Today* 33 (2), 16–24.

Dovchin, S. (2017b) Uneven distribution of resources in the youth linguascapes of Mongolia. *Multilingua* 36 (2), 147–179.

Dovchin, S. (2017c) The ordinariness of youth linguascapes in Mongolia. *International Journal of Multilingualism* 14 (2), 144–159.

Dovchin, S. (2017d) Translocal English in the linguascape of Mongolian popular music. *World Englishes* 36 (1), 2–19.

Dovchin, S. (2018) *Language, Media and Globalization in the Periphery: The Linguascapes of Popular Music in Mongolia*. New York: Routledge.

Dovchin, S., Sultana, S. and Pennycook, A. (2016) Unequal translingual Englishes in the Asian peripheries. *Asian Englishes* 18 (2), 92–108.

Dovchin, S., Pennycook., A. and Sultana, S. (2018) *Popular Culture, Voice and Linguistic Diversity: Young Adults On- and Offline*. Palgrave-Macmillan.

Higgins, C. (2009a) *English as a Local Language: Post-colonial Identities and Multilingual Practices*. Bristol: Multilingual Matters.

Higgins, C. (2009b) From Da Bomb to Bomba. In S. Alim, A. Ibrahim and A. Pennycook (eds) *Global Linguistic Flows, Hip Hop Cultures, Youth Identities, and the Politics of Language* (pp. 95–112). New York: Routledge.

Jacquemet, M. (2005) Transidiomatic practices: Language and power in the age of globalization. *Language and Communication* 25 (3), 257–277.

Jørgensen, J.N., Karrebæk, M.S., Madsen, L.M. and Møller, J.S. (2011) Polylanguaging in superdiversity. *Diversities* 13 (2), 23–38.

Kubota, R. (2015) Inequalities of Englishes, English Speakers, and languages: A critical perspective on pluralist approaches to English. In R. Tupas and R. Rubdy (eds) *Unequal Englishes: The Politics of Englishes Today*. London: Palgrave Macmillan, 21–42.

Lee, J.W. (2018) *The Politics of Translingualism: After Englishes*. New York: Routledge.

Leppänen, S., Møller, J.S., Nørreby, T.R., Stæhr, A. and Kytöla, S. (2015) Authenticity, normativity and social media. *Discourse, Context and Media* 8, 1–5.

Lindemann, S. (2005) Who speaks 'broken English'? US undergraduates' perceptions of non-native English. *International Journal of Applied Linguistics* 15 (2), 187–212.

Li Wei (2017) Translanguaging as a practical theory of language. *Applied Linguistics* 1–23; doi:10.1093/applin/amx039.

Mahboob, A. and Szenes, E. (2010) Linguicism and racism in assessment practices in higher education. *Linguistics and Human Sciences* 3, 325–354.
Major, G., Terraschke, A., Major, E. and Setijadi, C. (2014) Working it out. *Australian Review of Applied Linguistics* 37 (3), 249–261.
Maybin, J. and Tusting, K. (2011) Linguistic ethnography. In J. Simpson (ed.) *Routledge Handbook of Applied Linguistics* (pp. 515–528). New York: Routledge.
MN. (2016) He was killed for speaking Polish. *Mirror News*. See http://www.mirror.co.uk/news/uk-news/hekilled-speaking-polish-brothers-8738218 (3 February 2017).
Musgrave, S. and Bradshaw, J. (2014) Language and social inclusion. *Australian Review of Applied Linguistics* 37 (3), 198–212.
Nørreby, T.R. and Møller, J.S. (2015) Ethnicity and social categorization in on- and offline interaction among Copenhagen adolescents. *Discourse, Context and Media* 8, 46–54.
Pennycook, A. (2007) *Global Englishes and Transcultural Flows*. London: Routledge.
Pennycook, A. and Otsuji, E. (2015) *Metrolingualism: Language in the City*. London: Routledge.
Piller, I. (2012) Multilingualism and social exclusion. In M. Martin-Jones, A. Blackledge and A. Creese (eds) *The Routledge Handbook of Multilingualism* (pp. 281–296). London: Routledge.
Piller, I. (2016) *Linguistic Diversity and Social Justice: An Introduction to Applied Sociolinguistics*. Oxford: Oxford University Press.
Poynting, S. and Noble, G. (2004) Living with racism: The experience and reporting by Arab and Muslim Australians of discrimination, abuse and violence since 11 September 2001. Report to the HREOC, Centre for Cultural Research, University of Western Sydney.
Rampton, B. (2005) *Crossing*. Manchester: St Jerome Publishing.
Rampton, B., Tusting, K., Maybin, J., Barwell, R., Creese, A. and Lytra, V. (2004) UK linguistic ethnography: A Discussion paper. See www.ling-ethnog.org.uk.
Rastas, A. (2009) Racism in the everyday life of Finnish children with transnational roots. *Barn* 19 (1), 29–43.
Skutnabb-Kangas, T. (2015) Linguicism. *The Encyclopedia of Applied Linguistics* 1–6.
Sultana, S., Dovchin, S. and Pennycook, A. (2013) Styling the periphery: Linguistic and cultural take-up in Bangladesh and Mongolia. *Journal of Sociolinguistics* 17 (5), 687–710.
Sultana, S., Dovchin, S. and Pennycook, A. (2015) Transglossic language practices of young adults in Bangladesh and Mongolia. *International Journal of Multilingualism* 12 (1), 93–108.
TT (2016) Linguistic xenophobia and why it should be resisted. Tlang Team. See https://tlangblog.wordpress.com/2016/07/13/linguistic-xenophobia-and-why-it-should-be-resisted/ (accessed 10 February 2017).
Tupas, R. and Rubdy, R. (2015) Introduction: From world Englishes to unequal Englishes. In R. Tupas and R. Rubdy (eds) *Unequal Englishes: The Politics of Englishes Today*. Basingstoke: Palgrave Macmillan, 1–21.
Varis, P. and Wang, X. (2011) Superdiversity on the Internet: A case from China. *Diversities* 13 (2), 71–83.

6 Translingualism as Resistance Against What and for Whom?

Jerry Won Lee

Introduction

Perhaps among the most compelling axes of scholarship on the sociolinguistics of globalization is that of translingualism. Translingualism has been manifest through various iterations, including translingual practice (Canagarajah, 2013), translanguaging (Creese & Blackledge, 2010; García, 2009; García & Li Wei, 2014; Williams, 1994), transglossic language practices (Sultana & Dovchin, 2017; Sultana et al., 2015), polylingual languaging (Jørgensen, 2008; Jørgensen et al., 2011), fragmented multilingualism (Blommaert, 2010), metrolingualism (Otsuji & Pennycook, 2010; Pennycook, 2010; Pennycook & Otsuji, 2015) and linguascaping (Dovchin, 2017a, 2017b). While all these inquiries certainly do not necessarily invoke the expression 'translingualism', the common thread among this scholarship is the rejection of static boundaries of 'language' and 'culture' along with a recognition of the legitimacy of hybridity, which is frequently the subject of pathologization. As Canagarajah (2013) argues, translingualism is derivative of a postcolonial orientation to language and culture, which eschews expectations of uniformity and fixity along with the discursive hierarchization of language and culture. Thus, one of the foundational objectives of the translingual orientation in sociolinguistics is the resistance against the epistemological residues of colonialist logics, including top-down conceptualizations of language and culture.

There would appear to be, at first glance, much to commend in the resistant agenda of translingualism, especially if we acknowledge, following Piller (2016), the centrality of linguistic plurality to global social justice. For instance, the scholarship on Korean-English translingual practice counteracts the metadiscourses of monolingual normativity.

However, scholars have alternatively suggested that one of the inherent faults of translinguistics is the means by which it renders legible translingual practices according to mainstream epistemologies of 'difference' (Dovchin, 2017a; Lee, 2017; Pennycook & Otsuji, 2015). Further, as scholars such as Pennycook (1998) and Cameron (2012) have argued, the insistence of linguistic plurality for the sake of plurality is to risk losing sight of whose interests such pluralistic agendas serve. Likewise, translinguistics reflects the tendency to valorize the praxis of resistance while assuming that which is being resisted inherently warrants resistance. Put differently, translingualism perhaps reflects what Acosta (2014) has called a 'deadlock of resistance', in which 'resistance' becomes sedimented as a means unto itself, and imagined as an inherently commendable theoretical position or praxis to counter dominant epistemologies and ideologies.

In response to this critical stasis, this chapter considers the dubious practices and outcomes of resistant translingualism as it circulates within English language materials such as English textbooks in the South Korean context. I will offer an extended critical discourse and social semiotic analysis of one such textbook, in order to understand not its conspicuous linguistic hybridity but instead the innocuous cultural and ideological hybridity that inheres within the artifact. The central purpose of this chapter is not to simply dismiss the emancipatory potential of 'resistance' nor to eschew translingualism as a misguided theoretical paradigm within sociolinguistics. Instead, by uncovering the paradoxes undergirding the ideological architecture of the aforementioned artifact, this chapter further directs us to re-examine the resistant potentiality of scholarly paradigms, such as recent iterations of translingualism, which are premised on the inherent good of resistance.

Translingualism as Resistance in the Korean Context

The ubiquitousness of English in the South Korean context has been extensively documented in scholarship, with much work focusing on the resistant potentiality of translingual practice. For instance, J.S. Lee's (2004: 446) study of hybridization in Korean popular songs demonstrates how elements of English are woven into lyrics as a 'discourse of resistance' in order to 'challenge dominant representations of authority, to resist mainstream norms and values, and to reject older generations' conservatism'. Yet, this chapter is premised on the claim that all iterations of English in this sociolinguistic context are necessarily translingual and while not overtly resistant as some K-pop lyrics, inherently resistant nonetheless. In other words, scholarly documentation of such translingual practices positions them as resisting dominant language ideologies of monolingualism and native speaker idealization (Kachru, 2005).

To clarify, my usage of 'translingual' in the context of this chapter can be understood in at least two ways. First, English is translingual in the sense of its conspicuous hybridity in the form of the simultaneous copresence of 'English' and 'Korean' resources in a given space or utterance. Other scholarship, including works by Ahn (2017), J.S. Lee (2006), J.W. Lee (2014) and Kim (2012) have emphasized the resourcefulness of Korean-English hybridity, counteracting expectations of a monolingual orientation to language (Canagarajah, 2013). Second, English is translingual in the sense of its comparatively innocuous linguistic and cultural hybridity in the form of Koreanized English resources, which additionally reject ideologies that pathologize the blending of languages and cultures. English is, without question, technically a 'foreign' language in Korea, in spite of the fact that all public school students begin learning the language in grade 3. Korea is considered, according to the Kachruvian world Englishes paradigm, an 'expanding circle' country in that English was not implemented through colonial occupation by an English-dominant entity such as the UK or US (Kachru, 1992, 2005). Therefore, unlike 'outer circle' countries, such as India or the Philippines, English does not have any 'official' status in Korea. Certainly, I acknowledge the limitations to the Kachruvian world Englishes paradigm, as identified by Canagarajah (1999), Pennycook (2007) and others. My point is not to affirm its analytical or theoretical relevance but instead to rely on it as a point of departure in emphasizing the point that English has become so sedimented within the cultural milieu of Korea that it is worthwhile not only questioning the fluidity of 'outer' and 'expanding' circle boundaries, as Kachru himself has noted, but also reconsidering whether English may be legitimately considered a 'Korean' language as well (Lee & Jenks, 2017). For instance, scholars such as Shim (1999), Hadikin (2014) and K.J. Park (2009) have identified features distinct to Korean English. More recently, Rüdiger's (2017) work complicates the ontological stability of a uniform variety of Korean English by focusing on features of a particular cross-section of the population. In short, the scholarship documents and thus endorses the reality that everyday users translingually incorporate 'Korean' resources and conventions into their practice of 'English'. Whether we are describing conspicuous or comparatively innocuous enactments of hybridity, translingualism is a ubiquitous phenomenon in the Korean context.

Description of Study

This chapter focuses on an artifact whose ideological architecture offers a useful avenue through which to re-examine the emancipatory potential of translingualism as a 'resistant' ideal. The artifact in question is an English language textbook from South Korea for grade 7 students, the *YBM Middle School English 2*, 2012 edition (Bak *et al.*, 2012). The initial objective of the study was to analyze various instances of translingual practice in a larger sample of English language textbooks from Korea. It is important to note that the textbooks are distributed to teachers and students for use in the classroom and are therefore not sold in bookstores. As a result, researchers are not always able to readily acquire textbooks from vendors or distributors. In addition, the textbooks are revised each year and therefore have little to no resale value and are regularly disposed of. They are thus not commonly sold by third-party merchants such as used bookstores. Textbooks for the initial study were therefore selected on the basis of convenience:

Daekyo Elementary School English 3, 2010 edition
Daehan Gyogwasuh Elementary School English 3, 2010 edition
Hansol Gyoyuk Elementary School English 3, 2010 edition
Gyohaksa Elementary School English 3, 2010 edition
Chunganggyoyukjinheung Yeonguso Elementary School English 3, 2010 edition
Gyoyukgwhahakgisukbu Elementary School English 4, 2010 edition
Gyoyukgwhahakgisukbu Elementary School English 5, 2010 edition
Gyoyukgwhahakgisukbu Elementary School English 6, 2010 edition
Chunchaegyoyuk Middle School English 3, 2012 edition
Doosan Dongi Middle School English 1, 2012 edition
YBM Middle School English 1, 2012 edition
YBM Middle School English 2, 2012 edition
YBM Middle School English 3, 2012 edition

The initial coding process focused on conspicuous and innocuous patterns of linguistic practices that would be reflective of translingual practice. However, during my examination of *YBM Middle School English 2*, 2012 edition, I unexpectedly discovered a series of unusual ideological strategies that appeared to deviate from the curricular goals of the textbook. Therefore, I allowed the research to develop as 'a process' (Pennycook & Otsuji, 2015; see also Blommaert & Dong, 2010) instead of constraining the research and analysis according to a preconceived design. Such a 'methodology,' or perhaps 'anti-methodology', enabled me to recognize, redirect my analytical focus and to make sense of the 'unexpected' (Pennycook, 2012; see also Pennycook, 2007 for the significance of 'going with the flow').

Upon deciding which artifact I would focus on, I decided to rely on hybrid methodology of critical discourse analysis (CDA) (Fairclough, 1985; van Dijk, 1993) and social semiotic analysis (SSA) (Kress, 1993). I focus on manifestations of social power in the form of signs that construct and mediate inequitable social relations. CDA, popularized by the work of Fairclough (1985), involves an analysis of 'the role of discourse in the (re)production and challenge of dominance' (van Dijk, 1993: 249). Van Dijk (1993: 249–250) defines dominance as 'the exercise of social power by elites, institutions or groups, that results in social inequality, including political, cultural, class, ethnic, racial and gender inequality'. Following the spirit of CDA, I am interested in the way discourse manipulates social cognition, especially how text constructs 'socially shared representations – such as attitudes or ideologies – about important social issues' (van Dijk, 2006: 368). SSA is an integrated methodology with shared objectives of CDA, but more specifically focuses on the process of semiosis, or the relationship between signs and the objects they signify (Kress, 1993). The benefit of an SSA approach for ELT textbooks is the opportunity to consider how semiosis is, rather than a systematic process, motivated by the interests of the producer of signs. A hybrid CDA/SSA approach facilitates an analysis of text and image, of image as discourse and of the semiological nature of an English language textbook as a discursive space, helping to better understand how relations of social power construct and mediate social realities within.

Translingual Textbooks as 'Resistant' Documents

In Korea, English is taught in public schools beginning in elementary grade 3 with textbooks that have been approved by the Korean Ministry of Education (*Daehanminguk Gyoyukbu*). The centralized approval process helps to ensure the implementation of the Korean national curriculum (*Daehanminguk Gyoyukgwajung*), a standardized set of curricular goals and learning outcomes. Textbooks 'are developed within the framework of the national curriculum', which includes not only mandatory English language instruction, but also an understanding of the 'national culture' (Ministry of Education 2011).

It is important to recognize state-sanctioned English language textbooks such as the *YBM Middle School English 2* as *translingual* documents. Of course, one might make the argument that because this textbook teaches a normative 'inner circle' English (Kachru, 1992) it cannot be viewed as 'translingual'. One lesson, for instance, teaches students idiomatic expressions common in 'inner circle' contexts such as

'The walls have ears (someone may be listening)', 'I feel like a fish out of water (I don't feel comfortable)', or 'It's the apple of my eye (It's my favorite)' (Bak *et al.*, 2012: 31). Likewise, the textbook does not teach students English translations of idioms that are common in Korea.

In spite of features such as this, I argue that it is a translingual document insofar as it is reflective of discrete 'Korean' curricular priorities, as noted above. Materials such as textbooks, beyond mere artifacts that transmit disinterested knowledge about language and how to use language, are often politicized documents that can achieve ideologically determined ends (Apple, 2004; Benavides, 2009). English language textbooks, in particular, are not merely politically neutral artifacts for the teaching of the English 'language' alone, but they are indeed capable of reproducing and sustaining dominant ideology beyond the confines of the classroom (van Dijk, 2001). As Ndura (2004: 143) notes, English teaching materials have the potential to 'transmit overt and covert societal values, assumptions and images'. For instance, in Schneer's (2007: 605) study of the Japanese context, textbooks are found to perpetuate harmful 'stereotypes and an us-and-them mentality'. D.B. Lee's (2010) study demonstrates how materials and curricula from the Democratic Peoples' Republic of Korea (North Korea) tend to overtly enforce a commitment to government policy and to disseminate state ideology, including the vilification of outsiders from enemy countries. Gulliver's (2010) analysis of English language textbooks in Canada uncovers how the textbooks present an unbalanced and misleading image of Canada as a place of redemption and upward social and economic mobility for immigrants. Awayed-Bishara's (2015) study shows how English textbooks in Israel perpetuate a Western-centric ideology that marginalizes the Palestinian Arab minority.

Existing research based on critical analyses of English textbooks in South Korea has tended to focus on issues about Korean culture and identity in relation to Western ideals and norms. I. Lee's (2009) study shows how Korean textbooks tend to privilege Western cultural traditions, including music, literature and art while marginalizing non-Western cultures. K. Lee's (2009) study points to a similar conclusion, but emphasizes how people of the Anglophone world, in particular US Americans, are portrayed as ideal users of English. The role of monolithic English language ideologies in English textbooks in Korea was also noted in Song's (2013) study of how such materials privilege US American varieties of English and cultural norms. These investigations indicate that Koreans, by producing these classroom materials, are themselves responsible for perpetuating inequitable cultural hierarchies that privilege Western, Anglophone and US American ideals.

Resistance Against What and for Whom?

Certainly, *YBM Middle School English 2* falls into similar patterns of inadvertently marginalizing Koreans. For instance, the following excerpt is from one of the lessons:

> I am writing because of my MOM! She often says, 'Don't go to the PC room'. She doesn't let me have a cell phone and always tells me, 'Study, study!' My mom is so strict that I am often stressed out. (Bak *et al.*, 2012: 97)

The text reifies two Korean stereotypes: the *horangi umma* ('tiger mom') along with youth obsession with PC gaming culture. In another lesson, portraits of three influential artists are presented: Park Gyeongni (a Korean novelist), Pablo Picasso (a Spanish painter) and Charlie Chaplin (an English actor). Not only is the Korean woman artist outnumbered by two European male artists, but her name is misspelled as 'Park Gyeongri' (Bak *et al.*, 2012: 179). While there are admittedly different ways of transliterating Korean words and names into English, 'Gyeongri' is not reflective of how a Korean would pronounce the name and thus alienates and symbolically de-Koreanizes the one Korean woman artist presented in the lesson. In an activity for a different lesson, students are presented with a passage 'To Koreans, English is a foreign _____', in which students are expected to fill in the blank with 'language' (Bak *et al.*, 2012: 146). Such a statement contradicts the aforementioned world Englishes scholarship that emphasizes Korean ownership of English while simultaneously undermining the English used by Koreans.

In spite of these problematic elements of the text, *YBM Middle School English 2* additionally provides the opportunity to examine how English textbooks in South Korea can simultaneously be used as a resource to counteract dominant ideology. One of the most striking features is one of the lessons, titled 'What's on Dokdo?', which aims to affirm the legitimacy of Korea's claim over territory that has been disputed with Japan following the Korean peninsula's independence from Japanese colonial occupation (1910–1945). The title of the lesson is especially unusual when viewed in the context of the other lesson titles:

Lesson 1: My New Buddy
Lesson 2: Seeing is Not Always Believing
Lesson 3: Three Easy Saving Tips
Lesson 4: The Great Judge
Lesson 5: Share Your Worries with Dolly
Lesson 6: Be Thoughtful on the Internet
Lesson 7: Foreign Festivals in Korea
Lesson 8: What's on Dokdo

Lesson 9: A Teen Hero
Lesson 10: The Future in the Past
Special Lesson 1: Mason and the Baby Bird
Special Lesson 2: Eggs-periments

The ongoing territorial dispute over 'Dokdo', a series of islets in the Pacific Ocean comprising approximately 0.19 square kilometers, is among the most notable examples of continued postcolonial friction today. The islets, known as 'Takeshima' in Japanese, are located almost equidistant to the two countries, which prompts both countries to insist on the legitimacy of their respective territorial claim. The dispute became international news in 2008 when the Japanese government authorized the publication of history textbooks claiming Japanese ownership of the islets. The Korean ambassador to Japan was recalled, followed by a series of protests in Korea, including demonstrations that involved people cutting off their own fingers outside the Japanese embassy in Korea. Many Koreans have insisted that the islets were Korean territory even prior to Japan's annexation of the peninsula. Those who claim Korean sovereignty over the Liancourt Rocks view Japan's claim to the islets as a prolongation of its colonial-era political aggression, territorial expansionism and cultural hegemony.

In the 21st century, we are well aware of the atrocities of colonial occupation, characterized by the ruthless exploitation of allegedly 'inferior' peoples and their territorial resources, throughout recent human history. One consequence of this virtually ubiquitous and unanimous recognition, in large part through various developments in postcolonial theory, is the binarized construction of colonizer as evil and colonized as innocent, which leads to conclusions that coloniality is bad and anticoloniality is good. Yet, as Spivak (1999) has insisted, scholarly paradigms founded on the resistance to and vilification of a homogeneous colonialist entity are unable to attend to the 'sheer heterogeneity of decolonized space', for instance, by neglecting the silencing of women that is operationalized in the interests of both coloniality and anticoloniality. Acosta (2014) troubles the tendency to valorize decolonial resistance, which is premised on an exceptional precolonial subjectivity. Similarly, in regards to the Korean context in particular, Choi (1993) has problematized how decolonial efforts are mobilized to serve the interests of conservative political elites. Soh (2009) further argues that the discourse of anticoloniality implicates a historical aggressor (the Japanese) while failing to acknowledge the complicity of the colonized (Koreans) in the oppression of their own peoples, especially women.

If it can be established, then, that resistant ideals need not be unilaterally romanticized as good, we are in a position to more critically examine the resistant potentiality of translingual artifacts such as the *YBM Middle School English 2*. What is of interest in this chapter is not the anticolonial territorial claims themselves, nor is it the strength of one country's claim vs that of the other. Instead, it is the representational praxis by which the controversy is presented both translingually (in terms of a local regional issue re-presented in English) and anticolonially. It is worthwhile to proceed by exploring the very decision of the textbook to refer to the Liancourt Rocks by their designated Korean name, 'Dokdo'. While this observation may seem unsurprising, it is important to understand that the choice of name for territory as controversial as the Liancourt Rocks has become a highly politicized issue. The use of 'Liancourt Rocks' is considered a diplomatically neutral choice, as in the labeling on the US version of Google Maps. As one would expect, the Korean version of Google Maps labels the islets as 독도 (Dokdo), while the Japanese version of Google Maps labels them as 竹島 (Takeshima). For non-Korean and non-Japanese entities, however, decisions to choose the other two alternatives can be subject to scrutiny and representative of a political allegiance to one country over the other. For instance, recently, Microsoft users discovered that they were unable to type 'Takeshima', but were able to type 'Dokdo', when entering their home location for their profile information. Although it remains unclear whether Microsoft deliberately prohibited the input of 'Takeshima', the restriction was nonetheless interpreted as a political gesture by Microsoft and subsequently praised by some Koreans (S.M. Lee, 2007).

Although the nomenclature choice may appear to be a harmless decision, it represents a practice of what might be called appellative screening. I develop Burke's (1966) notion of 'terministic screen', which describes the method of using terminology to refer to a particular object or phenomenon and thus 'screening' other terminological alternatives. As Burke (1966: 45) writes, 'Even if any given terminology is a *reflection* of reality, by its very nature as a terminology it must be a *selection* of reality; and to this extent must function also as a *deflection* of reality'. By using the expression *appellative* screening, I draw attention not only to the use of terminology to select and deflect reality, but also to the outcomes of assigning a particular appellation to a particular object/phenomenon (in this case 'Dokdo' instead of 'Takeshima' or 'Liancourt Rocks'). In other words, referring to the islets as Dokdo is not merely an appellative choice but also an ideological one. While Burke (1966) argues that screening reflects, selects and deflects 'reality', I of course do not, by any means, presume the 'reality' of one particular claim over the other. In fact, Burke's (1966) point is that reality is socially constructed and negotiated through language. In this case, the very naming of the islets as Dokdo, in an English textbook for Korean grade 7 students, is an effort to construct the reality of the Korean claim to their ownership, while simultaneously deflecting considerations of alternative and competing claims.

Insofar as the manner by which the appellative screening of the islets as 'Dokdo' presumes Korean ownership, another feature, which I call specious territoriality, serves a similar purpose. By specious territoriality, I refer to the textbook's use of specious reasoning and fallacious logic in a manner that attempts to assume and 'prove' how the Liancourt Rocks are indeed Korean territory. At the beginning of Chapter 8 of the YBM textbook, students are provided with three 'true or false' questions as a warm-up:

(1) Dokdo is an island which is part of Korea.
(2) Dokdo has its own zip code.
(3) No one is living on Dokdo (Bak *et al.*, 2012: 155).

Of note is the fact that 'Dokdo' is referred to as having a zip code, or Zone Improvement Plan code, which is a trademark of the US Postal Service, which in turn reflects a curious, although probably inadvertent, Americanization of a uniquely Korean controversy. Further, although the ideological significance of referring to the islets as 'Dokdo' was noted above, what is particularly noteworthy about the true/false questions is the first one, which encourages students to choose the one 'correct' answer: it is 'true' that 'Dokdo is an island which is part of Korea'. This exemplifies what is commonly known as the false dilemma, wherein an individual is provided with only two choices without any consideration of alternatives or gray areas in between the choices. In this example, the false dilemma provides students with a dichotomous either/or choice and manipulates and indeed obliges them to agree with the 'correct' choice of the Liancourt Rocks as Korean territory. What is potentially at stake for the students is committing to an ideological position in the guise of a question that is purportedly designed to assess their English reading comprehension.

Another, arguably more egregious, instance of specious territoriality is, within the same chapter, an image accompanied by the following caption: 'Can you read this? It's Hangungnyeong. This marker makes it clear that Dokdo is part of Korea' (Figure 1 in the textbook). Shortly after Korea's independence from Japan, *hangungyeong* (韩国领), which translates as Korean territory, was engraved onto one of the Liancourt Rocks as a political declaration. Just two pages later, students are provided with an exercise in which they are asked to match images with the appropriate box of text. The image of the Hangungyeong declaration corresponds with text that reads, 'It shows that Dokdo is part of Korea' (Bak *et al.*,

2012: 165). The declaration portrayed in the images is written not in the contemporary Korean alphabet but in Hanja, or Chinese characters that have been borrowed in the Korean language. Contemporary usage of Hanja indexes an antiquarian, protonational past and is unfamiliar to most of the students using the textbook, as Hanja is no longer a part of the standard public education curriculum. The focus on this protonational register within the context of the textbook therefore has the effect of convincing students that the engraving was made many centuries ago, further legitimizing Korea's claims to the Liancourt Rocks. In addition, by stating that the engraving 'makes it clear' and 'shows' that 'Dokdo is part of Korea', the textbook relies again on fallacious reasoning. The engraving itself does not make it clear or show that 'Dokdo is part of Korea'. Rather, the engraving makes it clear and shows that *somebody has declared that* Dokdo is part of Korea. The exercise leads students to wager their desire to answer the question correctly, as a reflection of their emerging proficiency in English, in exchange for dubious logic.

The Liancourt Rocks controversy is a highly contentious issue with serious implications for diplomatic relations. It is therefore fascinating to consider, in addition to the manipulations in logical reasoning discussed above, that the controversy is presented in the textbook through a visual and textual register designed to align with the sensibilities of younger students. I call this feature of the textbook semiotic puerilization. Weninger and Kiss (2013: 710) have argued for the importance of a semiotic approach to the analysis of English textbooks, ultimately insisting on a redesign of teaching materials in accordance with the principle that '[i]mages need to be much more than mere visual reinforcement or space-fillers'. They argue that images tend to be used to reinforce culturally stereotypical images of peoples and that English teaching needs to focus on 'reflexive engagement with cultural information' in addition to linguistic competence (Weninger & Kiss, 2013: 712). On multiple pages, the two main islets that comprise the Liancourt Rocks, Dongdo and Seodo, are rendered as cartoon images (Figure 2 in the textbook). The anthropomorphized islets have been drawn to feature a friendly, smiling countenance and narrate the text that students are to read: 'Welcome to Dokdo. We are Dokdorang, the characters of Dokdo. We'll be your tour guides today' (Bak *et al.*, 2012: 162). The reimagination of Dokdorang as 'characters' who are 'tour guides' for the students helps to acclimate them to the Liancourt Rocks controversy at a young age. Their characterization represents a use of multimodal resources that facilitates the students' dialogic engagement (Chen, 2010) with the text and material while additionally being reframed in a manner that is more appealing or accessible to young children.

I am not simply trying to point out the obvious fact that English teaching materials, and teaching materials more generally speaking, will tend to be age-appropriate in their presentation and content. Yet from this textbook we see the possibility that, when the content is not necessarily age-appropriate, it is able to be reconceived in a manner that reveals the ideologically inflected nature, not only of the language being taught (English), but also of the subject matter within. The method of semiotic puerilization is a means of presenting an issue such as the Liancourt Rocks controversy that most young children will probably be indifferent to, in an accessible manner that normalizes the presumed Korean ownership of the islets. The semiotic puerilization strategies of *YBM Middle School English 2* raise the question of when it is appropriate to introduce resistant ideals to younger generations. Further, it provides a compelling indication of the representational and ideological outcomes when resistance becomes a means to an end.

As noted above, the Liancourt Rocks, in their entirety, comprise a total of merely 0.19 square kilometers (as a point of comparison, the city of Seoul alone is 605.2 square kilometers). In the map image provided (Figure 3 in the textbook), which has been zoomed to a 200 km scale, the Liancourt Rocks are not visible. In fact, Ulleung-do, a much larger island (approximately 73 sq. km.) that is almost 400 times as large as the Liancourt Rocks, is barely visible. When zoomed to a 50 km scale, Ulleung-do is clearly visible while the Liancourt Rocks are still too small to be registered on the map (Figure 4 in the textbook). It is not until the map has been zoomed to 5 km scale that one is able to clearly see the Liancourt Rocks (Figure 5 in the textbook). In an age when the general public has ready access to satellite images of world through applications and services such as Google Maps, it is easy forget how manmade maps can be used to serve political purposes. As Mignolo (2003) notes, maps have historically been distorted in order to represent a particular cartographer's interpretation of the world. For instance, the placement of a particular country at the center of a map suggests that country's supposed ontological centrality, whereas the placement of other countries on the peripheries of the map represents their marginal status in the eyes of the cartographer. Geographic representations are therefore subject to high degrees of ideological distortion.

The images of Korea provided in the textbook are representative of a caricatural geography, entailing an exaggeration of geographic features in a manner akin to that of a caricature. In the images of Korea presented in the textbook, the size of the Liancourt Rocks is represented as up to 40 times larger than its actual size (Figure 6 in the textbook). I acknowledge the fact that the exaggeration of geographical features is a common practice in maps that are used for illustrative purposes. For instance, in the US, it is fairly common to provide a map of the 48 contiguous states with two separate maps for Hawaii and Alaska with each larger and smaller than scale, respectively. In the textbook in question, providing a map of Korea to scale that includes the Liancourt Rocks would simply be impossible and would require multiple images, as I demonstrated above. Nonetheless, the caricatural geography of the Liancourt Rocks is not insignificant when understood within the context of the other features described above (appellative screening, specious territoriality and semiotic puerilization). The act of caricatural geography is, in this instance, problematic in that it hyperbolizes the geographic magnitude of the territory in dispute. Yet, beyond being merely misrepresentative and misleading, they are a means of emphasizing the ideological significance, a significance disproportionate to the geographic size of the islets, within the national imaginary of Korea.

Conclusion

Following the above analysis, it is appropriate to reconsider the unilateral romanticization of resistance in relation to not only *what* is being said but also *who* is saying it. Perhaps it is an object's locus of enunciation (Mignolo, 2003) that shapes the potentiality of solidarity and resistance within a particular discursive artifact. In Mignolo's (2003) conceptualization, the locus of enunciation, or place of speaking, involves a recognition of how one's personal histories, cultural backgrounds and ideological commitments shape one's current behaviors and perspectives. This is partially relevant to the present inquiry because it needs to be noted that different stakeholders, including materials developers, representatives of the Education Ministry, local teachers and students, among others, can and perhaps probably would have different views about and interpretations of the textbook and its content than an outside researcher would. However, more importantly, I adopt the expression here not to consider how an individual researcher's background provides certain affordances and limitations to their analysis, but to critically examine the implications of the locus of enunciation of particular artifacts, including resistant resources, for questions of loci of enunciation engender new avenues for interpreting discursive phenomena. For instance, to return to J.S. Lee's (2004) analysis of Korean-English hybridity as resistance, one is able to take into consideration the political economy of the contemporary mass media industry of Korea, driven by shareholders of multimillion dollar corporations, which raises the question of who serves to benefit from such a discourse of resistance. The resistant, hybrid lyrics of Korean popular music are potentially deromanticized when one considers how media elites can readily appropriate the sentiment of a populace enthralled by the symbolic upheaval of the very norms and values that the elite embody and will continue to profit from.

As I have attempted to demonstrate in my analysis, taking into consideration the locus of enunciation of an artifact like an English textbook expands our analytical capacities by going beyond exposing the ideological maintenance of inequitable social relations. Rather, such an approach poses the question of what it means that an English textbook, endorsed and sponsored by the state government, and thus given status as an 'official' document, deviates from its stated purpose (the teaching of English) toward a politically resistant agenda such as the challenging of the cultural legacies of Japanese colonial occupation. It is, to be sure, a 'resistant' discourse but it also does not align with the dominant narrative that romanticizes resistance either. In this sense, the document is somewhat paradoxical in that it is simultaneously resistant (against present-day legacies of colonial occupation) but also hegemonic (deployed in accordance with top-down, state-driven means).

The above analysis perhaps has some potential pedagogical implications as well. I of course do not wish to merely reiterate the point that teachers generally or even more specifically teachers of English as a foreign or second language need to be mindful of how their work is complicit in potentially facilitating the continued global hegemony of English. Further, I do not wish to reiterate the point, which is made compellingly in much of the scholarship I have cited throughout this chapter, that language teachers and practitioners need to be cognizant of the power of language teaching materials to advance suspect ideological agendas. Instead, I wonder if we might move beyond 'critical' analyses of language teaching materials that merely 'expose' the inner workings of dominant ideology. Is it possible to imagine an alternative endgame of criticality? Or are we entering into a *postcritical* moment in which we need to ask ourselves if classrooms can actually be transformed into spaces of 'resistance?'

YBM Middle School English 2 is an embodiment of a hybrid, translingual artifact that invites inquiry into the possibilities and limitations of translinguistics as a paradigm of resistance. To reiterate, translingual does not simply refer to the conspicuous hybridity of 'multiple languages' but can refer more broadly to any enunciation or artifact that resists the restrictive expectations of monolingualism and monoculturalism. Even if one is skeptical of this conceptualization of translingualism, it is undeniable that the artifact in question embodies the ideals of resistance, in particular, of anticolonial resistance. While it has become commonplace to romanticize resistance, *YBM Middle School English 2* provides an unusual case to consider who actually benefits from the praxis of resistance. To clarify, I should emphasize that the above analysis does not presume to be an empirical study that unveils a representation of 'how English is taught in Korea', nor does it presume to be reflective of a larger trend of dubious methods of ideological indoctrination. Its usefulness for the present inquiry, thus, is not in its representativeness but rather in the opportunity it offers to reconsider who the beneficiaries of resistance are and what is actually being resisted against. These considerations can be pursued, as I have attempted to demonstrate above, through a fuller engagement with *how* the discourse of resistance is deployed. To return more squarely to the question of translingualism, it is important to remind ourselves that it is a resistant, whether overtly or inherently, orientation to top-down, static conceptualizations of language and culture, derivative of colonialist epistemologies. If translingualism is to remain useful as a resistant praxis, then it is critical that we remain attentive to the mechanics and outcomes of resistance rather than presuming the inherent expediency of resistance, romanticizing the very act of resistance as a means to an (uncertain) end.

References

Acosta, A. (2014) *Thresholds of Illiteracy: Theory, Latin America, and the Crisis of Resistance*. New York: Fordham University Press.

Ahn, H. (2017) English as a discursive and social communication resource for contemporary South Koreans. In C.J. Jenks and J.W. Lee (eds) *Korean Englishes in Transnational Contexts* (pp. 157–180). Basingstoke: Palgrave Macmillan.

Apple, M.W. (2004) *Ideology and Curriculum* (3rd edn). London: Routledge.

Awayed-Bishara, M. (2015) Analyzing the cultural content of materials used for teaching English to high school speakers of Arabic in Israel. *Discourse and Society* 26 (5), 517–542.

Bak, J.E. et al. (2012) *Middle School English 2*. Seoul: YBM.

Benavides, O.H. (2009) Narratives of power, the power of narratives: The failing foundational narrative of the Ecuadorian nation. In D.J. Walkowitz and L.M. Knauer (eds) *Contested Histories in Public Space: Memory, Race, and Nation* (pp. 178–196). Durham, NC: Duke University Press.

Blommaert, J. (2010) *The Sociolinguistics of Globalization*. Cambridge: Cambridge University Press.

Blommaert, J. and Dong, J. (2010) *Ethnographic Fieldwork: A Beginner's Guide*. Bristol: Multilingual Matters.

Burke, K. (1966) *Language as Symbolic Action: Essays on Life, Literature, and Method*. Berkeley, CA: University of California Press.

Cameron, D. (2012) *Verbal Hygiene* (2nd edn). London: Routledge.

Canagarajah, S. (1999) *Resisting Linguistic Imperialism in English Teaching*. Oxford: Oxford University Press.

Canagarajah, S. (2013) *Translingual Practice: Global Englishes and Cosmopolitan Relations*. London: Routledge.

Chen, Y. (2010) Exploring dialogic engagement with readers in multimodal EFL textbooks in China. *Visual Communication* 9 (4), 485–506.

Choi, C. (1993) The discourse of decolonization and popular memory: South Korea. *Positions: Asia Critique* 1 (1), 77–102.
Creese, A. and Blackledge, A. (2010) Translanguaging in the bilingual classroom: A pedagogy for learning and teaching? *The Modern Language Journal* 94 (1), 103–115.
Dovchin, S. (2017a) The ordinariness of youth linguascapes in Mongolia. *International Journal of Multilingualism* 14 (2), 144–159.
Dovchin, S. (2017b) Translocal English in the linguascapes of Mongolian popular music. *World Englishes* 36 (1), 2–19.
Fairclough, N.L. (1985) Critical and descriptive goals in discourse analysis. *Journal of Pragmatics* 9 (6), 739–763.
García, O. (2009) *Bilingual Education in the 21st Century: A Global Perspective*. Oxford: Wiley-Blackwell.
García, O. and Li Wei (2014) *Translanguaging: Language, Bilingualism and Education*. Basingstoke: Palgrave Macmillan.
Gulliver, T. (2010) Immigrant success stories in ESL textbooks. *TESOL Quarterly* 44 (4), 725–745.
Hadikin, G. (2014) *Korean English: A Corpus-driven Study of a New English*. Amsterdam: John Benjamins.
Jørgensen, J.N. (2008) Polylingual languaging around and among children and adolescents. *International Journal of Multilingualism* 5 (3), 161–76.
Jørgensen, J.N., Karrebaek, M.S., Madsen, L.M. and Møller, J.S. (2011) Polylanguaging in superdiversity. *Diversities* 13, 23–38.
Kachru, B.B. (1992) *The Other Tongue: English Across Cultures* (2nd edn). Urbana, IL: University of Illinois Press.
Kachru, B.B. (2005) *Asian Englishes: Beyond the Canon*. Hong Kong: Hong Kong University Press.
Kim, E.J. (2012) Creative adoption: Trends in Anglicisms in Korea. *English Today* 28 (2), 15–17.
Kress, G. (1993) Against arbitrariness: The social production of the sign as a foundational issue in critical discourse analysis. *Discourse and Society* 4 (2), 169–191.
Lee, D.B. (2010) Portrayals of non-North Koreans in North Korean textbooks and the formation of national identity. *Asian Studies Review* 34 (3), 349–369.
Lee, I. (2009) Situated globalization and racism: An analysis of Korean high school EFL textbooks. *Language and Literacy* 11 (1), 1–14.
Lee, J.S. (2004) Linguistic hybridization in K-pop: Discourse of self-assertion and resistance. *World Englishes* 23 (3), 429–450.
Lee, J.S. (2006) Linguistic constructions of modernity: English mixing in Korean television commercials. *Language in Society* 35 (1), 59–91.
Lee, J.W. (2014) Transnational linguistic landscapes and the transgression of metadiscursive regimes of language. *Critical Inquiry in Language Studies* 11 (1), 50–74.
Lee, J.W. (2017) *The Politics of Translingualism: After Englishes*. New York: Routledge.
Lee, J.W. and Jenks, C.J. (2017) Mapping Korean Englishes in transnational contexts. In C.J. Jenks and J.W. Lee (eds) *Korean Englishes in Transnational Contexts* (pp. 1–19). Basingstoke: Palgrave Macmillan.
Lee, K. (2009) Treating culture: What 11 high school EFL conversation textbooks in South Korea do. *English Teaching: Practice and Critique* 8 (1), 76–96.
Lee, S.M. (2007) Xbox 다케시마 퇴출사건 어이없는 결말로 끝나. *Naver News*, 27 December. See http://news.naver.com/main/read.nhn?mode=LSD&mid=sec&sid1=105&oid=092&aid=0000017579 (accessed 31 August 2017).

Mignolo, W.D. (2003) *The Darker Side of the Renaissance: Literacy, Territoriality, and Colonization* (2nd edn). Ann Arbor, MI: University of Michigan Press.

Ministry of Education (2011) *Overview*, 13 April. See http://www.moe.go.kr/main.do (accessed 31 August 2017).

Ndura, E. (2004) ESL and cultural bias: An analysis of elementary through high school textbooks in the western United States of America. *Language, Culture and Curriculum* 17 (2), 143–153.

Otsuji, E. and Pennycook, A. (2010) Metrolingualism: Fixity, fluidity and language in flux. *International Journal of Multilingualism* 7 (3), 240–254.

Park, K.J. (2009) Characteristics of Korea English as a glocalized variety. In K. Murata and J. Jenkins (eds) *Global Englishes in Asian Contexts: Current and Future Debates* (pp. 94–110). Basingstoke: Palgrave Macmillan.

Pennycook, A. (1998) *English and the Discourses of Colonialism*. London: Routledge.

Pennycook, A. (2007) *Global Englishes and Transcultural Flows*. London: Routledge.

Pennycook, A. (2010) *Language as a Local Practice*. London: Routledge.

Pennycook, A. (2012) *Language and Mobility: Unexpected Places*. Bristol: Multilingual Matters.

Pennycook, A. and Otsuji, E. (2015) *Metrolingualism: Language in the City*. London: Routledge.

Piller, I. (2016) *Linguistic Diversity and Social Justice: An Introduction to Applied Sociolinguistics*. Oxford: Oxford University Press.

Rüdiger, S. (2017) Spoken English in Korea: An expanding circle English revisited. In C.J. Jenks and J.W. Lee (eds) *Korean Englishes in Transnational Contexts* (pp. 75–92). Basingstoke: Palgrave Macmillan.

Schneer, D. (2007) (Inter)nationalism and English textbooks endorsed by the Ministry of Education in Japan. *TESOL Quarterly* 41 (3), 600–607.

Shim, R.J. (1999) Codified Korean English: Process, characteristics and consequence. *World Englishes* 18 (2), 247–58.

Soh, C.S. (2009) *The Comfort Women: Sexual Violence and Postcolonial Memory in Korea and Japan*. Chicago, IL: University of Chicago Press.

Song, H. (2013) Deconstruction of cultural dominance in Korean EFL textbooks. *Intercultural Education* 24 (4), 382–390.

Spivak, G.C. (1999) *A Critique of Postcolonial Reason*. Cambridge, MA: Harvard University Press.

Sultana, S. and Dovchin, S. (2017) Popular culture in transglossic language practices of young adults. *International Multilingual Research Journal* 11 (2), 67–85.

Sultana, S., Dovchin, S. and Pennycook, A. (2015) Transglossic language practices of young adults in Bangladesh and Mongolia. *International Journal of Multilingualism* 12 (1), 93–108.

van Dijk, T.A. (1993) Principles of critical discourse analysis. *Discourse and Society* 4 (2), 249–283.

van Dijk, T.A. (2001) Critical Discourse Analysis. In D. Schiffrin, D. Tannen and H.E. Hamilton (eds) *The Handbook of Discourse Analysis* (pp. 352–371). Malden, MA: Blackwell.

Van Dijk, T.A. (2006) Discourse and manipulation. *Discourse and Society* 17 (3), 359–383.

Weninger, C. and Kiss, T. (2013) Culture in English as a foreign language (EFL) textbooks: A semiotic approach. *TESOL Quarterly* 47 (4), 694–716.

Williams, C. (1994) Arfarniad o Ddulliau Dysgu ac Addysgu yng Nghyddestun Addysg Uwchradd Ddwyieithog. PhD thesis, University of Wales.

7 Transgrammaring Bilinguals and 'Ordinary' English in Japanese Ethnic Churchscapes

Tyler Barrett

Introduction

English speakers who speak Japanese as a first language are often impacted by strict ideological 'either/or' binary beliefs about what constitutes 'proficiency' in English (or any language) in Japanese society (Gottlieb, 2012; Japan Times, 2005). As Kumiko Iwasaki, psychology and education professor at the Open University of Japan, states, 'We Japanese have a strong psychological barrier to speaking English ... We have an obsession that we have to speak English perfectly' (Pickles, 2017). Perfectionism is part of Japanese culture exemplified in strong beliefs that there is a 'right' way to do something, which means that in Japanese society many Japanese people will not communicate in English if they believe there is a chance they may not produce the right answer (Yukutake, 2017; Lund, 2015). However, while Japanese people may not want to risk speaking English in many parts of society, many Japanese people have been going to Christian churches to speak English. This given, in this study I examine traditional conceptualizations of 'bilingualism' and 'language proficiency' that seem to impact members of Japanese society in Japanese ethnic church 'churchscape' communities (Appadurai, 1996) where churchscapes are essentially global and local landscapes of Christian religiosity characterized by the movement and exchange of people, information and objects (Riedel & Runkel, 2015). Through an analysis of interview texts from Japanese ethnic church members, I present the idea of 'transgrammaring' as a possibility to legitimize proficiencies in 'ordinary' or common Englishes and subsequent beliefs about being bilingual, or more accurately, translingual (i.e. operating between languages) in transglossic (i.e. language is not particularly attached to specific domains; Dovchin *et al.*, 2018; Sultana *et al.*, 2015) churchscape contexts, as I attempt to answer the following questions:

- How do Japanese ethnic church members define the term 'bilingual'?
- Based on their definitions of the term, why do they (un)perceive themselves as being bilingual?
- Do Japanese ethnic church policies *de facto* impact beliefs about being bilingual?

Japanese Ethnic Church as 'Churchscapes'

Similar to Appadurai's (2001) conceptualization of 'scapes', 'churchscapes' are characterized by movements of people, information and objects pertaining to globally dispersed church communities in a globalizing world. Churchscapes are in essence interconnected 'imagined communities' and 'imagined worlds' (Riedel & Runkel, 2015; Appadurai, 1996: 33) where perceived social, theological and ecclesiological connections with other church communities, languages and cultures impact the way people participate in church services and related practices. On a global scale, churchscapes are connected through theological and ecclesiological threads of religious beliefs (e.g. Christianity) and are essentially 'a deterritorialized set of cultural phenomena' (Riedel & Runkel, 2015: 2758). In terms of local practices, while churches are initiated with intentions beyond the dissemination of theology and ecclesiology that include facilitating languages and cultures as people and churches do not come from 'nowhere', churchscapes are often characterized, impacted and transformed by the local. For example, as reported in the Colonial Church Chronicle and Missionary Journal of 1860 (before religious freedom was granted under the Meiji Restoration of 1868), missionaries were welcome in Japan *only* to teach English, 'Our missionaries had met with a very cool reception; and, with earnest efforts of our American Consul Harris, they would have had to go back again, like the Chinese merchants that had been sent off at the same time. *They were allowed to remain only because the desire to learn English*' (emphasis mine, The Colonial Church Chronicle and Missionary Journal, 1860: 7). Thus, considering such an entrance in which the religiosity of Christianity was rejected while English was accepted, and the subtle impact that Christian churchscapes have had upon Japanese society over the last 150 years, as less than 0.5% of Japanese people claim to be Christian in recent times (Kanagy, 2013), it seems appropriate to suggest that the 'Church of English' has perhaps had a greater impact upon Japanese society in terms of efforts to 'convert' Japanese people into English speakers than missionary efforts to convert Japanese people into Christians. Similar to the transcultural refashioning and re-appropriation of hip-hop in translocal spaces around the globe as described by Pennycook (2007), we might say that churches in Japan have been refashioned and reappropriated by and for Japanese people into translocal churchscapes where Japanese people can do church according to their preferences and have 'foreign' experiences learning English or by participating in church-related activities such as Black Gospel concerts (Christian, 2000), 'especially if the pastor is an English-speaking missionary' (Kanagy, 2013: 51).

Often connected with churches in Japan, Japanese ethnic churches outside of Japan in North America are also churches that have been refashioned and reappropriated into translocal churchscapes that suit the Japanese language and cultural needs of the Japanese Christian diaspora. Like Japanese churchscapes in Japan, often in terms of function, Japanese ethnic churchscapes are typically characterized by their language practices as they are focused on facilitating a Japanese language church experience, yet many directly and indirectly provide opportunities for attendees to experience English in services and through partnerships with English congregations. Japanese churches and Japanese ethnic churches are also characterized as places where church member beliefs, such as perfectionist beliefs about proficiency in English, are often perpetuated within the church communities as many first-generation church members carry such beliefs from Japan. In addition, concerning Japanese language practices in Japanese ethnic churches, it is important to mention that Japanese ethnic church members in North America often have family members who are native English speakers, including spouses and/or children and grandchildren who might be 'nissei' and 'sansei' (second and third generation) Japanese heritage speakers who identify differently than their Japanese parents and grandparents, and as a result, impact the translocal, transcultural and translinguistic structures of Japanese ethnic church communities through processes of what Mullins (1987) characterizes as 'de-ethnization' as choices are made about accommodating English for 'bilingual' or translingual and 'monolingual' church members within the Japanese ethnic church community (Barrett, 2015, 2016).

Bilingualism

While 'translingual' (i.e. operating between languages) is perhaps a more accurate term to describe the transfer of languages used by subjects in this study, the term 'bilingual' is used because it is a familiar term to subjects, perhaps because it is a loan word in Japanese (i.e. 'biringuaru'). Traditional definitions of 'bilingualism' often suggest that being bilingual means that a person has grown up speaking both languages and is able to 'effortlessly' use languages 'equally'. However, these strict beliefs are often tied to ideologies of monolingualism beliefs that include: 'native speaker usage is "authentic" and thus ideal, a person's birthplace correlates with proficiency, and the plurality of languages and varieties results in incomprehensibility' (Lee, 2014: 1). Less strict beliefs, albeit still traditional and limited in scope since they are inherently tied to 'either/or' binary perspectives of proficiencies in named languages, tend to emphasize degrees of proficiencies such as 'balanced bilingual', i.e. being equally proficient in both languages, and 'dominant bilingual', i.e. being more confident or proficient in one language than another (Myers-Scotton, 2008). However, being bound by either/or binary perspectives, these distinctions are grounded in perceptions that languages are separated from one another as commonly perceived in society and thus speakers who identify with these distinctions experience conceptual limitations about their language proficiencies and subsequent legitimacies. Hence, 'translingual' is a preferred term.

Perhaps a step in the translingual direction, traditional views of bilingualism also suggests that bilinguals should be recognized as being competent in two monolingual languages, although bilinguals often feel that they do not know one or the other language (Grosjean, 1985). Continuing in the translingual direction, although still perhaps bound by either/or binary perspectives, Grosjean (1982: 269), suggests that being bilingual is being able to use any language, in different contexts, for different purposes. Yet distinguishing languages as being homogeneous and separated causes language users to approach language contexts in an either/or fashion, which often results in bilinguals who perceive themselves as being more or less capable or proficient in a particular language and in particular contexts. Matsumoto and Juang (2003) suggest that the issue is that situations in society, such as in Japanese ethnic church communities, permit bilinguals to use a particular language and/or one variety over another, which often results in higher degrees of perceived proficiency which subsequently reinforces heteroglossic positive and negative beliefs about proficiency and legitimacy. Thus, societal contexts and beliefs perpetuated in society and by society (e.g. education and government policies) often influence and perhaps limit beliefs about being bilingual and perspectives about being translingual.

Language Proficiency

Continuing in our discussion of traditional concepts of bilingualism, it is important to mention that traditional concepts of language proficiency potentially impact beliefs about being bilingual and translingual. Arguably, and with limitations, language proficiency has often been validated by descriptive instruments (Pray, 2005) that include the Interagency Language Roundtable (ILR) (2017), which is commonly used to describe reading, writing, listening and spoken language proficiency levels that range from 0 (i.e. no proficiency) to 5 (i.e. speaking proficiency is functionally equivalent to that of a highly articulate well-educated native speaker and reflects the cultural standards of the country where the language is natively spoken); however, most native speakers do not have a Level 5 proficiency. Using this proficiency scale, a person might speak English at a Level 2 or 2+ (i.e. able to satisfy (most) routine social demands and limited work requirements) as many church members do in this study, and Japanese at a Level 4 (i.e. able to use the language fluently and accurately on all levels normally pertinent to professional needs) as many native speakers do, and be considered 'dominant bilingual'. While the ILR proficiency descriptions provide distinctions between proficiency levels, as we will see from the perspectives of subjects in this study, many bilinguals do not clearly define their own proficiencies and are often critical of their language competencies to the extent that many have negative self-judgments about their language abilities (Roy, 2010: 546). As Grosjean (1996: 32) states, 'some criticize their mastery of language skills, others strive their hardest to reach monolingual norms, while others hide their knowledge of their "weaker" language, and most simply do not perceive themselves as being bilingual even though they use two (or more) languages in their everyday lives'.

Transgrammaring

Having acknowledged traditional conceptualizations of 'bilingualism' and 'language proficiency', which is necessary as these terms are used throughout the study because they are concepts that subjects in this study are familiar with and perhaps a starting point for discussions beyond the binary toward translingual awareness, in the spirit of recognizing bilingual and translingual proficiencies and subsequent legitimacy beyond perceptions of binary limitations, I use the term 'transgrammaring'. Recognizing the benefits of expanding the heteroglossic boundaries beyond the binary between 'named' languages, similar to translanguaging, which is the process by which bilinguals make use of the many resources their bilingual statuses offer (García & Wei, 2014: 558–559), in this study I use the term 'transgrammaring' as an alternative way to analyze and present 'imperfect' and 'ordinary' English as sociolinguistic evidence that through processes of entextualization (Bauman & Briggs, 1990), where texts are lifted and recontextualized in communicative ways, Japanese ethnic church members who do not often perceive themselves as being bilingual because they do not perceive themselves as proficient in English, use 'Englishes' in a legitimate and 'ordinary' way to the extent that they actually are 'bilingual' or more accurately, 'translingual' in the transglossic (i.e. language is not particularly attached to specific domains) sense of the term (Sultana, 2015). Legitimacy of 'ordinary' Englishes and subsequent bilingual and translingual identities for Japanese ethnic church members is possible from transglossic perspectives that emphasize the normalcy of transcendence and transformation of voices from traditional linguistic and cultural boundaries in heteroglossic contexts where two or more voices are present in a single text (Sultana et al., 2015; Sultana, 2015) because languages are not tied to the local but operate globally (Dovchin, 2017). Such alternative patterns are particularly evident when subjects in this study combine English with the null-subject and pro-drop language of Japanese, wherein, for example, the omission of subjects and pronouns and the omission and hybrid use of function words or grammatical words (e.g. articles and prepositions) is characteristic of 'ordinary' English that has been traditionally described as being grammatically 'imperfect' or characterized as 'broken English' (Lindemann, 2005). Previous to this study, the term transgrammaring has not often been used in reference to hybrid grammar patterns that have been associated with two or more languages; however, transgrammaring has been used to describe approaches to teaching the English language (e.g. see Malmstrom & Weaver, 1973). Perhaps the most significant usage of the term as it pertains to this study is Greenberg's (1990) 'transgrammatical facts' that refer to 'properties of languages which will not appear in grammars' with respect to relationships between two languages and cross-linguistic generalizations. For example, borrowed words are linked to their origins while also being indicative of 'different phonological constraints or derivational formations from native words' (Greenberg, 1990). Further, he argues that grammar rules that are a product of a theory (e.g. generativists theory about universals) are artifacts of particular theories of particular named languages and are not often indicative of what is observable in surface-level [trans]language use. Thus, inspired by this notion of Greenberg's (1990) 'transgrammatical facts' as it refers to the universal and transferable aspects of languages that are not typically identified in traditional grammars that describe single named languages, in other words, finite grammars are inductively incapable of describing all of the infinite possibilities of language in use, cross-linguistic and otherwise (Pinker, 2004). In this chapter, rather than using the term 'code switching', 'fossilization' or 'broken English', because these terms are conceptually bound by perceived binary structures of two monolingual languages and proficiencies (as described in the ILR), after determining English proficiency levels of the subjects in the study in the traditional sense using the ILR criterion, I use the term 'transgrammaring' in Japanese ethnic churchscapes that are transglossic contexts to positively identify the transfer of L1 grammatical features from an L1 to an L2 in an effort to recognize the legitimate bilingual proficiencies of subjects in this study who do not perceive themselves as being bilingual.

Methodology

In this study I use ILR Spoken Proficiency level descriptions to provide a traditional assessment of observable patterns in Japanese ethnic church member interview texts which is useful in showing proficiencies particularly when church members' perfectionist ideological perspectives seem to prohibit them from acknowledging their actual proficiencies and subsequent bilingual legitimacies. ILR Spoken Proficiency level descriptions include but are not limited to the following:

- pronunciation
- depth and breadth of lexicon
- structural and grammatical precision

In addition, I use transgrammaring to suggest the potential for an ideological and epistemological shift through analysis of the discourse of participants in their interview texts in transglossic contexts where 'discourse to me comprises all forms of meaningful semiotic human activity seen in connection with social, cultural, and historical patterns and developments of use' (Blommaert, 2005: 3). Further, within this notion of discourse there are 'orders of indexicality' 'with stratified normative complexes that organize distinctions between, on the one hand, "good", "normal", "appropriate", and "acceptable" language use and on the other, "deviant", "abnormal", etc. language use. Discourse in this sense is defined by "the dominant lines for senses of belonging, for identities and roles in society"' (Blommaert, 2010: 6). The interview texts are lifted, decontextualized and recontextualized through processes of entextualization

(Bauman & Briggs, 1990) with the intention of making the familiar strange and providing an alternative perspective that can potentially impact traditional epistemological paradigms and ideological constraints. The following is a description of analysis criterion used to analyze the discourse of interview texts in this study:

- Textual repetitions and similarities: Use of the same words and references and borrowed words different from native words (Greenberg, 1990).
- Inner speech: Verbalized thinking in a particular language. In English it is often indicated by saying filler words 'um', 'uh' and 'ok' or repeating the question, as opposed to Japanese filler words that include *'eeto'*, *'ano'* and *'nanka'* (Pavlenko, 2014; Guerrero, 2006).
- 'We vs You' Discourse: Contextualization cues (e.g. use of pronouns 'we' and 'you') to indicate inclusivity and exclusivity (Gumperz, 1982).
- Grammar and fossilization: L1 lexical and grammar omissions and hybrid constructions in L2 production (e.g. omission of subjects, pronoun usage, verb conjugations, Japanese topic markers and particles used in English) (Thompson, 2001).

Analysis of Interview Texts

As described above, using a combined content and linguistic analysis or qualitative content analysis approach (Mostyn, 1985; Marying, 2000), I interviewed 23 participants aged 18–66 from a Japanese ethnic church community in Western Canada. Each church is characterized as 'monolingual', 'dominant bilingual' and 'balanced bilingual' according to its language policy *de facto* (Barrett, 2016). Subjects in this study were ethnically Japanese, spoke Japanese as a first language and English as a second language to varying degrees of proficiency, and most had come to Canada as adults. All participants and locations have been given pseudonyms to ensure anonymity. During the interview church members were asked 'Are you bilingual?' and other related questions. Analyses of the interview texts using ILR Spoken Proficiency descriptions demonstrate that a majority of church members were proficient in English in the traditional sense to varying degrees and thus 'bilingual' as demonstrated in their ability to participate in a 30–45 minute interview using mostly English, not to mention that all said they used English in their daily lives in Canadian society to varying degrees. Table 7.1 indicates the distribution of the ILR spoken proficiency levels of church members and their responses in parentheses to the question, 'Are you bilingual?' according to their church associations.

Table 7.1 ILR spoken proficiency distribution and the ordinariness of English (N = 23)

	0+	1	1+	2	2+	3	3+
Monolingual	Toshimi (No) Pastor Yoko (No)	Miko (Not really)		Shiho (Not quite) Yumi (Not really) Aiko (Kind of) Mari (Not quite)	Tomomi (Not in Canada; Yes, in Japan)		
Dominant bilingual		Jun (No) Pastor Yuichi (No)	Shu (No) Hana (No)	Natsuko (Yes) Keita (No) Ryu (Yes)	Kiko (No) Mae (No) Nana (No)		Ana (Yes)
Balanced Bilingual				Megumi (Yes) Pastor Kenta (Yes, kind of)	Sho (Yes) Yuiko (Yes)		

To determine their spoken proficiency levels, the recorded interviews were transcribed 'sic erat scriptum', i.e. as closely as possible to the speech that was produced. The transcripts were then coded and marked according to the assessment details described in the ILR Spoken Proficiency levels. After the transcripts were coded and marked, they were re-evaluated and compared with ILR Spoken Proficiency level descriptions. As Table 7.1 demonstrates, according to the assessment, church members' proficiency levels range from 0+ to 3+. Church members in the 0+ to 1+ range did not perceive themselves as being bilingual. Church members in the circled 2 to 2+ range were almost evenly divided in terms of seeing themselves as 'Yes ...' bilingual and 'No ...' and 'Not quite/Not really ...' bilingual. A one-way ANOVA test for independent samples test was run to determine the significance of differences between the three churches. There was no significant statistical difference at the $p < 0.05$ level for the three conditions [$F(2, 20) = 1.51424, p = 0.244144$]. In other words, within this small sample ($N = 23$), concerning ILR-rated spoken English proficiencies of church members, the three communities of church members were not statistically significantly different from one another, and thus statistically they can be looked at as one community. The circled range indicates the majority of community members who were capable of a 'limited working proficiency' in spoken English whether they perceived themselves as being bilingual or not. Thus, according to traditional proficiency descriptions, this circled area also represents the 'ordinariness of English' present within this Japanese ethnic church community (Dovchin, 2017). In other words, English proficiency is an ordinary phenomenon in this Japanese ethnic church community even when bilingual proficiency is not perceived by those who are proficient in both Japanese and English. Only one church member, Ana, was assessed as a 3+, which was not surprising because she was the only participant who began living and being educated in Canada at age 8 during the 'critical period'. In addition, both Mae's and Tomomi's ILR Spoken Proficiency levels during the interview were assessed as 2+, although neither of them perceived themselves as being bilingual in Canada, yet they both assisted the church as interpreters and translators in different capacities such as when non-Japanese guests attended the Japanese services and when writing church reports in English. Additionally, although most bilinguals do not have the capability of interpreting and translating (Grosjean, 1996), during the time I spent in the church community I witnessed Mae's and Tomomi's abilities to efficiently translate and interpret from Japanese into English, i.e. skills that are dependent upon listening and writing proficiencies, but unfortunately these proficiencies were not formally assessed and presented in the study. In light of identifying the spoken English proficiency levels of subjects in this study and the ordinariness of a 'limited working proficiency' in spoken English, in the following, I present an analysis of interview texts with respect to each churchscape in the church community where brackets are used to insert expected words that were not stated and translated texts.

'Monolingual' Mountain Japanese Churchscape

Mountain Japanese Church is situated in a mountainous region where about 10–15 Japanese women church members often bring their children to church. Some of them are/were married to English-speaking Canadians and others are married to Japanese spouses; however, their spouses do not attend the church. They meet in a church building facilitated by an English-speaking congregation. The church began as a Bible study group and has been meeting as a church for more than 20 years. The church functions entirely in Japanese unless someone who does not speak Japanese comes to visit.

As Table 7.2 indicates, as we might expect in a 'monolingual' church, five out of seven church members did not perceive themselves as being bilingual. When I asked Pastor Yoko, who has been living in Canada for

Table 7.2 Monolingual Japanese ethnic church ($n = 7$)

'No ...'	'Not really ...'/'Not Quite ...'	'Kind of ...'	'Yes ...'
2	4	1	1

14 years and who speaks Japanese at home and at work if she was bilingual, she said she was not. Her response was not surprising since the majority of our interview was in Japanese. She was, however, able to respond in English to basic personal questions such as, 'What language do you use at home, at work, at church and with your children?' Yet, soon after the interview began she made it clear that she could not speak English.

Interviewer: So when you came to Canada, what did Canadians speak at that time?
PY: Canadian no hitotachi ni hanashi koto ga arimasu ka? [Translated: Do I speak to Canadians?]
Interviewer: Yeah, donna kotoba, sono toki? [Translated: What language, at that time?]
PY: Easy English.
Interviewer: I see.
PY: But I can't speak English.
Interviewer: Ok.
PY: Hotondo nihongo, eigo wa dame desu (laughs). [Translated: Almost all Japanese, I can't speak English.]

Unlike Pastor Yoko, with the exception of Toshimi, all of the other church members demonstrated significant degrees of proficiency in English and appeared to be dominant bilinguals, although they conceptualized the term 'bilingual' differently. For example, when I asked Shiho about the term bilingual, she stated the following:

Interviewer: So, what is bilingual?
S: I think, they understand [a] couple languages in [their] head[s] and then they can switch when you have to use English, like Ryusuke, or Taishin, or my son Toshikazu [who] can switch in head, in their heads, to when you use that language.

Shiho, who has been living in Canada for 18 years, who speaks Japanese and English at home, and whose spouse is an English-speaking Canadian, demonstrates transgrammaring with the absence of an indefinite article, pronouns and plural nouns, but overall she demonstrates proficiency in English, especially when she self-corrects 'switch in head' to 'in their heads'. Yet, she uses 'they' to position herself as different from bilinguals. She references the children of the church and her son, Toshikazu, whom she perceives as able to speak both Japanese and English, i.e. as being bilingual. For these children who have grown up in two or more transglossic 'worlds', their bilingual or more accurately translingual identity is often a natural and stable phenomenon (Gérin-Lajoie, 2011: 7; Grosjean, 1982). Her perception of these children as bilinguals who are more proficient than herself is implicit in the divide between 'old and young culture' wherein the first generation sees the second generation as having new culture (Dovchin, 2017), which is as Mullins (1987) suggests a potential step toward de-ethnization.

Interviewer: Are you bilingual?
S: Um, not quite. [I'm] Still learning both (laughs). So, I came here when I was 20 and then I was still learning Japanese in the proper way. But, I didn't really learn, and then I came here and I just used like more, not uh slang, just uh conversation Japanese and English. So, I don't know both the really good way, the proper way. So, that's my problem, too. I need to learn both sides. If I see the Japanese people, I need to [show] respect to talk to all the people. But, I can't really use the proper way to speak them, so I just talking [talk] to them like a friend, but [a] little bit polite, that's all, so ...

Although she doesn't believe she uses Japanese in the 'proper way' or a 'really good way' and she states that not speaking in the 'proper way' is a 'problem', she also states that she needs to learn to use 'proper' Japanese, or honorifics, a higher variety in Japanese diglossia (Reischauer & Jansen, 1995). She identifies the importance of context, in terms of 'then I came here', as a factor contributing to her inability to speak either language in the 'proper way'. Proper in Japanese is connected to showing respect by speaking 'properly', which is said to be different than speaking in a lower variety when 'talking to them like a friend', which is indicative of the diglossic ideology of higher and lower varieties. Similarly, she again demonstrates dominant bilingual characteristics and transgrammaring when she omits pronouns and definite articles, and inserts definite articles and the progressive tense. Yet, arguably these constructions do not detract from the meaning, and she seems to be aware of the general rules *de facto*. Also, she uses English filler words 'um' and 'uh' instead of Japanese filler words such as '*eeto*', which seems to indicate proficiency in English. Similarly, Yumi, who has lived in Canada for 16 years, is married to a Japanese spouse and has a son who is 'getting Canadian (laughs) ...' with 'some language problem ...' because she speaks both Japanese and English to him, but 'his answer everything English', says she is 'not really' bilingual because she cannot communicate 'deeply' in English.

Interviewer: What is it to be bilingual?
Y: Hmm, How to say, to be? Uh, It's uh ...
Interviewer: the ability ... means what? What can they do?
Y: Uh, ok, maybe, choice, choice, [It means it is] easy to get the job. And also, *ne*, it's uh [means] more communication [with] the people. Yeah, I think so.
Interviewer: Are you bilingual?
Y: Actually, I feel not really because it's uh, I can't talk to the Canadian[s], only like uh, simple sentence, simple English, not communication deeply, that's why not I don't want to say, I can't say I am bilingual.
Interviewer: Ok.
Y: Yeah, feel uh, because I can speak to the Japanese people more deeply and uh more powerful[ly], more strong[ly], but [to] Canadian[s], so uh [to] English speaker[s], I can speak, but it's not deep. Yeah, this is the tough part.

Yumi perceives 'bilinguals' as having a 'choice' and being able to easily get a job and communicate with other people. While not direct 'we vs you' discourse, she distances herself by referring to 'the Canadians' and 'the Japanese', suggesting that perhaps she may perceive herself as different from both; however, during the interview she also acknowledges her personal transcultural shift when she states, 'I was born in Japan, and then Japanese culture is uh I still have keep, but uh already in here is 16 years, yeah, getting like a Canadian (laughs)'. Perhaps aware that the interviewer can understand basic Japanese she demonstrates translanguaging (García, 2009) when she uses the Japanese particle '*ne*' equivalent to 'right?' or 'isn't it?' She demonstrates transgrammaring when she omits and inserts the pronoun 'it', omits prepositions 'with' and 'to', inserts a definite article, omits the plural nouns 'Canadian' and 'speaker' and omits the adverbial endings in 'powerful' and 'strong'. She repeatedly uses the English filler word 'uh' and not Japanese filler words such as '*eeto*'. She states that she 'feel[s]' she is 'not really' bilingual because she cannot speak like a Canadian, which is consistent with Grosjean (1982), who suggests that bilinguals often do not 'feel' they are bilingual. She states she can only speak in simple sentences in English and that she cannot communicate 'deeply' with Canadian English speakers. In contrast to her English communication with Canadian English speakers, she states tht she can speak Japanese with Japanese people more deeply, more powerfully and more strongly. While she struggles to understand the question, 'What is it to be bilingual?' at first, she quickly adjusts and is able to answer the rephrased version of the question. She is able to describe her perceptions about being bilingual and complete the interview using mostly English. Based upon the comparatives she uses to describe her proficiencies in both languages (i.e. more deeply, more powerful, more strong), she appears to be a dominant bilingual who describes herself as being more capable in Japanese. Similarly, Aiko, who has been living in Canada for 14 years, who works as a nurse at an English-speaking hospital, and who believes she is 'kind of ...' bilingual, demonstrates dominant bilingual proficiency.

Interviewer: How about, what is the meaning of bilingual?
A: Bilingual, [it means] to speak couple language[s].
Interviewer: Ok. And uh, are you bilingual?
A: Kind of (laughs).

Unlike Shiho and Yumi who responded by saying 'Not quite ...' and 'Not really ...' bilingual, Aiko emphasizes the positive in her response 'Kind of ...'. When answering the question, she does not use 'we vs you' discourse and thus does not position herself as bilingual. She demonstrates inner speech in English when she repeats the last word of the question, 'bilingual'. She demonstrates transgrammaring when she omits the pronoun 'it (means) ...' and the 's' in the plural noun 'languages'. Further, while during the interview she mentions that she uses English at work, she also states she chooses to use only Japanese at home with the intention of providing an opportunity for her children to become proficient in Japanese.

A: ... we decided to talk to Japanese in [the] house and then you know, if [they are] using English, [then] no answer (laughs). Yeah, because I want to keep Japanese for [my] children, and then it's good for them, and I'm teaching [them] Japanese and also they are going to Japanese school in [on the] weekend and that's why. Just only in the house we [would] like [them] to keep [speaking Japanese].
Interviewer: Does the church help you do that?
A: Uh, yeah it's good help[s] to the children and they likes to come to the church and they are talking to Japanese [people] in there. Yeah, it's good. It's really good [for them] to keep [speaking Japanese].

Aiko demonstrates transgrammaring again when she omits definite articles and pronouns and inserts definite articles, the progressive tense and the preposition 'in'. In addition, she uses a neoglism 'keep' perhaps in place of saying 'keep speaking'. Unlike Aiko, Tomomi, who has lived in Canada for more than 15 years, communicates with her Canadian 15 year-old son only in English because as she says, 'I didn't teach him my first language, which is Japanese', and who works in the human resources department at an international center where her job is to communicate in English with visitors, situates her bilingual ability according to nation-states.

Interviewer: What is bilingual?
T: Bi means double, uh so, the the, when I hear the word bilingual, it automatically comes to my mind, the image of the person who speaks more than two languages. So, in Canada, when you say you have to be bilingual, that means you have to be able to speak English and French, not English and Japanese, in Canada.
Interviewer: So, are you bilingual?
T: In Canadian standard[s], no. But, in Japanese standard[s], yes.

She demonstrates transgrammaring when she inserts the pronoun 'it' and omits definite articles 'the' and the plural noun 'standards'. She uses the English filler word 'uh' which seems to suggest English proficiency. She distances herself from identifying with the term 'bilingual' in Canada and refers positively to her bilingual status in Japan, suggesting that she perceives her bilingual legitimacy as defined by national boundaries. Her response seems to indicate a transnational perception of herself in which her Japanese national identity legitimizes her bilingual identity. In addition, as previously mentioned, her view is interesting because she is the interpreter and translator for her Japanese church community and her fellow church members told me they perceive her as being bilingual. In addition, and to her credit, although contrary to her view of herself, Grosjean (1996) suggests that few bilinguals are proficient enough to be interpreters and translators.

'Dominant Bilingual' City Japanese Churchscape

City Japanese Church is located just outside of the city center and consists of about 30 ethnically Japanese adults and their English-speaking children in addition to about five non-ethnically Japanese people who attend intermittently. The church began as a Bible study group in 2009 and the congregation meets in the afternoons in the building facilitated by an English-speaking church. Pastor Yuichi and his wife Mae and their two daughters operate the church and work together with ethnically Japanese

Table 7.3 Dominant bilingual Japanese ethnic church (*n* = 11)

'No ...'	'Not really ...'/'Not Quite ...'	'Kind of ...'	'Yes ...'
7	0	0	3

board members to determine the policies and practices of the church. On Sundays, the church facilitates a service in Japanese for adults, a 'youth' service in English for the junior high school and high school students because as Pastor Yuichi states, the 'young generation is English-speaking generation ... they are easy to speak English'. There is also a Sunday school in Japanese for children in elementary school and younger.

As Table 7.3 indicates, 7 out of 10 church members stated that they did not perceive themselves as being bilingual; however, the assessment of their interview transcripts suggests that they are proficient in English to varying degrees. When I asked Pastor Yuichi, who had been living in Canada for eight years and who spoke Japanese at home and at work as pastor of the church if he was bilingual and he said he was not, it was somewhat of a surprise, although his English proficiency was limited, as indicated in Table 7.1, because I had spoken English with him on different occasions and much of the interview was in English. He responded to many of the questions in English, such as when he provided a transglossic description of his home linguascape.

Interviewer: What is the language you use at home?
PY: Everybody is mixed up, English, Japanese, but uh, for me, to me, Japanese.
Interviewer: Oh, everybody's mixed up?
PY: Mixed up (laughs), I'm good at Japanese ...
Interviewer: Oh, so not everybody speaks just Japanese, it's mixed, uh, what do you mean by mixed?
PY: Sometimes English, sometimes Japanese.
Interviewer: OK.
PY: I, but I speak, I always speak Japanese.

His responses in English and his use of the filler word 'uh' seem to demonstrate proficiency in English. He describes the languages used at his home as 'mixed', suggestive that his family is perhaps translingual, not bound by borders between speaking Japanese and English. Pastor Yuichi's family consists of his wife Mae and his two daughters, Kiko and Ana, and at the time of the interview they had lived in Canada for 10 years. Mae was educated in Japanese and Japan; however, she earned a Master's degree in English from a university in the US. Kiko, 24 at the time of the interview, arrived in Canada as a first year high school student and was working as a hair stylist speaking English in her workplace when I spoke to her. Ana, 18 at the time of the interview, arrived as an elementary school student and was preparing to enter university when I spoke to her. In their family, although Pastor Yuichi describes their languages spoken at home as 'mixed up', in spite of their different English education and experiences, only Ana stated that she believes she is proficient enough in English to be bilingual. During the interview Pastor Yuichi also provided a transcultural 'mixed up' description of the culture of Japan.

PY: I was born in Japan, but uh, Japanese uh, itself uh, our pop-culture mainly comes from America, United States, so Japanese itself uh, thinks itself, we are not Asian, we are Caucasian.
Interviewer: Oh.
PY: It's weird. (laughs)
Interviewer: (laughs) Do you think so? Why?
PY: Umm, my opinion, we Japanese [are] thinking, we long for American culture, movie or music, or uh, food, fast food, Starbucks (laughs) or I don't where.

He demonstrates transgrammaring with his mixed use of pronouns alternating between 'itself' and 'we' and absence of the linking verb 'are' in the progressive aspect construction 'we Japanese thinking' (Thompson, 2001). Pastor Yuichi provides a description of Japanese culture suggesting that Japanese people think of themselves culturally as 'Caucasian' as they 'long for American culture', which contrasts with his description of traditional Japanese culture.

PY: Yeah, we may think traditional culture and I, we, sometimes uh, feel that when we had a traditional festival, or matsuri [trans. 'festival'], or other culture, uh, tea ceremony, flower arrangement, we maintain, we are keeping some kind of old [Japanese] culture.

Similar to the previous comments, Pastor Yuichi demonstrates English proficiency with minimal variations from the standard variety. While he uses English to provide a transglossic description of his home and to describe the transcultural aspirations within Japanese society contrasted with traditional Japanese culture, he does not see himself as proficient enough in English to be bilingual. Perhaps his reluctance is associated with the way he positions himself as Japanese and different from other non-Japanese. Comparatively, his wife Mae and both of his daughters

Kiko and Ana are much more proficient in English, although only Ana perceives herself as being bilingual.

Interviewer: What is bilingual?
M: People who can speak Japanese almost perfectly, and English almost perfectly, I mean two languages almost perfectly.
Interviewer: What is almost perfectly? For example?
M: When um, what is almost perfectly ... they don't have any trouble speaking that language, fluency.
Interviewer: Are you bilingual?
M: No.

Mae clarifies that 'almost perfectly' means 'they don't have trouble speaking that language' and that 'bilingual' is synonymous with 'fluency'. Her inner speech, i.e. repeating the question 'what is almost perfectly' and use of the filler word 'um' is in English, which seems to indicate proficiency in English. However, Mae refers to bilinguals as '(other) people' and as 'they', which seems to affirm that she does not believe she is bilingual. Similarly, other church members do not perceive themselves as bilingual because they do speak English 'naturally' or 'perfectly'. For example, Nana, who came to Canada in 1997 when she was 23, who seems to be proficient in English, and who is married to an English-speaking Canadian, gave the following response:

Interviewer: Ok, If I say the word bilingual, what does that mean?
N: Bilingaru wa ['Bilingual' cognate + Japanese subject marker], speak two languages perfectly.
Interviewer: What is 'perfectly'?
N: (laughs) Um, perfectly, they understand almost perfectly, reading and writing, and conversation.
Interviewer: I see.
N: Hai. [Translated: 'Yes'.]
Interviewer: Are you bilingual?
N: No.
Interviewer: Why not?
N: Because I don't understand English perfectly.
Interviewer: Do you understand Japanese perfectly?
N: Um, I think, I don't know perfectly, but yeah, almost 100 percent.

Nana uses 'they' in reference to bilinguals, which affirms her direct statement that she does not perceive herself as someone who is bilingual because she does not speak or understand English 'perfectly'. However, when asked if she understands her first language, Japanese, perfectly, she states she does not, but that she understands it almost 100%. Nana demonstrates translanguaging (García, 2009) when she uses the cognate '*biringaru*' with the subject marker '*wa*' and the affirmative '*hai*' equivalent to 'yes' in her responses in part because she is aware that the interviewer can understand basic Japanese. Also, she uses the English filler word 'um', which seems to indicate proficiency in English. Similarly, another church member, Keita, a college student who has been in Canada for more than two years and who spent a year living in Seattle, states that he does not 'feel' like he is bilingual, either.

K: Bilingual is, well I don't feel like I am bilingual, but I use English and Japanese, so I think bilingual is like the person who can speak the language, two languages in fluency, naturally, I guess.

Keita states, 'I don't feel like I am bilingual', which is affirmed when he describes bilinguals as 'the (other) person who can speak the language' in contrast to himself, but he acknowledges he is able to 'use' English. He also uses the term 'fluency' and 'naturally', which refers to being able to speak with a high competency. His 'feeling' is consistent with Grosjean (1982: 269), who suggests that bilinguals often feel that they do not know one or the other language, when in fact being bilingual is being able to use any language, in different contexts, for different purposes.

In contrast, there were two ethnically Japanese members, Natsuko and Ryu, who perceived themselves as being bilinguals although their English proficiency levels were very similar to others in the church who did not perceive themselves as being bilingual. Both arrived in Canada as adults and had been living there for 12 years at the time of the interview. Natsuko is married to an English-speaking Canadian, speaks English at home except when she speaks Japanese to her daughter, usually attends an English-speaking church and attends the Japanese ethnic church once or twice per month. Given her background and experience in Canada, it is not surprising that she believes she is proficient enough in English to perceive herself as being bilingual.

Interviewer: Um, how about ... What is it to be bilingual?
N: What is it to be bilingual?
Interviewer: Yeah, what is the meaning of bilingual?
N: To speak two language[s].
Interviewer: Ok. Are you bilingual?
N: (laughs) Am I? Um, I would say, yes.

Natsuko demonstrates inner speech in English as she repeats the question 'What is it to be bilingual' and uses the English filler word 'um'. She demonstrates transgrammaring as she omits the 's' in the plural noun 'languages'. Similarly, Ryu, a trained chef who works as a baker and speaks only English at work and only Japanese at home, states that he perceives himself as being bilingual although his English is 'not really good, though...' although he can 'switch' quickly between Japanese and English.

Interviewer: So, how about the word, if I say bilingual, what does that mean, bilingual?
R: Uh, you know, just basic idea is use second, uh both langua-, uh second, two languages. So English, oh no it shouldn't be, not necessarily English English you know, own language from parents, or you know, the own country, plus other country world, could be English, could be French, could be Italian.
Interviewer: Are you bilingual?
R: Uh, yeah, I can say, I have to say [I am bilingual]. I know my English is still not really good, though I can switch my language[s] quickly.
Interviewer: Yes.
R: So [in] that case I potentially have bilingual.

Ryu demonstrates transgrammaring in his unorthodox phrasing by omitting the 's' in the plural noun 'languages', and omitting the preposition 'in'. He uses the filler word 'uh', which seems to demonstrate English proficiency. Even though he does not appear to be heavily impacted by perfectionist ideology, like many bilinguals, he is still critical of his bilingual ability (Roy, 2010: 546; Grosjean, 1996).

'Balanced Bilingual' River Japanese Churchscape

River Japanese Church is located near the city center and consists of about 30 first-generation ethnically Japanese adults aged 26–68, including Sho, age 36, who grew up in intermittently in Taiwan, Hong Kong and Japan speaking Japanese at home with his Japanese mother and Taiwanese father. The church began nearly 50 years ago as a Bible study group for first-generation Japanese people living in the area. As their families grew, the church grew to include an additional English-speaking congregation of nissei children and sansei grandchildren and other English speakers. As a result, on a given Sunday, following a joint 15 minute musical worship service in the main sanctuary where mostly English songs are sung, the church divides into two congregations wherein the Japanese congregation gathers in an upstairs room and the English-speaking congregation remains downstairs in the main sanctuary. Megumi, who holds a TESOL certificate and has worked in Japan as an English instructor, describes the bilingual character of the church as Japanese is used upstairs and English is used downstairs.

Interviewer: Um what language do you use at church?
M: Um, here [upstairs] mostly Japanese. But of course, downstairs, usually you know English speaker[s] [are] there, so … Um, downstairs so I use English. Yeah.

Megumi demonstrates transgrammaring when she omits the 's' in the plural noun 'speakers' and matching verb 'are'. She uses the filler word 'um' which seems to indicate proficiency in English. When I asked her what it means to be bilingual and if she is bilingual, she described being bilingual as 'the people who can speak and understand like both languages' and unlike others who use 'we vs you' discourse she states she is bilingual.

Interviewer: What does it mean to be bilingual?
M: Um, like [valleyspeak] the people who can speak and understand like [valleyspeak] both languages, not only English [or] Japanese, but [valleyspeak] like uh two languages.
Interviewer: Are you bilingual?
M: Yes. Actually, I can speak Korean, too, so maybe …
Fluently?
M: Um, kinda, I, I haven't find, found [self correction] a chance to right here so I mostly forgot, but uh yeah, I can read it, [and] I can speak for the daily conversation. [It] Should be that level.

Megumi demonstrates transgrammaring with her uses of the definite article, omission of the conjunction 'or' and omission of the pronoun 'it'. She states that she perceives that she is bilingual and that she is able to speak Korean in addition to Japanese and English, although she also states that she has 'mostly forgot' how to speak Korean, yet she states she can still read and speak it at a daily conversation level, which demonstrates she is aware of levels of proficiency. In addition, she uses 'valleyspeak', a characteristic of 'native' English speakers when she describes what it means to be bilingual.

Table 7.4 Balanced bilingual Japanese ethnic church (*n* = 4)

'No …'	'Not really …'/'Not quite …'	'Kind of …'	'Yes …'
0	0	1	3

Similar to Megumi, as Table 7.4 indicates, when asked the question, 'Are you bilingual?' unlike many of the members from other churches in this study, all four responded by saying 'Yes …' although Pastor Kenta stated, 'Yes, it's kind of'. Although they responded differently than many of the members of the other churches by saying, 'Yes …/Yes, it's kind of', their spoken proficiency levels were very similar to members of other churches in the study who did not perceive themselves as being bilingual, who demonstrated a 'limited working proficiency' in spoken English. When I asked Pastor Kenta, a native speaker of Japanese who speaks Japanese at home, who has been living in Canada for about four years and who had lived in the United States for 12 years, if he was bilingual, he stated that he is and he described 'bilingual' in the following way:

Interviewer: If I say bilingual, what is the bilingual definition.
PK: Bilingual definition is uh that's bilingual is [means speaking] two languages, and so [that means] two culture[s] and so it's lingual [means] the languages it include[s] their lifestyle[s].
Interviewer: Are you bilingual?
PK: Uh, yes, it's kind of.
Interviewer: And what languages do you speak?
PK: Uh, Japanese.
Interviewer: And others?
PK: English.

In his response Pastor Kenta describes his understanding of the word 'bilingual' as two languages connected to 'lifestyle'. Although he states he perceives himself as being 'yes, it's kind of' bilingual as a speaker of both Japanese and English, he demonstrates transgrammaring by using a 'subject + wa' type of framework when he states 'bilingual is two languages', as well as his omission of 's' in plural nouns 'cultures' and 'lifestyles', and the use of the pronoun 'it'. The filler word 'uh' seems to indicate proficiency in English. Similarly, Yuiko, who attends university in Canada, lived as an exchange student in the United States for a year during high school and has been living in Canada for three years, describes the meaning of bilingual as speaking two or more languages.

Interviewer: Ok. What is the meaning of bilingual, definition?
Y: Bilingual?
Interviewer: Yes.
Y: Uh, some like [valleyspeak] uh, speaking uh more than two languages.
Interviewer: Are you bilingual?
Y: Uh, I think so. But like [my] Japanese is stronger, of course.

Yuiko demonstrates transgrammaring when she omits the possessive pronoun 'my'. She uses the English filler word 'uh', which seems to indicate proficiency in English. Similar to Megumi, Yuiko uses 'valleyspeak' and while she states, 'I think so' to declare that she perceives herself as being bilingual, she also states that her Japanese is stronger. Yet she states that she comes to the church to attend the English service, but because she is Japanese she attends the Japanese service, too.

Interviewer: Do you come here for English or do you come here for Japanese, or both, or whatever?
Y: English.
Interviewer: Really? How did you end up in the Japanese service if you came here [for English].
Y: Just because I'm Japanese (laughs).

Yuiko attends both services owing in part to her role as the bass guitar player in both services, although she prefers attending the English service. Just as her role is divided, Megumi describes the heteroglossic language practices of the church as being divided too.

M: ... So, I just visit the downstairs, and the um, Pastor Yuichi's um, yeah, church so I can't compare [them] exactly, but uh, but here, like for example, like the worship together means part of [it is in] English. But uh, if I go to Yuichi's place, [I] feel like Japanese mostly, or something like that.

Megumi again demonstrates transgrammaring with her omission of pronouns 'them', 'it' and 'I'. She uses the English filler words 'uh' and 'um', which seems to indicate proficiency in English. Unlike Yuiko, Megumi prefers to attend the Japanese service and she also attends City Japanese church on occasion, which she describes as a place where she feels like it is 'Japanese mostly' in contrast to the upstairs/downstairs Japanese and English experience she experiences at River Japanese Church. For the members of the bilingual 'two-congregation' River Japanese Church, their views of perceiving themselves as bilingual may be a reflection of their positive bilingual experiences related to the fact that all three of them came to Canada as young adults. Similarly, Pastor Jim had spent 12 years in the US prior to coming to Canada. Yet, with the exception of Yuiko, they prefer regularly attending the Japanese congregation service even when the English option is very convenient, as in right downstairs.

Conclusion

Most church members in this study demonstrated significant English proficiencies as they were able to participate in an interview speaking English, i.e. they were able to communicate through understanding messages in English (Krashen, 1985). However, many of them did not believe that they were bilingual because they did not speak English 'perfectly' or 'deeply' or 'politely'. Most subjects who did not perceive themselves as bilingual used types of 'we vs you' discourse to distance themselves from the term 'bilingual'; thus, their beliefs about their own bilingual proficiencies were also embedded in their described conceptualizations of 'bilingual'.

Rather than characterizing their English from a deficit perspective, the analysis revealed that from a transglossic perspective where language is not particularly attached to specific domains, their transgrammaring patterns in 'ordinary' English included consistent and ordinary, albeit hybrid, constructions that included omissions of articles, pronouns, plural nouns, progressive tenses and prepositions. While there were examples of translanguaging (García, 2009) and transglossic transfer (Sultana, 2015) that included Yumi's use of the Japanese particle *'ne'*, Pastor Yuichi's 'mixed' phrasing, and Nana's use of the cognate *'biringaru'* with the Japanese subject marker *'wa'*, with the exception of Pastor Yuichi, these were not distracting in terms of hijacking comprehensible input and demonstrating English proficiency. Also, in terms of inner speech, all used English filler words that included 'um' and 'uh', in contrast to Japanese filler words such as *'eeto'* and *'ano'*, which seemed to indicate levels of proficiency in English. The 'ordinary' English spoken by subjects in this study was most frequently characterized by null-subject and pro-drop patterns often associated with Japanese (Thompson, 2001). Thus, owing to the regularity of these patterns and the comprehensibility of their responses in English, these patterns are authentic varieties of 'ordinary' English, and thus their 'ordinary' English is a legitimate variety and subjects who use 'ordinary' English should be recognized as legitimate English speakers.

However, recognition of speakers of 'ordinary' English has been a particular challenge because the omission of subjects and pronouns in Englishes have been traditionally described as being grammatically incorrect and as attributes of 'broken English' (Lindemann, 2005). Given the increasing awareness of transcultural flows as Pastor Yuichi indicated when he described Japanese society as having a pop-culture that comes from America in contrast to traditional Japanese culture and that Japanese people are culturally 'Caucasian', the implication is that younger generations in Japan are increasingly transcultural and exposed to transglossic realities to the extent that their attitudes toward being bilingual or translingual are changing and moving away from perfectionist ideologies.

Given the historical impact of churches in Japan and Japanese ethnic churches abroad, which are arguably broader contexts of language education, such churches play a role in impacting attitudes of Japanese society members at home in Japan and abroad in terms of facilitating English education opportunities and legitimizing beliefs about proficiency in English and being bilingual. In light of this role of Japanese ethnic churches, in this study there appeared to be reciprocity with the language policy *de facto* of each church and the potential beliefs about English proficiency and being bilingual of church members as the language practices and language needs seemed to dictate the characteristics of each churchscape. For example, in the monolingual church most members did not perceive themselves as being bilingual, and in the 'dominant bilingual' church most church members stated that they were not bilingual, yet they supported a potential bilingual or translingual church environment. In addition, they had already implemented an English class for the teenage and young adult bilingual/translingual members of the church whose first language was English, which indicated how the Japanese churchscapes have changed over time given the increased presence of younger nissei and sansei generations. Even church members of the monolingual church such as Shiho described the next generations as 'bilingual' because they were 'able to switch in head'. Yet arguably, despite the perfectionist ideologies they carried, Shiho and other subjects in the study were able to switch from Japanese to English in their heads too. Thus, as Dovchin (2017) points out, there is a significant gap concerning perspectives about language proficiency between older and younger generations. Finally, concerning the balanced bilingual church, a church that had developed into two congregations as a result of generational language differences, although they shared the same 'ordinary' English limited working proficiency abilities with members from other churches who did not believe they were bilingual, all four members perceived themselves as being bilingual. In addition to the fact that three of these four members had attended colleges in Canada where instruction was in English, it is likely that their beliefs about being bilingual were legitimized in part because they were younger and members of a transglossic churchscape where speaking both English and Japanese was an expected and legitimate cultural norm.

In short, Japanese ethnic churchscapes can be characterized as church spaces where flows of ethnically Japanese people construct their local communities, where church members experience language practices that can be characterized as 'monolingual', dominant bilingual' and 'balanced bilingual' in terms of each church's language policy *de facto*. Japanese ethnic churchscapes include Japanese and 'ordinary' English to varying degrees, particularly when accommodations are made for English-speaking nissei and sansei church members. Japanese ethnic churchscapes are identifiable by a 'movement of ideas' (Dovchin, 2017: 3; Appadurai, 1996) in which the 'perfectionist' beliefs carried by first-generation ethnically Japanese church members impact beliefs about what it means to be bilingual. While many first-generation church members demonstrate limited working proficiencies in English, they do not perceive themselves as being bilingual because they do not speak English 'perfectly' or 'deeply'. However, given the continuing transcultural impact of the globalizing world where English varieties and cultures continue to impact Japanese society, as this study shows, viewing language as a resource, as opposed to a deficit through the lens of transgrammaring, has the potential to impact Japanese ethnic church members' 'perfectionist' beliefs about proficiency and being bilingual and possibly 'translingual'.

References

Appadurai, A. (1996) *Modernity at Large: Cultural Dimensions of Globalization*. Minneapolis, MN: University of Minnesota Press.
Appadurai, A. (2001) Grassroots globalization and the research imagination. In A. Appadurai (ed.) *Globalization* (pp. 1–21). Durham, NC: Duke University Press.
Barrett, T. (2015) Perceptions about being Japanese and Christian in Canada. *International Journal of the Sociology of Language* 236, 237–260.
Barrett, T. (2016) Language policy in Japanese ethnic churches in Canada and the legitimization of church member identities. *Language Policy* 16 (4) 433–460.
Blommaert, J. (2005) *Discourse: A Critical Introduction*. Cambridge: Cambridge University Press.
Blommaert, J. (2010) *The Sociolinguistics of Globalization*. Cambridge: Cambridge University Press.

Bauman, R. and Briggs, C.L. (1990) Poetics and performances as critical perspectives on language and social life. *Annual Review of Anthropology* 19 (1), 59–88.

Christian, N. (2000) For Japanese, gospel music sets spirits a bit freer; They flock to Harlem to sing, and feel god. *New York Times*. See http://www.nytimes.com/2000/09/18/nyregion/for-japanese-gospel-music-sets-spirits-bit-freer-they-flock-harlem-sing-feel-god.html

Dovchin, S. (2017) The ordinariness of youth linguascapes in Mongolia. *International Journal of Multilingualism* 14 (2), 144–159.

García, O. (2009) *Bilingual Education in the 21st Century: A Global Perspective*. Oxford: Blackwell.

Dovchin, S. (2017) The ordinariness of youth linguascapes in Mongolia. *International Journal of Multilingualism* 14 (2), 144–159.

Dovchin, S., Pennycook, A. and Sultana, S. (2018) *Popular Culture, Voice and Linguistic Diversity: Young Adults On- and Offline*. Palgrave-Macmillan.

García, O. and Wei, L. (2014) *Translanguaging: Language, Bilingualism, and Education*. London: Palgrave Macmillan.

Gérin-Lajoie, D. (2011) *Youth, Language and Identity Portraits of Students from English-language High Schools in the Montreal Area*. Toronto: Canadian Scholars Press.

Gottlieb, N. (2012) *Language Policy in Japan: The Challenge of Change*. Cambridge: Cambridge University Press.

Greenberg (1990) *On Language: Selected Writings of Joseph H. Greenberg*. Stanford, CA: Stanford University Press.

Grosjean, F. (1982) *Life with Two Languages: An Introduction to Bilingualism*. Cambridge, MA: Harvard University Press.

Grosjean, F. (1985) The bilingual as a competent but specific speaker-hearer. *Journal of Multilingual and Multicultural Development* 6, 467–477.

Grosjean, F. (1996) Living with two languages and two cultures. In I. Parasnis (ed.) *Cultural and Language Diversity and the Deaf Experience*. Cambridge: Cambridge University Press.

Guerrero, M.C.M. (2006) *Inner Speech – L2: Thinking Words in a Second Language*. New York: Springer.

Gumperz, J.J. (1982) *Discourse Strategies*. Cambridge: Cambridge University Press.

Interagency Language Roundtable (2017) *ILR Speaking Skill Scale*. See http://www.govtilr.org/Skills/ILRscale2.htm

Japan Times (2005) Aso says Japan is nation of 'one race'. *Japan Times*. See https://www.japantimes.co.jp/news/2005/10/18/national/aso-says-japan-is-nation-of-one-race/#.Wow0FoP49pg

Kanagy, R. (2013) *Living Abroad: Japan*. Berkeley, CA: Avalon.

Krashen, S.D. (1985) *The Input Hypothesis: Issues and Implications*. New York: Longman

Lee, J.W. (2014) *The Sovereignty of Global Englishes: Translingual Practices and Postnational Imaginaries*. University of Arizona, UA Campus Repository.

Lindemann, S. (2005) Who speaks 'broken English'? US undergraduates' perceptions of non-native English. *International Journal of Applied Linguistics* 15 (2), 187–212.

Lund, E. (2015) Pronunciation anxiety: Many Japanese people don't want to speak English unless its perfect. *Japan Today*. See https://japantoday.com/category/features/lifestyle/pronunciation-anxiety-many-japanese-people-dont-want-to-speak-english-unless-its-perfect

Malmstrom, J. and Weaver, C. (1973) *Transgrammar: English Structure, Style, and Dialects*. Harlow: Longman.

Matsumoto, D. and Juang, L. (2003) *Culture and Psychology* (3rd edn). London: Wadsworth/Thomson.
Mayring, P. (2000) Qualitative content analysis [28 paragraphs]. Forum qualitative sozialforschung. Forum. *Qualitative Social Research* 1 (2), Art. 20. See http://nbn-resolving.de/urn:nbn:de:0114-fqs0002204
Mostyn, B. (1985) The content analysis of qualitative research data: A dynamic approach. In M. Brenner, J. Brown and D. Cauter (eds) *The Research Interview* (pp. 115–145). London: Academic Press.
Mullins, M.R. (1987) The life-cycle of ethnic churches in sociological perspective. *Japanese Journal of Religious Studies* 14 (4), 321–334.
Myers-Scotton, C. (2008) *Multiple Voices: An Introduction to Bilingualism*. Melbourne: Blackwell.
Pavlenko, A. (2014) *The Bilingual Mind and What it Tells us about Language and Thought*. Cambridge: Cambridge University Press.
Pennycook, A. (2007) *Global Englishes and Transcultural Flows*. London: Routledge.
Pickles, M. (2017) Japan turns to basil Fawlty in race for Olympic English. *BBC*. See http://www.bbc.com/news/business-39410915
Pinker, S. (2004) Clarifying the logical problem of language acquisition. *Journal of Child Language*. Cambridge: Cambridge University Press.
Pray, L. (2005) How well do commonly used language instruments measure English oral-language proficiency? *Bilingual Research Journal* 29 (2), 387–409.
Reischauer, E. and Jansen, M. (1995) *The Japanese Today*. Cambridge, MA: Harvard University Press.
Riedel, F. and Runkel, S. (2015) Understanding churchscapes. Theology geography and music of the Closed Brethren in Germany. In S. Brunn (ed.) *The Changing World Religion Map: Sacred Places, Identities, Practices and Politics* (pp. 2753–2782). New York: Springer.
Roy, S. (2010) Not truly, not entirely ... *Pas comme les Francophones. Canadian Journal of Education/Revue canadienne de l'éducation* 33 (3), 541–563.
Sultana, S. (2015) Transglossic language practices: Young adults transgressing language and identity in Bangladesh. *Translation and Translanguaging in Multilingual Contexts* 1 (2), 202–232.
Sultana, S., Dovchin, S. and Pennycook, A. (2015) Transglossic language practices of young adults in Bangladesh and Mongolia. *International Journal of Multilingualism* 12 (1), 93–108.
The Colonial Church Chronicle and Missionary Journal (1860) Volume 14. London: F. and J. Rivington.
Thompson, I. (2001) Japanese speakers. In M. Swan and B. Smith (eds) *Learner English: A Teacher's Guide to Interference and Other Problems*. Cambridge: Cambridge University Press.
Yukutake, A. (2016) Japan's perfectionism and lessons we can learn from lean startups. *Medium.com*. See https://medium.com/@atsushiyukutake/japans-perfectionism-and-lessons-we-can-learn-from-lean-startups-6789a6fff8f6

8 The Coding Catastrophe: Translinguralism and *Noh* in the Japanese Computer Science EFL Classroom

Kim Rockell

Introduction

Despite moves toward enhancing language educational culture in the wake of increasing globalization, native-speakerism and the unquestioning belief that English is the only language that should be permitted in the classroom still persist in English as a Foreign Language (EFL) classroom contexts in Japan (Canagarajah, 2013; Flores & Aneja, 2017; Houghton & Rivers, 2013: 1–16). In fact, much EFL activity in Japan is undergirded by underlying, conservative assumptions on the part of both instructors and students about the restricted use of language in this context, which reduce English to 'a language used and taught only in its own presence' (Pennycook, 2008: 4–5). These conservative assumptions about and expectations of language in Japanese EFL are supported by 'a monolingual orientation toward language by emphasizing how language boundaries are ideological constructs of European philology and the nation-state' (Lee, 2016: 177).

Meanwhile, such entrenched conservatism is contradicted by studies that show that Japanese EFL learners appreciated teachers who provided both source and target language in the classroom (Saito & Ebsworth, 2004). As Mishima (2016: 23) recommends, 'stakeholders in Japanese higher education may well need to revisit how their English-only policies are implemented and consider a possibility for a more nuanced approach to offering English-only classes' (Mishima, 2016: 23). According to Saito and Ebsworth (2004) with Japanese learners, not restricting first language (L1) can can also facilitate the immediate expression of 'complex feelings' and mitigate Japanese learners' communication apprehension and culturally influenced fear of a loss of 'face' or the 'risk of public humiliation', which might occur when being pressed but unable to respond to the teacher. Moreover, in the case of a non-Japanese instructor, working with a group of EFL students who may hold differing beliefs and expectations of classroom practice, it can help to clarify the teacher's intentions and reassure students (Saito & Ebsworth, 2004: 111–113, 119).

Following these lines of thought, this chapter seeks to illustrate how the application of translingualism is effective in negotiating the difference and sameness between students and instructors in the classroom. In the current research with English language students at the University of Aizu in the Tohoku region of Japan, I draw on *Noh* drama, a form of traditional Japanese theater with a 700-year history that combines poetry, drama, music, song and dance (Choo, 2004; Komparu, 2005) in English, using a research methodology involving participant observation and linguistic ethnography. The combination of performing arts and language education is of pedagogic value (Rockell, 2015; Rockell & Ocampo, 2014). I thus argue for the effectiveness of a translingual approach to teaching that permits EFL instructors to draw on linguistic resources, unrestricted by prescriptive notions governing their use. By providing some examples of translingualism through their own teaching, instructors can promote an environment that helps to coax Japanese students out from behind their 'wall of silence' (King, 2013: 71). From there, translingualism helps to guide students from this unfamiliar place and toward a more outgoing, communicative orientation where the sharing of personal opinions, thoughts and feelings also becomes a genuine possibility.

Theoretical Framework

In considering the way diverse linguistic resources are combined in a Japanese university computer science EFL classroom, this study draws on the theoretical concept of translingualism (Canagarajah, 2013; Lee, 2016; Pennycook, 2007). The term translingualism has gained recent prominence in response to calls for a reconceptualization of language and new ways of understanding language diversity (Dovchin *et al.*, 2018). The continuing intensification of global flows of ideas and information, as well as increasing mobility of populations and individuals around the world, has made earlier thinking about combining separate languages less workable. In response, scholars recognized that fixed ideas about language boundaries need to be re-thought, affirming the relevance of the vibrant use of diverse language and resulting in a 'recent blossoming of work under various "trans" labels' (Dovchin *et al.*, 2018: 27, 194). The translingual trend helps us to comprehend 'the rising complexity of recombinant linguistic and semiotic practices' that have emerged globally (Dovchin, 2015: 441–442). This thinking values the 'fluidity and negotiability of language boundaries' (Lee, 2017), and moves beyond simplistic notions such as 'bi/multilingualism' and 'code switching' (Otsuji & Pennycook, 2010).

The term *translingual practice* is presented by Canagarajah as an overarching term that encompasses earlier ways of describing communicative modes that combine linguistic resources in various ways. Here, two key concepts that underlie the use of this term can be emphasized: 'Firstly, communication transcends individual languages. Secondly, communication transcends words and involves diverse semiotic resources and ecological affordances' (Canagarajah, 2013: 6–7). The inclusion of a wide range of semiotic resources in the second concept is a consequence of the first concept's inclusive orientation (Canagarajah, 2013). In the contemporary global context, translingualism has come to be seen as 'not the occasional language uses of exceptional communities, but rather the everyday language practices of the majority of the world' (Pennycook, 2010: 133). This idea is echoed by Lee (2017: 4), who points out that, 'many communities, especially in the context of late modernity, are coming to be characterized by such communicative practices'. The reader may infer that, based on 10 years' experience of EFL communities in Japan, I do not consider them, in general, to belong to the large group to which Lee refers. Hence, the application of translingualism in Japan has the potential to bring its communities into line with a broader, global communicative flow and divest them of notions of 'homogeneity and hygiene that govern assumptions about language and how language should be used' (Lee, 2017: 6). This shift in thinking may be very helpful in preparing speakers to process the 'intense and constant interaction at a transnational level' (Wei & Hua, 2013: 44) so characteristic of the present era.

Meanwhile, the development of increasingly nuanced social linguistic theoretical perspectives such as translingualism has the potential to inform English teaching practice. They support an approach that more appropriately reflects the situation of contemporary young people and their ability to 'transverse linguistic and cultural boundaries' (Dovchin *et al.*, 2018: 191). They also strengthen English ability while promoting respect for linguistic resources other than English (Pennycook, 2017: 104). Such a new way of thinking about language has been found to generate more communicative interaction in the classroom than a stringent insistence on English only and separation of languages within a classroom language ecology (Creese & Blackledge, 2010: 3; García & Wei,

2014: 63–77). In fact, translingualism has been found to be a creative and practical way of language teaching that increases variety while building on or cultivating pre-existing linguistic resources. In challenging hierarchies and introducing new identity positions associated with language, like the behaviors associated with the related term translanguaging, it increases the sense of inclusion, encourages participation and assists in the development of less formal relationships between the participants (Creese & Blackledge, 2010: 103–106).

In the EFL classroom, the combination of English and Japanese linguistic resources and other linguistic and semiotic resources helps to avoid a common classroom situation where English is viewed by students as an external object dominated mainly by the teacher. At the same time, it draws attention away from a 'preoccupation with particular linguistic characteristics' such as notions of purity, and encourages a refocus on the 'relational and emerging nature of language and identity' (Dovchin *et al.*, 2018: 195).

Thus, translingualism can be of great benefit to such EFL contexts because its inclusive ethos does not discourage the communicative impulse, whatever form it may take (Creese & Blackledge, 2010: 3; Dash, 2002: 7). Further, the notion of drawing on 'a wide set of possible resources to achieve communication' (Dovchin *et al.*, 2018: 27) is most appropriate when considering how speech combines with gesture and dance when English learning and drama join together, as occurs in the current project. Encouraging students to engage in translingual meaning-making processes in this way may help to develop 'resourceful speakers', who can access resources and are 'good at shifting between styles, discourses, registers and genres' (Dovchin *et al.*, 2018: 208–209).

Notwithstanding the insights offered by social linguistic theory on the clear value of translingualism in English language teaching in a way that permits rather than discourages the use of L1, at the present time these approaches have yet to be fully incorporated into teachers' pedagogical practices (Flores & Aneja, 2017: 460). In recognition of the foregoing, the current project sets out to further demonstrate the benefits of a translingual approach in the EFL classroom.

Research Methodology

The data used in this chapter derive from an ethnographic classroom research project involving the creation, rehearsal and performance of a Japanese *Noh*-style play in English by a group of computer science students at the University of Aizu, Japan in the Tohoku region (conducted between

30 September 2016 and 30 September 2017). While *Noh* in English do exist (Emmert, 1994; Hensley, 2000), their performance in a language education context, and in particular the focus on translingualism, is a somewhat new exploratory approach. While significant work has examined translingualism in relation to performing arts such as popular music (Alim *et al.*, 2009; Dovchin *et al.*, 2018), the direct link between translingualism and traditional performing arts within the EFL classroom, where activities such as classical drama are thought to stimulate group interaction and improve oral production, remains unexplored (Gaudart, 1990; Gilbert, 2002; Gill, 2016). In the current study, English, traditional Japanese *Noh* theater and a cyberspace narrative are brought together in a Japanese university English language classroom. Students are encouraged to render English with the visceral immediacy of *Noh*-style vocalization, body posture and *suriashi* (sliding feet) walking style. This presents a very explicit challenge. Traditional *Noh* stories often deal with dramatic and tragic themes. The disaster presented in this project is the story of Marco Marsala, a hosting provider who believes he has deleted his entire company's website and the websites of his clients by mistakenly entering the incorrect code on his computer server. This theme also helped to move *Noh* into cyberspace with the intention of capturing the interest of student participants. This relocation into cyberspace was represented visually by replacing the *kagami ita* 鏡板 or mirror board (Ishii, 1994: 53), the back wall painted with the image of a large pine tree, with a representation of the global Internet (partially visible behind the actors in Figure 8.1). The traditional *Noh hayashi* 囃子 or instrumental group was replaced by drum apps on students' cell phones with bluetooth speaker sound reinforcement. In this English *Noh* script, which I entitled 'The Coding Catastrophe', the roles and grouping, and terms that refer to them in traditional Japanese *Noh* such as *shite* (protagonist), were retained. The *shite*, Mr McMorsel (a character based on Mr Marsala), travels to the cloud in an attempt to retrieve the lost data. He returns transformed into a robot and performs a robot dance, which traces the shape of bash script rm-rf.[1] In this way, he is able to save his professional reputation. The use of a written *Noh*-script maintains the integrity of one layer of English, which is also capable of being the object of multilingual commentary.

Meanwhile, choosing the translingual approach in this rehearsal was a natural choice for me as an instructor, since it was almost surreal and impractical to conduct the rehearsal only in English. It was much more convenient and my students and I felt more motivated through integrating rich linguistic (Japanese- and English-oriented linguistic resources) and other semiotic resources (e.g. referencing of traditional Japanese *Noh* drama-related music, dance, gesture etc.) during the rehearsal. Here,

Figure 8.1 Margaret Price filming a rehearsal of 'The Coding Catastrophe' in the University of Aizu UBIC 3D theater 2017

translingualism provided a framework for considering the teacher's strategic application of language as well as other semiotic resources that occur spontaneously in the classroom. Having already taught for a period of three years at the same institution, and lived in Japan for almost 10 years before commencing this project, I was not only already familiar with some of the students' backgrounds in a way that helped inform the sociohistorical implications of the text, but was also already fluent in Japanese myself. As preparation for the creation of an English *Noh*, I also studied traditional Japanese *Noh* chant with a local teacher for two years prior to commencing this research project. Consequently, translingualism was the most practical linguistic choice in this EFL classroom environment.

The 30 student participants, all identifying as Japanese, of whom only two were female, were aged between 19 and 20 years of age, were also important in the current project. Individual participants are referred to by common Japanese names or simply as 'student' in order to preserve anonymity. They were all members of the advanced English elective course Computer Assisted Ethnomusicology, available to third year students. Meanwhile, I acted as a participant–observer and guided rehearsals, during which photographic images and audio-visual video recordings of classes, rehearsals and the final performance were taken. In similar work in ethnomusicology it is common for a researcher to participate in ensemble performance and, since the researcher also performs, their voice or instrumental sound is considered part of the overall data examined

(Baily, 2008; Barz & Cooley, 2008; Titon, 1996). Similarly, in the current project, the instructor's voice forms an integral part of the *Noh* rehearsal and performance and is hence included as part of the data considered.

The inclusion of the instructor's voice as might occur in the case of ensemble or choir participant–observation data in ethnomusicological work also helps reach an understanding of the pedagogic function of translingualism. Since an assistant took responsibility for the practical and technical difficulties involved in the recording process, I was free to act without hindrance in the role of instructor. This made it possible to capture helpful examples of the way translingualism can be applied by teachers. Here, the teacher's voice is instrumental in helping to foster classroom relationships, guiding students to engage communicatively and supporting their expression of inner thoughts and feelings. Indeed, since the instructor's voice also has a ubiquitous classroom direction function, it would be difficult to capture natural data in this context where the instructor's voice in not present to some extent. For these reasons, the inclusion of the instructor's voice in data presentation became both a necessary and an informative feature in this project.

Moreover, video-recording facilitated the consideration of semiotic resources beyond words such as gestures in the data analysis, and which fall within the purview of the 'transtextural analytic framework', which is explained in the following section (Pennycook, 2007; Dovchin, 2015). Audio-visual recordings were done with the assistance of documentary filmmaker Margaret Price, who also helped with set design and logistics. These audio-visual recordings made it possible to review language data that occurred during class rehearsals as well as observe physical movements, postures and gestures that accompanied speech. The recordings were also used to make a short film about the project. This film and other photographic images were presented as work in progress at the Tiempo 4 All 1st International Conference on Intercultural Dialogue through the Arts in Fukuoka, Japan in 2017. In addition, diary methods to record the general patterns of all language occurring during the 90 minute lectures or *koma*, as well as details of specific interactions that arose while introducing and rehearsing the *Noh* play, were used.

Data Presentation: 序破急 *Jo-ha-kyū* [Introduction–Exposition–Denouement]

In reporting on the production of 'The Coding Catastrophe' here, three sets of language data are examined taken from the beginning, middle and final part of an English *Noh* rehearsal. These correspond to the idea of *Jo-ha-kyū* or introduction, exposition and denouement found in *Noh* as well as many other traditional Japanese art forms (Malm, 1959: 110–112).

Jo data was retrieved during the beginning of class in the regular classroom when the English *Noh* was initially introduced; *Ha* data was retrieved during negotiation of the movement to the University's UBIC 3D theater,[2] and *Kyū* data was retrieved during the last part of the *koma* while rehearsing the English *Noh* in the 3D theater. The data from this project was analyzed employing a transtextual analytical framework (Pennycook, 2007; Dovchin, 2015). This framework reaches beyond the text itself to include the sociohistorical history, physical location, associations with other texts and speakers' metalingustic interpretations of their own texts (Pennycook, 2007: 53–54). Such a broad and nuanced consideration of the textures replete with meaning that are woven throughout and around the text itself provides a key to understanding the rich flow of interaction that emerges in translingual practice. It helps us to bear in mind that texts are not independent, hermetically sealed units, but rather belong to 'larger frameworks of meaning' (Pennycook, 2017: 53), necessarily connected to environment influences, transactional dynamics, personal histories and complex interactive timeframes. Each of these facets within the transtextual analytic framework helps to reach a holistic interpretation of text. Sociohistorical elements provide insights into speakers' motivations and orientation toward the present. The consideration of the particularities of location and environmental factors are an important part of transtextual analysis because they shed light on how speakers relate, explore and share ideas under the constraints set in place by particular local conditions. In addition, these can be augmented by the information that speakers provide, reflecting on their own language practice (Dovchin, 2015). In the current project, this was possible by taking advantage of one of the many short breaks that occur in the course of a 90 minute rehearsal and garnering students' feedback.

Extract 1

序 *Jo* [Introduction] – Out from behind the wall: Creating group solidarity

Language guide: Japanese and languages other than English – *italicized*; English – regular font; elided material that might aid comprehension – [in brackets]; non-linguistic features such as utterances, situations or physical gestures – ((in double parentheses))

Teacher–student interaction introducing *Noh* in the usual EFL classroom	Translation
1. PA System: *So re mi do*	C, G, A, F ((in contemporary English language notation))
2. Teacher: Good Morning!	
3. Takeshi: (Giggles) … *Saiko datta!*	((giggles)) … It was great!
4. Hiroki: *Honto? Ikkinakatta. Baito ga atta*	Really? I didn't go cause I had part-time work
5. Teacher: OK, guys so this is our *mihon* or script. Write your names *wasurenaide ne*!	OK, guys so this is our script. Write your names [on them] Don't forget, OK!
6. Students: ………………	((Students silently mark their names))
7. Teacher: Now let's try the opening *shidai*. *Se – no* …. *kumikomi* embedded, embedded, embedded!	Now let's try the opening chorus. Here we go … Embedded, embedded, embedded, embedded!
8. Students: embedded, embedded …	Embedded, embedded … ((chanting hesitantly))
9. Teacher: *Motto ooki koe de*! *Gambatte! Se – no…*	In a louder voice! Do your best! Here we go …
10. Students: Embedded, embedded!	Embedded, embedded, embedded!
11. Teacher: Great! That's better! Now in *Noh* we have different roles like *waki*, *shite*, *jiutai* and *hayashi*. Today we need to choose who is *waki* and who is *shite*.	Great! That's better! Now in *Noh* we have different roles like main actor, supporting actor, chorus or chanters and instrumental group. Today we need to choose who is the main and who is a supporting actor.
12. Takeshi: *E–? Dame dame dame! Zettai yaranai!*	Now just hang on a minute! No way, no way, no way! I definitely won't do that [be a main or supporting actor].
13. Teacher: *Dekirun jyan!*	You can do it, I reckon!

The pretextual history of language occurrences *Jo*3 and *Jo*4 is associated with two classmates, Takeshi (19) and Hiroki (19), who are both enrolled in the third year advanced English elective course Computer Assisted Ethnomusicology at the University of Aizu. They are both also members of the campus *keion saakuru* or light music club. As they enter the English language classroom, they discuss the *gakusai* or university festival, held the previous weekend. Synchronous with their utterances, the notes *so re mi do* (*solfège* for the last of four melodic-sub phrases, which encompass the range of a major sixth) are broadcast electronically[3] (Harrison, 2016). This can be heard at the beginning and end of class at almost all educational institutions throughout Japan, including the University of Aizu. The teacher's active greeting in English, which directly precedes the classmates' conversation, meets with no response, and functions to bookend or mark off the beginning and end of the class period in the same way as do the Westminster Quarters.

When introducing the English *Noh* to participants for the first time, the teacher speaks English in *Jo5*, but leaves key *Noh* terms such as *mihon* (script), *shidai* (opening chorus) and *waki* (main actor or protagonist) in Japanese. There is some redundancy here, as in the sentence example *Jo5*, where the teacher says *mihon* or script, giving an English equivalent of *mihon* directly after the Japanese term. Using the Japanese terms directly, without translation, conveys respect for *Noh* and its conventions, recognizing that using the terms' English glosses and referencing Western theater traditions might be inadequate to capture the unique, local character of Japanese, *Noh*. The idea is that, coming from the teacher, an outsider who is learning Japanese traditions, respect for *Noh* implies a respect for things Japanese generally and by association, for the students themselves. Also in *Jo5*, the teacher switches to Japanese directly after the directive 'Write your names', to nuancing it with *wasurenaide ne*! (Don't forget, OK!). This is delivered in a light and playful way that aims to soften the authority of the command and engender a sense of solidarity with the student participants. In *Jo6*, the students comply silently with the directive without further comment. In *Jo7*, the chorus is set into commencement with a direct translation of the word embedded (*kumikomi*), presented here by the teacher (and later by one member of the *jiutai* [chorus of chanters], with the rhythmic support of a virtual drum app downloaded on his cellphone). The teacher also uses the Japanese exhortation *Se no* instead of English equivalents *Here we go!* or '3, 4 …' because of their functional efficiency in coordinating Japanese group activity. This was a conscious, split-second decision based on a decade's experience of using both the English and Japanese forms of these commands in educational settings with Japanese learners of English. To exhort a more full voiced chant, after the students' half-hearted effort in *Jo9*, the teacher uses Japanese directly, in a firm, insistent tone of voice. When the students respond positively with louder chanting of the *shidai*, the teacher reverts to an all-English comment when delivering positive feedback and praise in *Jo11*. Also in *Jo11*, like the word *mihon* [script], other key *Noh* terms are included directly in the teacher's instructions and explanation with no English translation. Students are asked to make a choice, which might result in increased personal exposure or prominence. This creates a heightened sense of anxiety and excitement, which immediately precedes Takeshi's emotional outburst in *Jo12, E–?Dame dame dame! Zettai yaranai!* (Now just hang on a minute! No way, no way, no way! I definitely won't do that!). Here, Takeshi did not appear to be using the language to convey a decision to the teacher, nor addressing other student participants, but rather to process his own transitory emotional excitement by voicing it out loudly. In *Jo13*, the teacher responds to Takeshi's outburst immediately with words of encouragement in Japanese, delivered in a slightly rough tone, *dekirun jyan*! (You can do it, I reckon!). This kind of intonation references the style of talking used by young male street gangs and presented on Japanese television. This, like most of the Japanese language used by the teacher while working with this class, is used with the intention of creating a sense of group and peer solidarity with the students, intending to communicate through linguistic competence an understanding of the students' world and local environment. In response to such language delivery, the students in this class frequently responded with light laughter or smiles, adopted more relaxing-looking body postures and readily engaged in classroom activity. Here, translingualism positions 'English' in more or less favorable ways so that group solidarity is secured, while their common ground is (re)gained through entertaining and humorous means (Dovchin *et al.*, 2018). Dovchin *et al.* (2018: 168) note that, through transglossic interactions, the speakers may act in ways through which 'group members bond together to either express their positive imaginations and identifications toward the "other", or belittle and exclude the "other" in a satirical and humorous manner through reasserting and encouraging each other's interactions in the group – (re)establishing the group/peer solidarity'.

Extract 2

破 *Ha* [Exposition] – guiding external encounters and negotiating transition

Language guide: Japanese and languages other than English – *italicized*; English – regular font; elided material that might aid comprehension – [in brackets]; non-linguistic features such as utterances, situations or physical gestures – ((in double parentheses)); heavy katana style pronunciations of English words – regular font and spelled approximating their pronunciation.

Relocating to the UBIC 3D Theater for dress rehearsals	Translation
1. Teacher: *Sumimasen; suri-ji-siyata-wo youyaku shittain desu ga ...*	Excuse me; I'd like to book the 3D theater.
2. Administrative Staff: *E? Hai. Jya moushikomishou wo* ((does writing hand gesture))	Uh? Oh, right. Well, [please fill out] these forms ((does writing hand gesture)).
3. Teacher: *E? Zenbu? Un, wakarimashita* ((writes almost identical information in Japanese on five separate forms)) *Douzo*	What? All of them? OK, I understand ... Here you are.
4. Administrative Staff: Dear Rockell, I send forms. Please confirm it. ((Sends Email containing English translations of the five forms))	Dear Rockell, I have sent you [English translations of] the forms. Please check them and confirm that you received them.
5. Teacher: PLEASE GO DIRECTLY TO THE UBIC 3D THEATRE ((writes directive on white board)) OK, *yosh*, Let's go, let's go, let's go! Bring your bags.	OK, alrighty, Let's go, let's go, let's go! Bring your bags.
6. Students: ((silently follow directive and begin to walk to 3D theater))	
7. Teacher: So, how was the *gakusai*?	So, how was the university festival?
9. Takeshi: Um, is beri enjoy	Well, I really enjoyed it
10. Passing Professor: Good Morning!	
11. Teacher and Takeshi: Good Morning!	
12. Takashi: *Chigau yo!* ((response to excited conversation with fellow students))	No it isn't! ((response to excited conversation with fellow students))
13: Passing Chinese exchange student: *Meiyou la, nage laoshi jiu shi...*	I didn't! ((or 'there isn't/wasn't'). That teacher is ...
14. Teacher: *Moshi moshi, sumimasen, suri-ji-siyata-nan desu kedo, mada aitenasasou desu ga ...*	Hello, excuse me but it's about the 3D Theater. It seems that it hasn't been opened yet ...
15. Administrative staff: *Hai, sugu ikimasu.*	OK, I'll head over there straight way.

After introducing the play in the standard classroom (see 序 *Jo*), the dynamic nature and volume level of *Noh* chanting and space required for dance and other physical expression in *Noh* meant that it was favorable to move to the UBIC 3D theater. This relocation called for a complex negotiation involving both written and spoken Japanese and English as seen in 破 *Ha* above. In *Ha*1, the teacher asks to reserve the room using standard Japanese. In *Ha*2, the administrative staff member in charge of the rooms is caught off guard and surprised, as indicated by the short utterance *E?* (Uh?). In going on to direct the teacher to fill out the Japanese room-booking forms, the administrative staff member does not complete the whole spoken sentence, which is delivered while passing the forms to the teacher. Instead, the idea of 'fill out' is suggested by a hand gesture that indicates writing, following on directly from the utterance. In *Ha*3, the teacher acquiesces to the request, but expresses mild displeasure at having to duplicate written information on multiple forms with the back-throat grunt *Un* (OK). This is followed by *Ha*4, where the administrative staff member has translated the forms into English and sent them to the teacher's university email address for confirmation. As shown in *Ha*14, despite the intricacies of the room booking process, the room is not actually open when the students arrive at the venue. It requires the teacher to make a further follow-up phone call in spoken Japanese and oblique request to open the room: *mada aitenasasou ga ...* (It seems that it hasn't been opened yet ...). In *Ha*5, full capital letters are used in a written message for the benefit of late students, asking them to move to the 3D theater. The teacher's spoken directive in English includes the Japanese word *yosh*! This is used with the intention of spurring students into action with a sufficient degree of dynamism to effect an efficient relocation. Students comply silently and while walking downstairs and outside toward the 3D theater. In *Ha*7, the teacher mixes Japanese and English in an attempt to encourage small talk, asking about the recent *gakusai* (university festival). In *Ha*8, Takeshi responds in katakana English and directly following this in *Ha*9, a non-Japanese professor, who happens to encounter the group as they walk outside, delivers a cheery greeting in English, which is responded to by the teacher and Takeshi in *Ha*10. Japanese students are also involved in private conversations in Japanese. Takeshi takes part in one with students walking near him, causing him to retort excitedly the denial *chigau yo!* (No it isn't!). Further linguistic complexity is added by passing Chinese exchange students in *Ha*12, where their conversation is clearly audible briefly but not directed to any of the English *Noh* group, nor toward the teacher. As explained above, an extra phone call in Japanese is required for the room to be unlocked and the administrative staff member responds affirmatively in *Ha*14, promising to come and unlock the room immediately. In this section, during the physical relocation that occurs in *Ha*, the teacher and students encountered persons from outside their regular class group. During these encounters, the teacher provides an example for students by using both English and Japanese in an uninhibited manner. Translingualism is also seen to be useful to facilitate logistic and administrative processes. As well as providing an example, the teacher also involves students in the process by drawing them into conversation drawing on both English and Japanese linguistic resources. This extract highlights the rich linguistic complexity that is required and generated even in the performance of apparently straightforward tasks. Responsible for the students and acting on their behalf in real time and in their presence, the teacher uses translingualism effectively as they transfer to new physical space. In doing so, students are able to observe how translingualism can be an invaluable, practical tool, which also helps when dealing with unexpected social encounters – guiding external encounters and negotiating transition.

急 *Kyū* [Denouement] – Sharing Personal Thoughts and Feelings

Language Guide: Japanese and languages other than English – *italicized*; Japanese kana or kanji – (in parentheses); English – regular font; elided material that might aid comprehension – [in brackets]; non-linguistic features such as utterances, situations or physical gestures – ((in double parentheses)); heavy katana style pronunciations of English words – regular font and spelled approximating their pronunciation.

Continuing to rehearse in the UBIC 3D Theater	Translation
1. Teacher: OK *shite, wak*i, *daijoubu kai?* From the bottom of page 3. *koko, koko ...*	OK, main actor(s),[4] supporting actor(s), Are you OK to go? From the bottom of page 3, here, here ...
2. *Waki* Students: Mr McMorsel!	
3. *Shite* Students: Is it a real human voice? Or maybe robot?	
4. Teacher: You are lost in cyberspace through your Internet mistake	
5. *Waki* Students: You are lost in cyberspace through your Internet mistake	
6. Teacher: Good, good. What's the problem?	

7. Takeshi: I can't see ... ((gestures at the tatami mat))
8. Teacher: You can't see ... anything. That's why in the traditional *Noh* they have a *nantoka bashira*, kind of pillar to guide them. OK, so how is your experience of English *Noh*? Please let me know. You can use English or Japanese. *Dochidemo ii desu yo!* ((Teacher hands out paper for students to write their responses))

That's why in the traditional *Noh* they have some kind of pillar, a kind of pillar to guide them. OK, so how is your experience of English *Noh*? Please let me know. You can use English or Japanese. Either is fine! ((Teacher hands out paper for students to write their responses))

9. Student: *Eigo is muzukashii* (英語 is ムズカシイ)

English is difficult.

10. Student *Hatsuonya onseihou, koe no to–n nado ga tokushu teki de omoshiroi* (発音や発声法、声のトーンなどが特殊的で面白い)

The pronunciation, vocalization method, voice tone etc. are special and interesting.

11: Student: Ingirisu ando Japanizu habu diparento shiraburu

English and Japanese have different syllables

12: Teacher ... OK. Good, good. *Jya, raishuu gambarimashou ne!*

OK. Good, good. So, let's all do our best next week OK!

In 急 *Kyū*, the teacher and participants enter the UBIC 3D theater. As rehearsal commences in *Kyū* 1, the teacher directs the main and supporting actors (more than one of each in order to maximize speaking opportunities) to begin chanting. As was the case in *Jo*11, terms for actors' roles *shite* and *waki* remain in Japanese. *Daijoubu kai?* (Are you OK [to go]?) in Japanese, seeks to call students' attention without undue strictness and *koko, koko* (Here, here!) is uttered quickly by the teacher while simultaneously pointing at a place in the script. In *Kyū*2–*Kyū* 4, students chant a verse from the middle section of the play:

> Mr. McMorsel!
> Is it a real human voice?
> Or maybe robot?
> You are lost in cyber-space
> Through your Internet mistake

This verse and the rest of the script follow the syllable patterns of *tanka* poetry (5–7–5–7–7), which is commonly found in *Noh* texts. The text in enunciated with heightened speech and in the call-and-response rote learning method used in traditional *Noh* training. The *waki* are seated at the side of the stage and the *shite* are center stage wearing Steve Jobs and Horiemon *Noh* masks that they have made themselves for the play. As is the case with traditional *Noh* masks, visual access is difficult for inexperienced performers. One *shite* appears a little off-balance, prompting the teacher to ask if there is a problem in *Kyū* 6. In *Kyū* 7, the *shite* responds with the beginning of a sentence in English, providing an object to complete the sentence with a circular gesture, pointing at the surrounding floor area. The teacher interprets the gesture and in *Kyū* 8 provides a fully interpreted English sentence, directing it to the whole group. This is followed by an explanation mixing Japanese and English. *Nantoka* (some kind of) is a casual way of introducing the idea of *hashira* (柱) or pillar, and this is followed directly by a translation of the same short phrase 'a kind of pillar' in English. Following on in *Kyū* 8, the teacher elicits feedback from student participants, emphasizing in Japanese that responses in either English and or Japanese are all welcome. English or Japanese, *dochidemo ii desu yo!* (English or Japanese, either is fine!). *Kyū* 9, *eigo* is *muzukashii* (英語 is ムズカシイ) or English is difficult is a rare example of recombination of linguistic resources by a student in the Japanese-English language classroom. While combination with English in various permutations often appears in Japanese popular music, in over 10 years of teaching in Japan, this is the only deliberately presented example I have ever encountered in an educational context. The written sentence combines Japanese *kanji*, English and a less common presentation of the word *muzukashii* (difficult) in katakana for emphasis. As is clear from data sets *Jo*, *Ha* and *Kyū*, the teacher frequently combined English and Japanese. However, when students used Japanese, it was usually as a private, embedded language and not directed toward the teacher. Here, the appearance of a mix of Japanese and English within a sentence, on the part of a student, can be read as a crack beginning to appear in the wall of non-mutual permeability, and minuscule but potentially very meaningful de-objectification of English. In *Kyū* 10 and *Kyū* 11, students respond in full sentences in both Japanese and English, respectively. Their awareness of contrasting prosodic features that appear in these languages has been stimulated and is characterized positively in *Kyū* 10 and negatively in *Kyū* 11. Finally, in *Kyū* 12, the teacher pauses, and then continues, addressing the negative characterization closing the rehearsal with a positive statement, which is delivered in English and Japanese. In the *Kyū*, translingualism is seen to effectively facilitate interaction and help to provide students with immediate clarifying explanations, offering information while maintaining a friendly tone. It is effective in mediating the teacher's authority so as to appear more approachable and invite a communicative response from students. It provides an avenue for responding in a way that is sensitive to the inevitable technical difficulties that students may experience during dramatic rehearsals and performance. At the same time, it generally supports an open and welcoming platform that invites students to express themselves more intimately – sharing personal thoughts and feelings.

Conclusion: Translingualism as an Effective Tool in the EFL Classroom

In this project, I applied a translingual strategy that drew on diverse linguistic and semiotic resources involved in a Japanese EFL classroom context. This translingual teaching practice emerged primarily in three main ways as follows. The first was as an affective strategy to help students overcome shyness and develop relationships. Here, translingualism helped to draw students out from 'behind the wall' and forge stronger bonds both amongst themselves and with the instructor. It helped to remove barriers and bring the instructor closer to the students, becoming a more integrated participant in the flow of classroom activity. Second, translingualism was used for functional efficiency in coordinating group activity, guiding external encounters and negotiating transition. In this respect, translingualism helped to spur students into action and direct their attention and when explaining details. It became particularly important during the physical relocation to a new building during the project, where moving the lesson to another venue was only possible with the application of bilingual literacy on the part of the teacher. In this process, although an effort was made to use only English or only Japanese when approaching authorities with respect and negotiating contractual obligations, translingual resources were still very much required. Third, this translingual approach helped to bring students to the point where they were comfortable sharing personal thoughts and feelings. This was a very positive result given the reticence and tendency toward shyness the students often displayed earlier in the project. Permitting an immediacy of emotional expression also facilitated the expression of ideas about the difficulty of English. These results proceeded because translingualism enabled the instructor to show respect toward Japanese culture and students as individuals, soften authority, engender a sense of solidarity and demonstrate an understanding of the students' position. These findings are in line with Saito and Ebsworth's (2004) argument, that learners were better able to negotiate the immediate expression of emotion and benefit from teachers' explanations when L1 was not restricted (Saito & Ebsworth, 2004: 111–113, 119).

Additionally, translingualism contributed to meaning-making. Here, the use of other semiotic resources such as gestures to expand or complete an idea commenced in English, which can be considered through the lens of a transtextural analytic framework. Students used gestures for meaning-making and sentence completion during the project and administrative staff also drew on these semiotic resources, although in this case as a way to actually reduce the amount of their spoken communication in English. This may have occurred because, unlike in classes and rehearsals, the underlying assumption of the dynamics of this particular cross-cultural encounter appeared to be that only English should be used when speaking to non-Japanese. The combination of English and *Noh* also helped to increase students' linguistic and cultural awareness. As *Noh* moved into English, the underlying structure of the script, syllable patterns and key *Noh* terminology in Japanese drama remained unchanged. Although it was revealed that some participants were uneasy with the aesthetic results of this process, at the same time, as a result of having their attention drawn to various prosodic anomalies, they became more attuned to prosodic features. These students, however, generally characterized the combination of English and *Noh* positively. An increased sense of interest by this group of younger-generation Japanese in traditional Japanese *Noh* was a further positive outcome of the research. When asked directly in writing whether they were interested in *Noh*, only a third of the participants answered 'yes' at the beginning of the project while at the end half of the class claimed positive interest. Written comments in Japanese included the following:

- I hadn't heard about it [*Noh*] before but when I tried it in class I found it really interesting. [以前までは聞いたことがなかったが授業にやってみてとても面白かった。]
- This time I thought that as a traditional Japanese art *Nohgaku* is a wonderful thing. [能楽は日本の伝統芸能としてとても素晴らしものだと今回で思いました。]
- Although I was not very interested in *Noh*, I became a little interested through taking part in the (computer-assisted ethnomusicology) lessons. [あまり興味がなかったが授業を通じて少し興味がもてました。]

This alone speaks in favor of incorporating performing arts-based projects, such as English *Noh* within education, using the kind of re-combinatorial blending of language practices described here.

In general, by setting the tone and providing an example of translingualism in the classroom, and not overly dominating overall classroom language practices, the strategic combination of *Noh* and English began to break down the condition of non-mutual permeability between Japanese and English, so frequent in a Japanese EFL environment. By allowing students to express their emotions in Japanese, it was possible to prevent them from further 'building the wall'. However, much more needs to be done so long as English continues to be viewed by students as an exacting, external object made up of sonic and orthographic rules and conventions, as a barrier or hurdle in the path of students' various other life goals.

The *Noh* script developed in this project can be re-used with other groups of EFL students. However, in future work it would be useful to explore how allowing students more freedom in choosing themes and encouraging them to co-create a translingual *Noh* script themselves might further impact interactive social patterns of language use and linguistic diversity. English *Noh* in cyberspace may have been a catastrophe for Mr McMorsel. However, for me and my students who chanted vigorously while the robot danced bash script '*rm-rf*', translingualing in English *Noh* was affirmed to be an extremely positive approach, illustrating the efficiency that translingualism can bring to EFL in Japan.

Acknowledgments

This project was part of a broader linguistic ethnographic research project funded by General Research funding at the University of Aizu. I am very grateful to Associate Professor Sender Dovchin for her encouragement and support in developing the chapter while she was extraordinarily busy with her own professional and family commitments. I must also express gratitude to the two anonymous reviewers who offered very constructive suggestions. I would also like to thank Margaret Price for her invaluable assistance and the student participants for taking up the challenge to perform a drama in English, and I am forever indebted to Yoshika Sato Sensei for her patient guidance in my first steps learning traditional Japanese *Noh*.

Notes

(1) Bash is a Unix shell and command language. The r in the code stands for 'remove directories and their contents recursively'.
(2) The regular classroom plant restricts the freedom of movement and there is a no open space in which the chorus of chanters can assemble in kneeling position as occurs in traditional *Noh*. This was one reason for moving the class to the 3D theater.
(3) The melody is the Westminster Quarters, originating in the church of St Mary the Great in Cambridge, England.
(4) The Japanese noun form can refer to either a singular or plural entity and here the teacher is not sure how many actors are ready to come on stage at this time.

References

Alim, S., Ibrahim, A. and Pennycook, A (eds) (2009) *Global Linguistic Flows: Hip Hop Cultures, Youth Identities, and the Politics of Language*. New York: Routledge.

Baily, J. (2008) Ethnomusicology, intermusability, and performance practice. In H. Stobart (ed.) *The New (Ethno)musicologies* (pp. 117–134). UK: Scarecrow.

Barz, G.F. and Cooley, T.J. (2008) *Shadows in the Field: New Perspectives for Fieldwork in Ethnomusicology*. Oxford: Oxford University Press.

Canagarajah, S. (2013) *Translingual Practice: Global English and Cosmopolitan Relations*. New York: Routledge.

Choo, L.B. (2004) They came to party: An examination of the social status of the medieval noh theatre. Paper presented at the Japan Forum.

Creese, A. and Blackledge, A. (2010) Translanguaging in the bilingual classroom: A pedagogy for learning and teaching? *The Modern Language Journal* 94 (1), 103–115.

Dash, P. (2002) English only (EO) in the classroom: Time for a reality check. *Asian EFL Journal* 4 (4), 1–20.

Dovchin, S. (2015) Language, multiple authenticities and social media: The online language practices of university students in Mongolia. *Journal of Sociolinguistics* 19 (4), 437–459.

Dovchin, S., Pennycook, A. and Sultana, S. (2018) *Popular Culture, Voice and Linguistic Diversity: Young Adults On- and Offline*. Berlin: Springer.

Emmert, R. (1994) Nō: Exploring its non-Japanese possibilities 1. *Contemporary Theatre Review* 1 (2), 137–144.

Flores, N. and Aneja, G. (2017) 'Why needs hiding?' Translingual (re) orientations in TESOL teacher education. *Research in the Teaching of English* 51 (4), 441.

García, O. and Wei, L. (2014) Translanguaging and education. *Translanguaging: Language, Bilingualism and Education* (pp. 63–77). Berlin: Springer.

Gaudart, H. (1990) Using drama techniques in language teaching. *Language Teaching Methodology for the Ninetees Anthology Series* 24, 230–249.

Gilbert, A.G. (2002) *Teaching the Three R's Through Movement Experiences*. ERIC.

Gill, C. (2016) Maximising Asian ESL learners' communicative oral English via drama. *Advances in Language and Literary Studies* 7 (5), 240–246.

Harrison, J. (2016) *Bells and Bellringing*. London: Bloomsbury.

Hensley, C. (2000) No business like Noh business. *American Theatre* 17 (1), 34–38.

Houghton, S. and Rivers, D. (2013). Introduction: Redefining native-speakerism. *Native-speakerism in Japan: Intergroup Dynamics in Foreign Language Education* (pp. 1–16). Bristol: Multilingual Matters.

Ishii, M. (1994) The Noh theater: Mirror, mask, and madness. *Comparative Drama* 28 (1), 43–66.

King, J. (2013) *Silence in the Second Language Classroom*. Berlin: Springer.

Komparu, K. (2005) *The Noh Theater: Principles and Perspectives*. Warren, CT: Floating World Editions.

Lee, J.W. (2016) Beyond translingual writing. *College English* 79 (2), 174.

Lee, J.W. (2017) *The Politics of Translingualism: After Englishes*. Abingdon: Routledge.

Malm, W. (1959) *Japanese Music and Musical Instruments*. Tokyo: Tuttle.

Mishima, M. (2016) Searching for the best medium of instruction: Japanese university students' views on English-only instruction in EAP courses. *The Journal of Rikkyo University Language Center* 36, 15–27.

Otsuji, E. and Pennycook, A. (2010) Metrolingualism: Fixity, fluidity and language in flux. *International Journal of Multilingualism* 7 (3), 240–254.

Pennycook, A. (2007) *Global Englishes and Transcultural Flows*. London: Routledge.
Pennycook, A. (2008) Translingual English. *Australian Review of Applied Linguistics* 31 (3), 30.31–30.39.
Pennycook, A. (2010) *Language as a Local Practice*. Abingdon: Routledge.
Pennycook, A. (2017) *Global Englishes and Transcultural Flows*. London: Routledge.
Rockell, K. (2015) Musical looping of lexical chunks: An exploratory study. *JALT CALL Journal* 11 (3), 235–253.
Rockell, K. and Ocampo, M. (2014) Musicians in the language classroom: The transference of musical skills to teach speech mode of communication. *ELTED* 16(Spring), 34–37.
Saito, H. and Ebsworth, M.E. (2004) Seeing English language teaching and learning through the eyes of Japanese EFL and ESL students. *Foreign Language Annals* 37 (1), 111–124.
Titon, J.T. (1996) Knowing fieldwork. In G.F. Barz and T.F. Cooley (eds) *Shadows in the Field: New Perspectives for Fieldwork in Ethnomusicology* (pp. 87–100). New York: OUP.
Wei, L. and Hua, Z. (2013) Diaspora: Multilingual and intercultural communication across time and space. *Aila Review* 26 (1), 42–56.

Index

Aboriginal 84
Afghans 51
American 9, 107, 120, 135
Anglophone 41, 107
Anglos 54
Appadurai 22, 45, 119, 120, 144
Arab 24, 107
Arabic 24
Authenticity 34, 35, 43, 70, 72, 73, 79, 95, 100

Bakhtin 3, 13
Balanced bilingual 122, 126, 127, 138, 140, 143, 144
Bangladesh xiii, xiv, 1, 2, 3, 6, 7, 9, 10, 11, 12, 13, 14, 15, 16
Barbados 26
Barrett xv, xvi, 119, 121, 126
Bilingual xv, 33, 35, 40, 41, 119, 120, 121, 122, 123, 124, 125, 126, 127, 128, 129, 130, 131, 132, 133, 134, 135, 136, 137, 138, 139, 140, 141, 142, 143, 144
Bilingualism 86, 119, 121, 122, 123
Binary 66, 68, 73, 119, 122, 123, 125
Blommaert xiii, xv, 2, 5, 34, 42, 43, 50, 57, 62, 66, 67, 68, 69, 80, 86, 89, 94, 97, 98, 102, 105, 125
Bourdieu 50
British 25
Broken English 124, 125, 143

Canada xiii, 30, 107, 126, 127, 128, 129, 130, 132, 133, 134, 135, 136, 137, 140, 141, 142, 144
Canadian 26, 30, 39, 40, 41, 43, 126, 128, 129, 130, 131, 133, 136, 137

Canagarajah 67, 68, 81, 86, 102, 104, 147, 148, 149
Center 17, 68, 69, 80
Chinatown 20, 21, 25, 26, 29, 30, 34, 37, 39, 40, 41, 42
Chinese 25, 26, 32, 33, 34, 35, 36, 37, 38, 39, 40, 41, 43, 77, 91, 112, 120, 158, 159
Christian 119, 120, 121
Church of English 120
Churchscapes xv, 119, 120, 121, 125, 143, 144
Cicourel 52, 53
Cityscapes 23
Code-switching xiii, 125, 149
Critical Discourse Analysis (CDA) 106

Decontextualization 4, 5
Democratic People's Republic of Korea 107
Discourse 2, 4, 5, 17, 29, 30, 42, 44, 48, 49, 50, 52, 57, 58, 61, 62, 66, 76, 77, 79, 88, 103, 106, 109, 114, 115, 116, 125, 126, 131, 132, 139, 142, 150
Discourse of resistance 103, 114, 116
Dokdo 108, 109, 110, 111, 112
Dominant bilingual 122, 123, 126, 127, 129, 130, 132, 133, 134, 143, 144
Dongdo 112
Dovchin xiii, xiv, xv, xvi, 2, 3, 22, 68, 84, 85, 86, 87, 88, 89, 90, 91, 102, 103, 120, 124, 127, 130, 143, 144, 148, 149, 150, 151, 153, 154, 157, 165

EFL vi, x, xvi, 23, 147, 148, 149, 150, 151, 152, 155, 163, 165

Emoticons 1, 5
English ix, x, xi, xv, xvi, 4, 6, 8, 10, 11, 21, 22, 23, 25, 26, 29, 30, 32, 33, 34, 35, 36, 37, 38, 39, 40, 41, 43, 55, 56, 66, 74, 75, 76, 78, 79, 84, 87, 88, 90, 91, 92, 93, 94, 95, 96, 98, 99, 102, 103, 104, 105, 106, 107, 108, 110, 111, 112, 113, 114, 115, 116, 119, 120, 121, 123, 124, 125, 126, 127, 128, 129, 130, 131, 132, 133, 134, 135, 136, 137, 138, 139, 140, 141, 142, 143, 144, 147, 148, 149, 150, 151, 152, 154, 155, 156, 157, 159, 160, 161, 162, 163, 164, 165
Englishes x, 104, 108, 119, 124, 143
English language learners 23
Entextualization 3, 4, 5, 6, 7, 10, 15, 16, 124, 125
Ethnic churches 121, 143
Ethnic shops 48, 50, 51, 54
Ethnomusicology x, 152, 155, 164
Ethnographic xiii, xiv, xv, xvi, 6, 52, 85, 89, 90, 150, 165
Ethnography 6, 28, 89, 148
Ethnolinguistic 26

Facebook 1, 5, 6, 8, 11, 29, 76, 92
Fairclough 106
Far East 25, 70
Fluidity 104, 149, 68, 85, 87, 99
Fossilization 125, 126

Gakusai 155, 158, 159
Garfinkel 48, 50, 62
Gee 48, 62
Germans 70, 71
Global xiii, xiv, xv, 1, 5, 16, 17, 22, 66, 67, 68, 70, 73, 74, 78, 79, 80, 81, 94, 102, 115, 119, 120, 148, 149, 151
Globalization 17, 22, 43, 44, 68, 74, 75, 81, 84, 85, 99, 102, 147
Goffman 47, 48, 50, 54, 57, 60, 62
Google Maps 110, 113
Greeks 54
Grosjean 122, 123, 128, 130, 131, 133, 137, 138
Gumperz 53, 126

Hangungyeong 111
Hanja 112
Hashira 162
Hong Kong 26, 81, 138
Hybrid 68, 85, 86, 87, 106, 114, 115, 124, 126, 142
Hybridity xiii, xv, xvi, 43, 72, 85, 102, 103, 104, 114, 115
Hymes 54

Identity ix, xi, xv, 2, 5, 6, 15, 17, 39, 40, 49, 50, 51, 55, 57, 59, 62, 66, 67, 69, 72, 73, 79, 80, 94, 97, 107, 130, 133, 150
Identity construction 55, 62
Ideologies v, x, 5, 6, 7, 16, 23, 45, 48, 66, 67, 71, 72, 78, 80, 81, 88, 103, 104, 106, 107, 122, 143
Indexicalities 86
Indigenous 84, 88, 89
Inner speech 126, 132, 136, 138, 142
Interaction order 54, 56, 62
Interactional sociolinguistics 48, 53
Interagency Language Roundtable (ILR) 123, 125, 126, 127, 128
Interlocutors 1, 2, 6
Internet ethnography 6
Interpretive phenomenological analysis (IPA) xiv, 28, 44
Intertextual 7, 9
Intertextuality 57, 58
Interviews xiii, xiv, xv, 29, 69, 70, 77, 81, 87, 127
Iranian 59, 60
Irish 25
Italian 25, 30, 34, 35, 138

Jamaica 26
Japan xiii, xv, xvi, 108, 109, 111, 119, 120, 121, 127, 133, 134, 135, 139, 143, 147, 148, 149, 150, 152, 153, 156, 162, 165
Japanese ethnic churches 121, 143
Jewish 24, 25, 37, 39
Jo-ha-kyū 153, 154

K-pop 103
Kachru 104, 106

Kagami ita 151
Kanji 160, 162
Katakana 159, 162
Kazakhstan xiii, xiv, xv, 66, 67, 68, 69, 70, 71, 72, 73, 74, 75, 76, 77, 78, 79, 80, 81
Keion saakuru 155
Kensington Market 20, 21, 25, 26, 29, 30, 35, 36, 39
Koma 153, 154
Koreans 70, 71, 107, 108, 109, 110
Korean Ministry of Education 106
Kumikomi 155, 156

Language policy xiv, 70, 74, 75, 80, 126, 143, 144
Language proficiency 119, 123, 143
Liancourt Rocks 109, 110, 111, 112, 113, 114
Linguicism 88
Linguistic xiv, xv, xvi, 1, 2, 3, 4, 5, 6, 7, 10, 16, 17, 20, 21, 22, 23, 24, 28, 29, 38, 40, 43, 44, 48, 50, 57, 66, 69, 77, 78, 84, 85, 86, 87, 88, 89, 90, 91, 92, 93, 98, 99, 102, 103, 104, 105, 112, 124, 126, 148, 149, 150, 151, 152, 154, 157, 159, 160, 162, 163, 164, 165
Linguistic discrimination v, 84, 85, 87, 88, 90, 92, 93, 98
Linguistic diversity xiii, 21, 165
Linguistic ethnography 89, 148
Linguistic injustice 88
Linguistic landscape xiii, 20, 21, 23, 24, 29, 44
Linguistic racism 87
Linguascaping xiv, 20, 21, 22, 23, 25, 29, 41, 43, 44, 102
Local xiii, xiv, xv, 1, 3, 5, 14, 15, 16, 17, 22, 66, 67, 68, 70, 72, 76, 78, 79, 80, 81, 85, 86, 87, 88, 89, 93, 94, 95, 98, 99, 110, 114, 119, 120, 124, 144, 152, 154, 156, 157

Meaning-making 1, 2, 3, 4, 5, 6, 10, 20, 27, 150, 164

Mediated discourse analysis (MDA) xiv, 48, 49, 50, 55, 56, 61, 62
Mediational means 48, 49, 50, 53, 55, 56, 57, 58, 62
Microsoft 110
Mihon 155, 156
Mississauga 25
Mongolia xiii, 22, 79, 81, 89, 90, 91, 92, 93, 94, 95, 96, 97, 98, 99
Monolingual 97, 102, 104, 121, 122
Multicultural 50, 51, 72, 93
Multilingual 21, 22, 23, 50, 86, 93, 151
Multimodal xiv, 1, 2, 3, 4, 5, 6, 7, 16, 17, 23, 29, 50, 53, 112
Multiperspectival approach 52
Muslims 84

Nissei 121, 138, 143, 144
Noh vi, xvi, 147, 148, 150, 151, 152, 153, 154, 155, 156, 159, 161, 162, 164, 165
Noh hayashi 151
North Korea 107
Northern Territories 84

Pennycook x, xi, 4, 6, 7, 22, 43, 48, 66, 68, 85, 86, 102, 103, 104, 105, 121, 147, 148, 149, 153, 154
Periphery xvi, 17, 68, 69, 80
Persia xiv, 47, 48, 49, 50, 51, 52, 53, 54, 56, 57, 58, 59, 60, 61, 62
Persian Shops 47, 62
Phenomenology 21, 27, 28, 29, 30, 41
Philippines 104
Pinker 125
Polish 30, 84
Portuguese 25, 26
Post-textual 7
Pre-textual 6, 7, 9, 14, 155
Psychogeography 24, 29

Raciolinguistics 88
Resemiotization xiv, 3, 4, 5, 6, 7, 10, 15, 16, 17
Russian 66, 70, 71, 74, 75, 76, 77, 78, 79, 80, 90, 91, 92, 93, 94, 95, 96, 98, 99

Sansei 121, 138, 143, 144
Scales xvi, 66, 67, 68, 70, 71, 73, 75, 76, 79, 80, 81
Scapes 22, 45, 120
Scollon xiv, 36, 42, 48, 49, 50, 52, 53, 54, 56, 61
Semiosis 49, 106
Semiotic xiii, xiv, xv, xvi, 1, 3, 4, 5, 6, 10, 16, 17, 21, 29, 41, 42, 44, 48, 49, 50, 52, 54, 62, 66, 67, 68, 86, 95, 103, 106, 112, 113, 114, 125, 149, 150, 151, 152, 153, 163, 164
Seodo 112
Service encounter xiv, 47, 48, 49, 50, 53
Service interactions xiv, 47, 48, 49, 50, 53
Shidai 155, 156
Shite 151, 155, 160, 161, 162
Social justice 102
Social semiotic analysis xv, 103, 106
Sociolinguistics ix, x, xiii, 2, 3, 20, 29, 48, 53, 62, 66, 67, 69, 85, 102, 103
Sociolinguistics of globalization ix, xiii, 62, 85, 102
South Korea xiii, xv, 105, 107, 108
Soviet Union 66, 69, 70, 71, 79
Subtextual 6, 7, 12, 13
Sultana xiv, xvi, 1, 2, 3, 6, 16, 85, 87, 102, 120, 124, 142
Superdiversity 29, 50
Suriashi 151
Sydney xiv, 47, 50, 51, 52, 90

Takeshima 109, 110
Tanka poetry 161
Tatars 71
Text xv, 3, 4, 7, 23, 24, 29, 37, 38, 42, 48, 52, 106, 108, 111, 112, 119, 124, 125, 126, 128, 152, 154, 161
Textbooks xv, 92, 103, 105, 106, 107, 108, 109, 112
Thailand 25, 32, 33

Tohoku 148, 150
Toronto v, x, xiv, 20, 21, 24, 25, 26, 29, 30, 33, 34, 36, 39, 42, 44
Translation 3, 4, 8, 11, 95, 107, 155, 156, 157, 158, 160, 162
Translingualism xv, xvi, 84, 85, 86, 87, 88, 90, 94, 98, 99, 102, 103, 104, 105, 115, 116, 147, 148, 149, 150, 151, 152, 153, 157, 160, 162, 163, 164, 165
Translinguistics 86, 103, 115
Translocal 4, 5, 121
Transmodal 4, 10
Transnational 22, 29, 45, 86, 133, 149
Transtextual 4, 154
Transglossia xiv, xvi, 3, 16
Transglossic xiv, 3, 4, 6, 16, 17, 102, 120, 124, 125, 130, 134, 135, 142, 143, 144, 157
Transgrammaring v, xv, xvi, 119, 123, 124, 125, 129, 130, 131, 132, 133, 135, 138, 139, 140, 141, 142, 144
Transgrammatical facts 124
Turkish 54, 74

Ukrainians 71
United States (US) 135, 140
Uyghurs 71
Uzbeks 71

Van Dijk 106, 107
Vietnam 25
Virtual space xiii, xiv, 1, 2, 3, 4, 5, 15, 16, 17
Vygotsky 49

Waki 155, 156, 160, 161
World War II 25
West Indians 26

YouTube 23

For Product Safety Concerns and Information please contact our EU Authorised Representative:

Easy Access System Europe

Mustamäe tee 50

10621 Tallinn

Estonia

gpsr.requests@easproject.com

www.ingramcontent.com/pod-product-compliance
Ingram Content Group UK Ltd.
Pitfield, Milton Keynes, MK11 3LW, UK
UKHW021822220426
5349IPUK00003B/43